# The Unquiet Path

## my pilgrimage in Brittany

Wendy Mewes

Drawings by Lucy Kempton

The Unquiet Path
published by Red Dog Books
ISBN: 978-1-3999-9854-3

© Wendy Mewes 2024

The right of Wendy Mewes to be identified as the author of this
work is asserted in accordance with sections 77 and 78 of the
Copyright Designs and Patents Act 1988

British Library Cataloguing-in-Publication Data
A catalogue record for this book is available
from the British Library

Red Dog Books is based in Somerset and in Brittany.
Enquiries should be addressed to the editorial office at
Red Dog Books, 29690 Berrien, France.
email: reddogbooks@orange.fr
www.reddogbooks.com

For Roselle Angwin,
my kind and generous friend
who knows a thing or two about writing,
with love

# Thanks

First and foremost, my heartfelt thanks to Roselle Angwin for her comments on the text, and her friendship. The book has been enhanced by Liz Ridgway's wonderful cover painting and the evocative drawings of Lucy Kempton. I am indebted to them both for their thoughtful creativity.

I am very grateful to faithful friends David Wright, Alan Montgomery, Lucy Kempton, Julia Kirby and Phil Watson for their practical support and stimulating company on the route. I have also derived many general benefits from the writing talk of Françoise Bacq, Fabienne Bozec, Barbara Hahn and Odile Simon.

Arnaud Lampire and Laurine Mourot at the Association Mon Tro Breizh deserve many thanks for their support and the exceptional work they have done on waymarking and guide-booking a definitive route for this pilgrimage (even if I didn't follow it!). My appreciation also to Anne-Marie Le Port, President of the Association de la Chapelle des Sept Saints in Erdeven, for a warm welcome when I attended the Pardon at their chapel.

Finally a big thank you to Annie Jaubert and the staff at the Abbaye Saint-Jacut-de-la-Mer, where I have been relying on my writing retreats in the last few years to get things finished. A wonderful spirit of place breathes there.

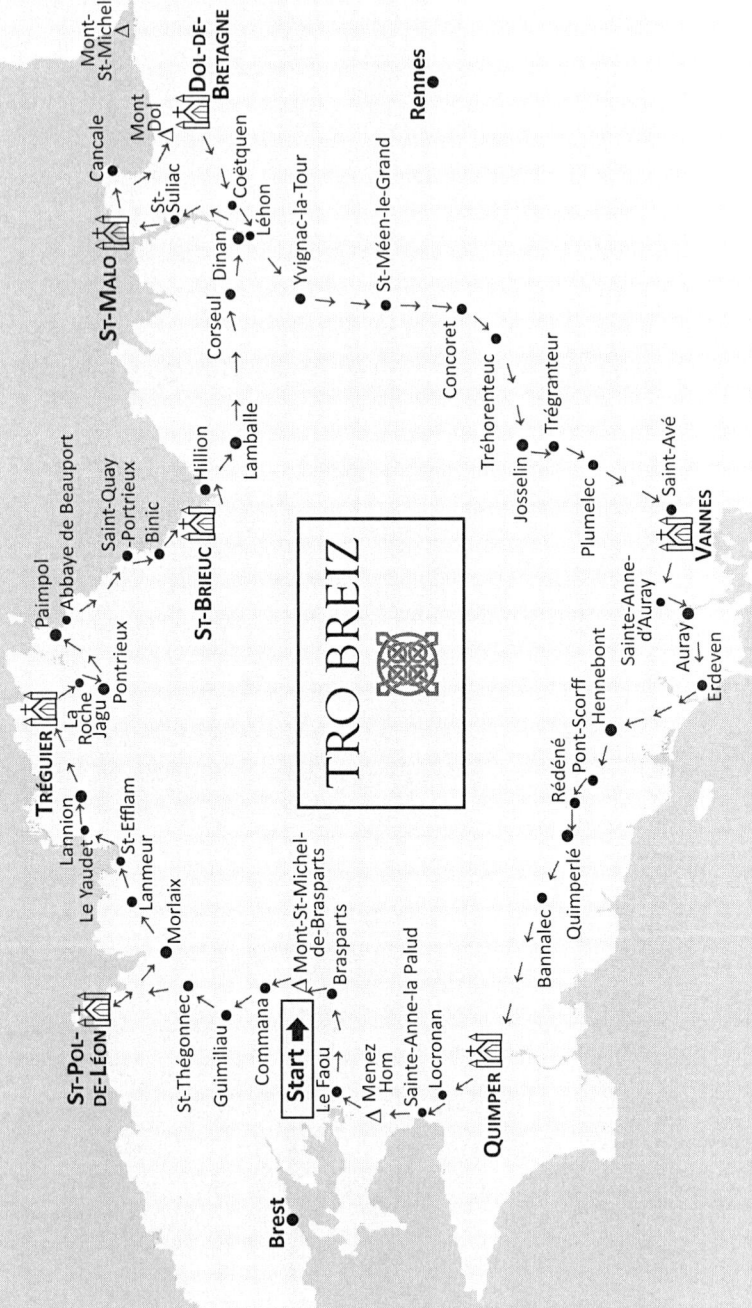

# Contents

# Introduction

It seemed such a ridiculous idea in 2016 when my health was at a low ebb. Walking the dog was a challenge, so almost 1000km on a pilgrimage trail was an impossible goal. If I managed a few miles in one day, the next would be for recovery. My first attempt to organise on such a great scale and get started was a dismal failure. I had a heart attack in 2017, quickly followed by a virulent attack of head shingles. The next time, in 2019, I soon wondered if the Christian aspect of the Tro Breiz was really something I wanted to spend so much time with, and diverted my attention to other projects. But I couldn't shake the idea, because it became clearer and clearer to me that the Tro Breiz goes right to the heart of Brittany, and way beyond the confines of official Catholicism. It is the story of a still living past, of origins, ancestors and settlement, themes personally relevant and important. Eventually in 2023, under better circumstances, I resolved to make the adventure happen once and for all.

The logistics were still horrendous, as I can't walk long distances or more than two or three days at a time, and carrying a heavy pack is impossible without triggering my arthritic feet into violent protest. Quite apart from other health problems, as I get older the physical struggle becomes ever more challenging. I wanted to walk alone whenever possible, but needed friends to help with transport, given a dearth of bus or taxi services in some of the deeply rural terrain the route crosses. Many times in the end I had to walk a pitifully small distance and then turn round and walk back to the start. But fortunately the plan of taking at least a year proved kind, and with the exception of one 10km train journey and a few lifts to ease the pain when road walking, I made it to the very end.

What separates a pilgrimage from a long walk is the search for sacred. For something completely outside ourselves that nevertheless generates the profoundest spiritual satisfaction. It may not be conventionally 'religious' at all. Anything that gives meaning to our lives and enhances the level of our daily existence may be worthy of awe. To make a journey to a place that enshrines something so significant to us creates a pilgrimage. But pilgrimage is a microcosm of the whole life journey, and can often seem a combination of pedestrianism and progress, false starts and fanfares. My own Tro Breiz is a homage to Brittany's history and culture, a way of connecting with the land and its ancestral heritage at a penetrating level. It is also a symbolic personal ending to a long quest, to overcome my physical limitations, forcing another kind of strength to step up and lead me home.

Walking is what has forged my close relationship with landscape in Brittany. In the last twenty-five years, I've covered a fair few thousand kilometres, often very slowly, in the cause of research, understanding and sometimes no more than the pure pleasure of feeling Breton earth under my frail feet. Such a long, growing journey has opened endless imaginative links to my adopted land, this so familiar beloved territory. But there is something in this whole history of the Dark Age migrations and the layers of legends they have laid down into the bedrock of Brittany that grabs at my attention, and shakes me up enough to go out and try crazy things like walking the Tro Breiz.

Tro Breiz (journey around Brittany) is the modern name for what may be a very ancient pilgrimage, connecting the seven cathedrals of the seven founding saints of Brittany. That is to say, mainly evangelists from Great Britain, who arrived in the centuries following the fall of the Roman empire. The fragmentary nature of the evidence makes a definitive analysis impossible, but certainly something called the Journey of the Seven Saints (*pèlerinage des sept saints*) existed in medieval times, and people of all sorts undertook some kind of pilgrimage between these religious centres, honouring the relics, which were thought to have healing powers, and memory of the saints, who were at the origin of the Brittany that was to emerge as a recognisable state in the 9th century. For a Breton pilgrim, completion was a step on the way to paradise.

The connection between these seven holy places forms a circular route for pilgrims travelling around the core of Brittany, giving a journey of about 1000kms in its most direct form. The Tro Breiz (or Breizh in modern Breton) was revived in the 1990s by the association Chemins du Tro Breiz, which continues to this day. They organise annual pilgrimage walks covering one of the seven stages and focusing on the religious context, with services, prayers and ritual along the way. More recently another association, Mon Tro Breizh, has begun to waymark a specific route in the distinctive black and white of the Breton flag, and produce guidebooks. As their name reflects, this is more about individual journeys, whatever the motivation.

I decided to follow a guidebook of 2014 (Le Guide du Tro Breiz, published by Coop Breizh) with text and photos by Yvon Autret and Bernard Rio, which had been my original inspiration for pursuing this pilgrimage. This uses a fairly direct itinerary between the seven cathedral towns, which seemed more manageable for me than making diversions to every possible religious site. Where necessary, I relied on IGN® maps to change and adapt the directions. Only a few waymarks from this out-dated route remain in situ. Some of the paths were already familiar to me from research for other books, notably Wayfaring in Brittany, but I tried not to over-prepare, so as to come fresh to each day's experience. Nor did I slavishly follow the printed maps when actually walking, retaining the right make spontaneous decisions and thus to get lost on occasion.

To understand the history of western Brittany, awareness of the famous Breton saints is vital, even if they were neither Bretons (given no such entity as Brittany existed in the Dark Ages) nor saints (in any official sense, being unrecognised by the Vatican). These holy men and a few women came in their hundreds to what was then Armorica, the land by the sea in Celtic parlance, from Great Britain, mainly Wales, Ireland and Cornwall, during the centuries after the collapse of Roman rule, arriving as individuals or in small groups mostly from the 6th to 7th centuries CE. Whether this and an earlier period of emigration was in general terms a response to the incursions of the Anglo-Saxons into Britain, or Pictish aggression on the western coasts or even something less tangible like pressures on land availability is unclear, but a degree of religious exodus from the monasteries of Wales and Ireland especially brought Brittany into focus as a relatively close destination.

Their purpose was settlement and evangelisation, winning acceptance (although it was not always plain sailing) against a background of triumphant miracles and healings performed in the contest against paganism. They were arriving in a place long-connected by trade and other ties with Great Britain, so it was hardly a case of virgin territory. An earlier wave of incomers from the 5th century were already in situ. The territory of Domnonée existed in England and was established in the 6th century as a kingdom in northern Brittany. The name for the south-west was Cornouaille, cognate with Cornwall. Traffic between the two sides of the Channel was commonplace. Some arrivals even found relatives already established here and able to offer a helping hand.

Grants of land by local rulers enabled the establishment of the saints' oratories, monasteries and primitive church buildings, which provided the nucleus for gradual development of larger centres of population, emerging into the later record of history as many towns and villages still in existence today. Some of these connections are obvious, like the towns called Saint-Malo or Saint-Brieuc, some less so, such as Locronan, the holy place of Saint Ronan. In fact, the presence of the saints is ubiquitous in toponyms, fixing their stories firmly in the landscape, and the implications of settlement remain one of their greatest legacies.

The traditional seven founding saints, with their differing stories, give the flavour of the whole phenomenon, and their seven cathedrals still stand in later medieval form even if not all the original patrons have kept hold of their status. So we have Saint Pol or Paul Aurelien with his centre at Saint-Pol-de-Léon, Saint Tugdual (or more accurately Tudgal) at Tréguier, Saint Brieuc at his eponymous town, likewise Saint Malo, then Saint Samson at Dol-de-Bretagne, Saint Patern at Vannes and Saint Corentin at Quimper. The cathedral at Tréguier is now associated with Saint Yves, the patron saint of Brittany, with traditional Catholic (non-Breton) saints taking over Saint-Brieuc (Étienne or Stephen), Saint-Malo (Vincent of Saragossa) and Vannes (Peter).

While there is no shortage of information of various kinds about the Breton saints, evidence for the actual Tro Breiz pilgrimage is sketchy. The medieval journey called the *Pèlerinage des Sept Saints* existed, apparently followed by thousands of people over the centuries, but there are no personal accounts surviving and it is unsure exactly what routes were established between the cathedral towns, although the use of Roman roads would have been important. Dom Lobineau in 1707 says that he had seen traces of a paved route called the Way of the Seven Saints for this 'once famous' pilgrimage near Dinan, probably on an old road to Broons.

Anne de Bretagne, Duchess of Brittany and Queen of France (twice), undertook a tour of shrines in 1505, although it was probably equally a political progress in the days when the best publicity was personal appearance. She started from her château in Nantes, and visited Vannes, Quimper and Saint-Pol-de-Léon as well as other eminent shrines such as Saint-Jean-du-Doigt and Le Folgoët in Finistère, with Saint-Brieuc a point of call on the return. We do not know the full itinerary. Two historians of her time make reference to the seven founding saints. A manuscript of Alain Bouchart actually presents a stylised illustration with the named saints shown in a line, and Pierre Le Baud in his *Chronicles* not only mentions the immigrant bishops, but also tantalisingly speaks of a circuit called the Tour de Bretagne (Journey around Brittany), the origin of the modern name in Breton: Tro Breiz.

The Celtic/Breton saints settled the coastal areas and interior of this western part of the peninsula, bringing their similar language to merge with the existing Gaulish to form Breton. Much of the east of later Brittany, away from the Channel coast, was already firmly under the control of the Roman church, with bishops established at Nantes and Rennes. This is also the area which naturally came under the greatest influence of the Franks and later the French, and had its own language, Gallo, a *langue d'oïl*, ultimately derived from Latin. There is still a marked difference between the two halves of the region of Brittany. Pockets of Breton-speaking that lingered in the eastern area reflect the early settlers in the Age of Saints.

Whether the Christianity brought to western Brittany by their efforts was some distinctive Celtic form as practised in such lands in Great Britain is a complex question. One piece of evidence on this is a remarkable letter surviving from the early 6th century, in which western priests are chided by eastern bishops (of Rennes, Angers and Tours) for letting women participate in the administration of the mass, handling the chalice and 'daring' to offer the blood of Christ to the people. They are also reprimanded for using portable altars and moving from house to house for this office. This shows these practices were regarded as outside the official Catholicism of Rome.

Another indication of discrepancy is the use of the Celtic tonsure (front of head shaved, hair long at the back, possibly derived from Druidic practice) which was forbidden at the Abbaye de Landévennec in 818 as part of the command of Louis Le Pieux, emperor of the Franks, to bring the monks into strict line with the Benedictine rule. The pronounced asceticism of many of the holy incomers was another perceived Celtic characteristic. Some were wanderers, seeking lonely places to devote themselves to solitary prayer, others underwent rigorous bodily deprivations of food and sleep to hone their spiritual acumen. Closeness to the natural world of rural Brittany in the west was also a contrast with developed urban religion. Saints thrived in the countryside.

The Breton saints have always had their status through the *vox populi* or popular acclaim, and their stories are inextricably mixed into the culture of western Brittany, staunchly founded on the strong oral tradition underpinning all Celtic countries. The godliness of their lives and the exercise of miracle-working, particularly in the context of healing, accounted for the tenacity of reverence from the people their personae have maintained through the centuries. They were also powerful intermediaries between poor sinners and the might of God, and religious exponents more relatable on a personal level. The *Lives* or *Vitae* of the most significant figures, the celebrity saints one might say, were not written down until centuries after their deaths, and often these focus on moral edification in the formulaic pattern of hagiography, although interesting details can be extracted to give a sense of individual personalities, undertakings and journeys.

Legends and folklore place the saints in their particular territories, and many are still celebrated now with Pardons (saints' day festivals) when their relics are honoured, banners are carried in processions, their special canticles sung in Breton and the places associated with their stories given attention. In other words, the Breton saints are still living in the memories of the local population as each generation renews and enhances their own heritage. Their sites spread along the Tro Breiz route, particularly chapels and sacred springs or *fontaines*, giving context to these intrepid survivors and illuminating the countryside. Behind all the historical development of Brittany lies the shadowy shape of the Breton saints.

Pilgrimage is a very old story of aspiration, preparation, journey, arrival and aftermath. These are the common elements that connect a variety of motivations among the wide assortment of people who decide to set out on the road. In the modern world there may be less emphasis on the religious commitment of faith, replaced by more personal incentives such as self-discovery, or reconciliation with trauma and loss. The long walk provides an opportunity for the sort of quiet contemplation and inner engagement that is often elusive in everyday life, the time for reflection that brings change. The sense of quest is usually intensely personal. I wanted to challenge my feeble physical abilities to live up to the determination and commitment that drive most of my work. I also wanted to celebrate a quarter of a century working in the compelling world of Brittany's formative years. I looked forward to exploring the shape of sacred, this circular journey a series of experiences like beads, or sometimes precious stones, on a necklace.

Conversely it is the notion of companionship and shared purpose, the positive sociability of the route that appeals to many others, with its guarantee of a place in some form in community. The pilgrimage becomes a recreational experience, with human contacts the lasting legacy of the whole undertaking. Pilgrim is a kind of recognised status that can ease the path of the individual, but that works rather better on well-established routes like the Compostela. The Tro Breiz may one day benefit from the same kind of infra-structure to give security and a sense of *communitas* on the route. I have to say that I met not one single pilgrim on the paths, except for talking with those about to embark on an organised week's walking from Dol-de-Bretagne.

In a more general spiritual impulse, the traveller looks to immerse him or herself in something greater than ego-driven desires, to become absorbed in the inevitable elemental encounters of life in the open air, the history of the landscape through which the pilgrim passes, the developing relationship with the physical actuality of the outdoors, with nature and the natural world. All these differing motivations can lead to the same appreciation of achievement at the end of the road. Although my journey was broken and prolonged, each tiny sliver of progress mattered physically and emotionally. Spiritual experiences for me as a non-Christian passionate pagan, were sporadic, but intense and moving when they came, sometimes from surprising sources. The whole thing wrung me out, but ultimately left the fabric of my being in considerably better condition.

Because our knowledge of the more famous pilgrimages like the Compostela trail is based on accounts of the participants from the early medieval period up to the present day, personal perspectives and emotional reactions dominate. (We do not have such material for the Tro Breiz until very recent times.) Relegated to a lesser rôle is the spirit of place that binds all the itineraries of these individuals. The pauses at shrines, springs, rocks and viewpoints are more than a backdrop to particular exploration, they are the essence of the experience which sets an individual in the context of their changing environment. This is what gave me the most satisfaction on my journey and persisted most strongly in my memory, the palpable communication of the landscape itself. This served to reinforce the sense of my own rootedness in my homeland.

Places have their own intrinsic quality which is the essence of attraction, even when this is overlaid by the sum of later human endeavour, those earlier travellers who forged the route and the emotional connection of their journey. It gives a depth to certain spots which may have been sacred for millennia, long pre-dating organised religion, honoured for a recognition of their own exceptional native character. I call this the personality of place. The simple structures of nature-based worship – stones, water, trees – become more complex in energy as not only footfall but the creation of stories add layers. The human instinct for interpretation can both change and obscure the essence of a place: it provides for both enlightenment and fabulation.

Finally, what on earth have I in common with those old Breton saints who have figured largely in my work over many years and hold such a special place in my affections? It is not the astounding faith for which they were so highly regarded by contemporaries, and their miracles do little more than mildly exercise the imagination. I think it is at the level of endeavour that I feel admiration, the many times when things went awry on the way to settlement and success. The ineptitude of some, the skill, patience and determination that saw others forge communities from scratch. And what they represent overall, symbols of the beginning of a recognisable Brittany, a Celtic essence.

Sometimes even saints got things wrong. It is at that human level that they seem most relatable now. Saint Malo quarrelled with his parishioners, Saint Herbot had difficulty dealing with women and frankly preferred the company of cattle, Saint Ronan didn't seem to get on with anyone at all. While many of the hundreds of saints remain simply names, mere ciphers, some emerge vibrantly as real people through the detail of their stories. Samson would be a wise choice in a crisis, Gildas in circumstances requiring resuscitation. I have most sympathy for the reluctant bishops like Pol and Corentin, who really would have rather been left alone in isolated spots to enjoy a life of peaceful devotion. Solitary misfits is a profile I can easily identify with although, as yet, no ambitious political figure has called me to high public office. The solace of landscape has proved its worth, then and now.

The seven founding saints anchor this pilgrimage of the Tro Breiz but the journey passes through the land of hundreds of others. Their stories have seeped into the earth, blossomed in the trees and permeated the stone of Brittany. Their images rise up again in the statues and banners paraded on their festive days even today. Their legacy is a great network of towns and villages that started out as tiny communities created by incomers from over the sea. And as I walked, what began to emerge as a recurrent theme of my thoughts and experience was the whole question of settling and settlement, not only in a physical context but also in the mind and heart. This, together with all the resonant echoes of the land of saints, made this knotty journey something of an unquiet path.

# 1 Setting out: a sacred hill, the realm of air and a simulated cave

The beginning is magical. I stand on the sacred summit of Mont-Saint-Michel-de-Brasparts. Sweeping views range across the crests of the Monts d'Arrée, highest hills in Brittany, and the Yeun Elez below, a boggy expanse that houses the entrance to the Celtic underworld. Here beats the very heart of Breton legend, here linger the ghostly figures of mysterious black dogs, dangerous nocturnal washerwomen and dodgy gnomes. My starting point for this journey has been chosen carefully, a site whose tradition long predates Christianity, a crucible for pagan forces, worship of older gods and Druidic rites. Long before that too, considering the wavy neolithic alignment of stones that runs across a plateau below my vantage point. It is also home territory to me, a terrain that draws me endlessly onto the craggy skin of the moors with its far-reaching vistas over history and geology.

Today I am embarking on the Tro Breiz, that elusive medieval pilgrimage, and my own personal journey around Brittany, a kind of summary of twenty-five years work exploring the bottomless well of the region's eventful culture. I am neither Catholic nor Christian, but pilgrimage today, especially post-pandemic, is more fluidly regarded. It is my intention to be thoughtful, despite what will be first and foremost an extreme physical challenge, supported by the memory of loved ones. And also an act of homage to the land that has given me so much.

Many of the sacred sites along the way were honoured and valued thousands of years before the birth of Jesus Christ. But those Dark Age Breton saints who brought

Christianity to the west of the Armorican peninsula hold a stirring imaginative pull, given their combination of ambivalent instincts, all too human weaknesses, semi-magical workings and a formative role in the establishment of what would later become Brittany. They are also still a vibrant cast in contemporary culture, characters on the cusp of legend and history whose flimsy origins have proved no barrier to providing a fixed point of reference for Bretons even today. They are, in a certain fashion, the opening lines of a wonderful story.

Because of its circular shape, pilgrims committing to this particular journey probably set out from home towards the first religious landmark on the route. We do not have any detailed and conclusive evidence of any complete itinerary of the Tro Breiz, only tantalising glimpses. My chosen starting point is half-way between two of the seven cathedrals: Quimper to the south and Saint-Pol-de-Léon to the north where I am heading. The top of Mont-Saint-Michel-de-Brasparts or Menez Mikel to give its Breton name, is a suitably dramatic natural setting to nail my commitment. The traditional Catholic saint is a late-comer to this spot, which was once called Motte de Cronon, presumably in common with other distinctive summits a place for worship of the Sun God.

It is one of the seven sacred hills of Brittany. From here I can see right around a ring of crests and right across the vast marsh in the sunken middle. The TV antenna to the right of lumpy Roc'h Trévézel is a landmark symbolic of more modern preoccupations. Just beside that is a small protuberance called Roc'h Ruz, the Red Rock, which technically is the topmost point of Brittany. Straight ahead across the reservoir is a decommissioned nuclear power station, ironically founded soon after the whole area was declared a regional park for its bleak beauty in the 1960s.

The Monts d'Arrée are a place of many conflicting energies. The heights are the realm of Air, with huge skies and competing winds, an outdoor cathedral for more elemental forms of religion than the churches and chapels that highlight the Tro Breiz. It is also the landscape that makes me feel at ease in myself. The moment my foot treads on those rough skittering moorland paths, I am most content, fitting naturally into a skein of earth and atmosphere that can sustain my spirit like nothing and nowhere else. Here I shed the restrictive layers of imposed identity - a foreigner, a woman, an ill-fitting loner - and enter a simplicity of being that is *my* element. For me, the open air has always meant more than any man-made structure or a peopled environment. Natural outsider I may be, but here I have found my place, and I knew it on my very first journey to Brittany. The stony scrambles and sunken ways of this wild land are my spiritual paths. Not desolation but inspiration.

Before me now, this eerie landscape has been rendered doubly so by the results of last year's awful summer fires, leaving a sea of bleached quartzite gleaming like some lonely moonscape against the dark shadow of biblical scorched earth. It lies naked, stripped of proper clothes, a skinned animal. Splotches of bright moss and grass stalks show regeneration but there are no leaves on the branches of stunted heathland trees, and much of the traditional flora of the *landes* like gorse and broom is nothing but a tangle of blackened stems. There is still a whiff of smoke in the air after all this time. It is a sight both heart-breaking and fearfully thrilling. Some new primal identity rises from the destruction of the familiar old, the unseen substructure forced shockingly into the limelight. But the unmistakable character of the landscape - these little hills are the last stand of what were once huge mountains like the Alps - remains deep, harsh and mystical.

It is April 7, painful anniversary of the recent deaths of two beloved souls. Two stabilising influences torn away, leaving a gaping hole I am still struggling to patch. But I chose this day to start with them in mind, to bring some kindred spirits along on this first step of my Tro Breiz journey, an adventure that will honour and respect ancestors from a much more distant past, exploring the bonds that hold us up and tie us down. The weather is beautiful, but it is not a moment for the quiet contemplation I had envisaged to mark the start. On the summit, workmen are putting a new roof on the iconic hill-top chapel, hammering nails into the fresh timbers.

First constructed in 1672, it was granted indulgences by Pope Innocent XI, acknowledging a role on pilgrimage routes, but the chapel fell into disuse after the French Revolution, being found in a ruinous state when Jacques Cambry visited in 1795. A small pilgrim's shelter was established in 1842, and two annual Pardons to celebrate Saint Michael were held. But the chapel also came to serve practical purpose as a shepherds' hut, offering protection in the serious weather conditions of this isolated spot. During WW1 pilgrimages came here to pray for peace: in 1917 people from all surrounding villages arrived in procession, singing canticles and reciting prayers. In WWII the chapel survived German occupation, when the summit was used as a radar site with a massive antenna.

I'm lingering over these views and the pilgrim past, but my young dog is over-excited before we have begun, leaping and circling on his lead, wanting to be off. He has probably heard long before me the strange noises assaulting the air from the other side of the hill. A long, ragged line of maybe fifty teenagers and a handful of adults comes caterwauling across the moor. There is a sort of singing, but also yells and cries that sound like anguish. I sit on a rock to wait as they stagger in dribs and drabs up the last steep ascent. As I finally walk away across the moor, I turn back to see a line of silhouetted figures round the rim of the hill, yelling and gesticulating, like some primitive declaration of war.

The discordant noise echoes all around and then fades away, finally to be replaced by welcome silence and aloneness, although this is a very early reminder about the nature of the task: there is no possibility of controlling conditions, and taking what comes is an essential skill to be mastered. Pilgrimage is only a romantic practice from the comfort of an armchair. Being on the road is hard for everyone at some point, whether the struggle comes from mind, body or emotional upheaval. For many these trials can be relieved by company, a fundamental part of medieval pilgrimage, as Chaucer so memorably portrayed in the Canterbury Tales, and today anecdotes of solidarity and friendships formed on the Camino routes to Compostela fill the many accounts of individual journeys.

I am a solitary walker by choice, but will follow some of this pilgrimage with friends and rely on others for back-up transport.

Crossing the little road that runs on to Saint-Rivoal, I notice the first Tro Breiz marker on a post, all shiny and new with its black and white slashes. It is labelled Mon Tro Breizh, an appellation designed to emphasise the individualistic nature of this journey for each and every pilgrim, whether 'religious' or not. Same path, different journeys. We continue along a track turned stream, already ascending gradually towards the next summit of Tuchenn Gador. On the moor again, the wind pushes past, asserting its power over travellers shorn of all protection. Views to the north-west open up, the first sense of a world beyond this heart of Finistère. One short steep climb on sliding stones is a good preparation for most of what is to come on today's walk. I see what I think is a newly installed cross on the skyline far ahead and feel a moment of outrage at this imposition on a wild site, but it turns out to be a barren tree...

The natural formation of rocks on the top, gleaming with points of quartzite, resembles a group of decrepit old people, leaning on each other for support. Looking north, I can see to Roscoff and Saint-Pol-de-Léon, my first goal. Menez Hom, another of Brittany's special sacred hills lies to the south-west near the Atlantic coast, and the hazy line of the Black Mountains or *Montagnes noires* defines the south. In a nearer context it's a bit daunting to see ranges of scabrous hills ahead, a symbolic reminder of awaiting trials and tribulations. For me they actually represent the comfort of home scenery and I already feel on this first expedition a gnawing reluctance to leave the beloved known, the place that for me brings harmony between outer and inner landscapes. My dog scrabbles down the steeper face of the hill, dragging me precariously behind him. Dangerous sheer drops into quarries line the path, as we manage the rough descent into the Elorn valley.

Walking a pilgrimage is to be always on a line somewhere between past and future, with a long history of earlier others forging the trail for whatever reasons, and the future route to be walked, the ultimate goal ahead, to be achieved. Here in the Monts d'Arrée, my primary thoughts go back to the neolithic people who have left their monuments all around and may have been the original pioneers of certain rough interior paths still in existence. Theirs were the hands that began to clear these summits of wooded cover with the new demands of settlement and permanent exploitation of the land.

If some of the alignments and burial chambers were sites of seasonal ritual for extended gatherings, then they were at the same time creating their own pilgrimage trails to places of spiritual and social significance, deepening experience through the travelled way, precursors of all pilgrims. The barrier of this hill range would also have been crossed for commercial links with the north coasts and then Britain across the Channel, at that time relatively recently separated from the European land mass. The traffic of status goods and utilitarian tools was well-established in that epoch, as archaeological finds show, a reminder that movement and communication have always been the essentials of human existence.

In recent times, the journeying of the *pilhaouerien*, impoverished rag-and-bone men from Mont d'Arrée villages like Botmeur, La Feuillée and Loqueffret that could not provide a living on poor land for an entire family, has also incised a history of dire poverty and endurance on the stony pathways. Away for months at a time when there was no agricultural work, they travelled widely in western Brittany, hawking cheap pottery in exchange for anything that could be sold on at profit. They passed over the moorland heights with two-wheeled carts and skinny horses, although some also travelled on foot bearing huge loads on their back. It was a life of grinding effort for modest reward. Emile Souvestre records a song showing the *pilhaouer*'s sense of alienation even from his own community: *le pillawer n'ai ni foi ni paroisse* (he has neither faith nor parish). It was also said that they never knew if they were returning home to a coffin or a cradle. These men without monuments - were their lives in the 19th and early 20th centuries any more well-provided for than their stone age forebears?

At the bottom of the valley, it's hard to make the connection between the little stream we cross and the huge Elorn river that widens into the Rade de Brest not 40 kilometres to the west. Sluggishly dribbling up out of the boggy mess a few hundred metres to my right, the flow is soon lively and strong, the neophyte river rushing on towards its other persona as an extensive inland sea. From a stagnation of mud and marsh to a vast body of water that joins the vaster Atlantic Ocean, emblem of the transformation that is a basic ingredient of pilgrimage. Development is often a less scary prospect than change.

The paths here are degraded and slippery, requiring attention to footholds at every step, with ferns already pushing across the narrow defiles. The ascent ahead is steep but finally we reach the ridge path at a crossroads of routes, relieved to have springy grass underfoot instead of scree. Up on the shoulder of this last line of peaks, the view ahead is a revelation. It is like emerging into a different world, about to come down from the savage hills, as many did, starving or steeped in alcohol in the 19th century, hoping for salvation of some sort in the more prosperous region of Léon to the north.

In place of raw rocky hillsides and prickly gorse, I look down on fields, trees, white village houses, the church spire of Commana, and towns further north towards the channel coast. It all speaks of wealth and a richness of land that contrasts painfully with the beloved territory I am about to step out of rather reluctantly. A final line of schist crests thrust their jagged profile towards this garden of Eden, showing a cutting edge, the Monts d'Arrée defiant to the last. The great physical and psychological barrier created by this hill-range is truly apparent now as I stand on the separation point of two worlds.

Far below lies the bright square of a parking area beside the dark mouth of a neolithic passage grave that once saluted these very hills in its placing. To the left Lac Drennec is a quiet recreational oasis in the richer landscape. A tortuous narrow stream-bed forms most of the descent, and as I drop down into the tree-line, the route turns off the rough track for raised wooden walkways of the Korrigan Trail, a nature study of the claggy *tourbières* forming the valley bed. Still descending, the route passes a small green field, bright as a jewel, its size and oval shape revealing its origin as a *quevaise* holding, a unique land system of this area.

Both the Cistercian Abbaye du Relec and the Commanderie of La Feuillée (Knights of Saint John) worked their lands in the Monts d'Arrée by this method of giving units capable of sustaining a family, with a farmhouse, storage buildings, courtyard and field in return for some labour and produce. The unusual element was a security of tenure in the terms and the passing down of the property through inheritance, even to females. Those were significant things, a plus in the preservation stakes of such precarious existence as peasants endured.

I come out of the trail opposite the megalith of Mougau Bihan, an *allée couverte* or passage grave dating to c3000 BCE, of impressive size (14m long), with one long chamber covered by five enormous capstones and a small separated *cella*. Inside are some fine carvings of paddles, goddesses' breasts (perhaps) and a hafted axe on the end stone, even if the specific significance is elusive. From here I look back up to the heights of the Monts d'Arrée, conscious that the landscape is little changed from when the monument was erected, with a marshy valley of plants found then and now below the cleared heights. The name of the monument means 'little cave' in Breton, giving us a linguistic link between natural places and the construction of a simulated cave for burial and ritual purposes.

From time to time the axe carving is spray-painted with a florescent pink cross, a curious contemporary reaction against paganism, harking right back to times when Christianity felt the need to physically attack the symbols of older religious practices. In the 5th century the Council of Arles decreed against the pagan cult of stones, trees and springs. Two hundred years later, idols were to be destroyed but sacred places taken over by the new faith. Many standing-stones and burial places were lost to destruction or to adaptation later with the addition of carved crosses. But the cross-fertilisation of Christianity and paganism is a fundamental characteristic of Breton faith and culture. Traditions of the long past are important for their own stake in the continuity of rural life, with transmutation more acceptable than rude substitution.

From the lithic mystery of this monument, I will soon move firmly into a different world dominated by the hand of organised Christianity, and a more obvious aspect of pilgrimage begins. The transition is marked by the beautiful wayside *fontaine* or sacred spring dedicated to Saint Jean (John the Baptist), whose statue stands in a niche above the water, with an adjacent *lavoir* where clothes were washed until well into the 20th century. Enclosed by slate walls and shaded by trees, it is a place of peace and quiet these days, a simple tribute to nature's life-giving force. This echoes the ethos of Mougau Bihan, also built with local materials in some form of reverence to celestial or ancestral powers. One can see the connection in spiritual terms.

But the simplicity of the *fontaine* is quite a contrast to what is to come, for I am now only a short distance from the village of Commana and so about to enter Parish Close country.

## 2  Fearing failure: spring flowers, a secular saint and a seductive siren

The dour profile of the church of Saint Derrien in Commana reflects the weather in this portal village of the Monts d'Arrée, which is a breezy place at the best of times. The spire, undecorated except for a chain of rough stony hooks, has a sober air, robust windbreak for the flurries it must withstand during inclement months. Indeed, the whole enclosure has an air of cold sturdiness, from the heavy gateway, a bone-house decorated by impressive gargoyles and two calvaries, in what remains of the graveyard. The church's southern entrance porch is a truly impressive example of Renaissance work in the cluttered world of parish close finery, with a tiny figure of the patron saint above, but the church is best known for what waits inside: the fantastically elaborate gilded altarpiece of Saint Anne.

The Breton phenomenon of the *enclos paroissiaux* or parish closes is not unique to northern Finistère, but the greatest and most varied concentration is here. It is a cultural form deeply set in the values of rural society. The most striking examples of these architectural religious ensembles lie on my route beyond Commana, but here in the village the essential elements are clearly present. A walled precinct separates sacred and profane spaces, with the monumental entrance gate stepped and blocked by a slab to keep animals out. Then there are the church itself, an ossuary building where the bones of the dead were kept, and a calvary showing the crucifixion, sometimes decorated with a narrative frieze. Each parish close is essentially the kingdom of death with a promise of resurrection and after-life for the faithful.

This basic pattern can be as simple or ornate as local funds permitted, with some parishes hiring the best of sculptors for the statuary that is a memorable feature, particularly on the calvaries which were used as teaching aids by priests and sometimes illustrated by dozens of figures, mainly in scenes from the Passion. The Château de Kerjean not so very far away, built during the second half of the 16$^{th}$ century, had instigated a trend for the new decorative features of the Renaissance, and the same workmen took on many church projects. Local artisans' workshops were bang up to date with the latest European styles when commissioned. The closes have more to tell than the journey of a Christian into heaven: they also provided the focus of local pride and family life with Sunday rituals, festivals, rites of passage and even a certain amount of commerce – like auctioning off donated livestock - within the precinct.

The name of the village of Commana is made up of the Breton *koum* (valley or stone trough) and Ana/Anne, perhaps with reference to a story that a statue of Mary's mother was found in this spot. This would explain her cult here (although the church is technically under the patronage of Saint Derrien). The huge altar in the north transept is a major homage. It represents Anne and her daughter Mary with the baby Christ between them, but unfortunately, when I arrive, the main figures are missing, removed for restoration, leaving a gaping hole in the middle of this refulgent spectacle. Even without them, the Baroque bravado almost hurts my eyes.

To someone unfamiliar with Roman Catholicism, this object may come as something of a shock for the sheer extravagance of gold and intense colour, the dazzling coverage of every inch by people, animals and vegetation giving a sense of movement and vitality. Cupids pick bunches of grapes, birds hide in the twisting foliage and the faces of biblical luminaries appear in burnished cameos. It is easy to imagine how to peasants living in primitive cottages with none but the most basic of facilities, this must have seemed like another world, a foretaste of the splendour of heaven. It touches the same enchantment as the world of legends.

It's a first indication on this Tro Breiz journey of the astonishing richness to be found inside grand churches in poor Breton villages, where giving to God and communal pride were more highly valued than individual ostentation. Modest private houses and extravagant religious public buildings were the order of the day in the 16th and 17th centuries. The closes were not just religious precincts, but a manifestation of social cohesion and parish identity. There was also a strong element of local rivalry: having more modern or more flamboyant décor or a taller bell-tower than the neighbouring village was a factor in the ambitions of each *fabrique* (church council). Donations must have been high in Commana to commission a work like this tribute to Saint Anne. The painting and gilding were carried out by Pierre du Mesmeur from Huelgoat, who in 1682 was paid the mighty sum of 1500 pounds – over 30,000 euros today.

Commana church also provides an introduction to the shadier side of the world of saints, with the patronage of

Saint Derrien, a knight from Great Britain who went on pilgrimage to the Holy Land with his companion Neventer. According to legend, their adventures in passing through Brittany on return involved rescuing the lord of La Roche Maurice from drowning after he attempted suicide from the battlements to avoid seeing his family given in tribute to a flesh-eating dragon. Such were the stresses of everyday life in those times. Despite the good offices of the knights, he refused to convert to Christianity, but conceded that a church should be built for those who willingly chose the new religion. (It is not at all clear how this might have led to the far off Commana connection.) But here the holy family seem to have had little trouble in pushing aside an obscure saint like Derrien.

The vague details, uncertain connections, nuggets of history wrapped in the fantastical become a familiar story in the narrative of saints in Brittany, especially of those just passing through, like Derrien. He leaves traces of his presence in place-names – the village of Saint-Derrien, hamlets called Lander(r)ien (= the holy place of Derrien) – and sacred springs dedicated to his cult, but of the man himself, there is little sign. Association with Jerusalem pilgrimage combined with triumph over a ravaging beast in the Elorn valley is enough to foster the popular acclamation of sainthood in this area and hazy memories surviving the march of time. But we shall meet plenty of others with better back-stories that leave a firmer impression of individuality. There is no shortage of saints in Brittany – the traditional number is one thousand.

A day later I make an early start north from Commana in dim light, with mist hanging over the Monts d'Arrée behind me. Getting out of the village involves a few minutes of barking dogs – mine not least among them – breaking the soft silence that seems to hang like garlands in the air. Once free of houses, small empty roads lead off into the countryside, plunging down a valley and up to Pen-ar-Quinquis before rolling on towards the well-kept hamlet of Kerverous, a pretty place with a large stepped *calvaire* handy for a brief rest. The inhabitants of this tiny community are going about their everyday lives. No-one speaks or looks my way. Would it be any different if I carried a staff and wore a large hat with scallop shell symbol of the Compostela pilgrimage? Probably not. I feel very much an outsider, and don't linger.

This countryside is choppy and varied, mild hills and sweet valleys with spongy ground underfoot around their defining streams. There's plenty of mud too, but it hasn't deterred the spring flowers as I pass not only luxurious stands of bluebells, but a group of early purple orchids right in the bog. After another ascent and descent at Botrez, the lovely winding valley of the Penzé offers a long run of wooded path above the river. When this way finally drops to the wide flow, there's a rough wooden bridge to cross, but on the other side numerous trees and thickets have been felled. Left to lie in vast irregular piles, the footpath along the other bank is completely covered. It takes a long time to work through, mostly carrying the dog whose short legs keep slipping into deep spaces between the massed trunks. Finally free of obstacles, we criss-cross the water on a series of bridges before coming up into the centre of Loc-Éguiner-Saint-Thégonnec, past a medieval motte which may once have surveyed the river-crossing of the old Roman road from Carhaix to the north coast.

I've always liked this small village, with its cumbersome double-barrelled name, emanating an air of simple sanctity in the low double-naved church (1566) above a green valley. The interior has an odd domestic tinge with photos of the Pope and another prelate in frames on a lace altar-covering, like family members proudly displayed on a sideboard in the living room. Double the conventional number of *fontaines* too, with one dedicated to Saint John the Baptist and another to the eponymous Equiner, plus a *lavoir* with inscribed gravestones used in the surround. The name Loc-Equiner means in Breton 'the holy place of Saint Eguiner', but he is one of the nebulous ones; maybe, if he existed, an Irish evangelist who arrived in Brittany on a stone boat. His statue in the church is appropriately nondescript.

There's also an Iron Age *stele* in the cemetery which once did service elsewhere as a marker on the local Roman road, but by now I am more interested in sitting down, and find a weird picnic table made of bricks. My sandwich is enhanced by the restful view over this agreeably peaceful dell. Someone has placed a woven ring of hazel twigs on the surface of the table, as if it was a sacred offering at an altar in an open-air pagan shrine. Yet another dimension of sacred, which seems fitting as I very much have the sense that Christianity is adapting itself to the patterns of nature here. The Tro Breiz is to throw up a lot of unsung places like this, and many will dwell in the memory for their intimate appeal well beyond the more vaunted highlights.

I do not relish the second stage of my day's journey to the goal of Guimiliau, through unremarkable landscape. It seems more and more a managed and ordered world, far removed from the primitive terrain of the Monts d'Arrée. Here faith is directed and larger-scale agriculture controlled for profit and prosperity. It was ever thus. Haut Léon, or the territory I am walking through today, was the centre of a widespread cloth-making industry in the 16-17th centuries, with all stages of the process performed locally from growing the flax, cutting and soaking it, extracting the thread, bleaching and finally weaving lengths of fabric that could be transported to the port in Morlaix for international trade, mainly with England. As a result, rural society here was dominated by a rich peasant aristocracy (later known as *juloded*) who called the shots on how villages and parish closes were run. The intensely decorative character of the churches is a reflection of the wealth accrued from this commerce.

That old familiar struggle with arthritic pain in my left foot begins after an initial long uphill drag on the road, relieved only momentarily by the sight of a beautiful house with *apoteis*, a jutting gable, a style found often in this area, where perhaps it was once a weaver's house with workroom upstairs. Below, the extension added an extra space, often dominated by a wooden chest serving as a table with built-in benches, a chance for a family to gather together for meals rather than fitting around the hearth as best they could. It seems such a small extra dimension, but the social development may have been significant. In examples of such preserved houses that can be visited, a spoon rack hangs above with implements of varied size, a Goldilocks detail to vivify the familial nature of the ritual.

Gradually, trudging along to the Croix de la Garenne in its little hedged precinct, I lose all powers of observation in the necessity of grim endurance. Negativity slips a treacherous arm around my shoulder in faux sympathy. There you are, it's all too much. Never mind, it was a ridiculous plan to start with. I ask myself seriously, how is this ever going to work? Only a short distance from home and already the threat of failure hangs wearily over me. What delusion to think I can manage another 900 odd kilometres! Later, on this vast route of the Tro Breiz I will have to walk day after day, simple logistics dictate that. At this moment, it seems utterly impossible. Future tribulations fill my mind to the detriment of present surroundings, and I walk along stiffly like an automaton, hoping to find a little relief in muscular rigidity.

But Guimiliau is like a magic potion, one that will revive me and re-instil courage. It is the most engaging of villages, and the parish close provokes an emotional reaction which is tied up in a knot of saint lore, stony finesse and a kind of femininity well beyond the reach of the Virgin Mary. There's also a Tro Breiz information point or shop nearby, decorated inside with brightly coloured mini-statues of the saints, selling walking sticks and branded clothing, all incongruously established in an ancient house with huge beams and fireplace. No energy for that today, nor the excellent centre of interpretation for the parish closes just beyond the church. I once worked very hard on the translations of that permanent exhibition. Now I'll settle for communing with the *enclos* from the resting-place of a low wall, clinging on to the knowledge that any minute a familiar car will clunk into sight by the *mairie* to fetch me and my canine companion, and I will not need to leave the village on foot, at least today.

The parish (*gui*) of good king Miliau brings us into the murky Dark Age history of violence, greed and political rivalry that enlivens much of the legendary Breton 6th century. It also brings a lot of confusion, as Miliau, a strong, popular ruler, was traditionally leader in Cornouaille, with a northern border of the Monts d'Arrée, so quite off piste here. For that reason some think the Miliau of Guimiliau was perhaps not him at all but an immigrant monk of that name from Great Britain. But the story of noble Miliau, to become a secular saint, and his little son Mélar or Méloir is so important in the Breton canon that the geography has been glossed. He is shown above the door and on his altarpiece every inch a king, with crown and sword, and on a precious woven banner surviving from the 17th century like a country gentleman with felt hat and thin moustache.

Entering the modest monumental gate, attention is inevitably diverted from the church by the spectacular calvary which looks as if a large crowd of people have been tipped onto it from above and stuck fast. Here is a clear example of the narrative power of these devices, a lithic cartoon frieze to materialise the last days of Christ and his sufferings before a triumphant resurrection. It was designed as a lesson open to all of the faith, literate or not. The priest could persuade with outdoor larger-than-life visual aids, like any teacher using powerpoint in a classroom. But the closer details tell other stories too. There's a stone vignette of Katel Golett, the Breton girl who was too fond of drinking and dancing and so pulled down into the mouth of hell by demons. Her terrible fate is a salutary lesson, but the sculptor obviously lingered lovingly over the shaping of her large bare breasts.

The entrance to the church is likewise rich in details, so many that the surprising, seductively smiling siren tucked into the pediment over the porch often goes unnoticed. There are a lot of intriguing carved details in

this *enclos*, like the bizarre cockerel and baby in the entrance and a pair of wrestlers in hairy tights guarding the doorway. It's almost like fun, if you add Noah, drunk as a lord, being supported by his sons on the outer arch, and the peeping pairs of animals on the ark. The heavy seriousness of the Catholic message is relieved by such small touches that emphasise the humanity at the heart of every story. The parish closes reflect contemporary society which built them in numerous ways, from fashions and hairstyles of many figures, to references to people or events that may be totally obscure to us now. I can't imagine that some very distinctive faces were not directly modelled on locals, for good or ill.

Amongst the conventional altars are representations of Saint Joseph (his cult revived by Louis XIV in 1661) and the Virgin Mary giving the beads of the rosary with all their attendant prayers to Saint Dominic. Much more Breton is that devoted to the local hero, Miliau. The dedicated altarpiece inside the church shows his terrible fate at the hands of his own brother Rivod, who wanted to seize the kingdom for himself. A painted panel shows the murdered man holding his severed head in his hands, whilst his wife shields him protectively. This is an interesting link to the fate of Miliau's son, Mélar, a child at the time his father died. He too was destined for a dreadful death on the orders of his uncle, and this tragic fate will materialise in mysterious circumstances at a destination further along the Tro Breiz route.

Another day unfolds, showery and cold. But pilgrimage is walking in any weather, going on against all obstacles. So I keep telling myself. Another day, another attitude. Suffering as authentification might be some kind of badge of honour in the end. The trees are not yet in leaf, but soft yellow flowers of tender gorse and newly ploughed fields speak of full spring to come. Beside the road lies the *fontaine* dedicated to Marie-Amice Picard, a Breton mystic from the nearby hamlet of Kergam. She bore the stigmata and was said to suffer the actual pains of martyrs on their anniversaries. Her extreme behaviour eventually led to accusations of witchcraft, but she was supported by powerful religious admirers. She died on Christmas day in 1652 and is buried in the cathedral of Saint-Pol-de-Léon. Lauded by some and scorned by others, her life trod a weird line between accepted practice and moral outrage, a whole new dimension of the religious experience.

I glance back to wonderful views of the northern crests of the Monts d'Arrée, Roc'h Trévezel and little Roc'h Ruz in clear profile on either side of the communications mast. A decided pang strikes me to be finally leaving these beloved familiars, but it's some consolation to remember that they are not going anywhere even if I am. There are new things to be seen and felt. The cord can stretch without being cut. I'm also in a rhythm of walking now that is bodily comfortable and although I know I need a rest I won't stop yet, scraping up some physical determination after yesterday's time of doubt. It's important not to break the continuum. Through the fields of bright rape flowers I come to a lovely sunken way, the tree trunks bending gracefully to shelter the path. It descends to the river Penzé, that staple of my march northwards, but I turn off for a short detour just beforehand and climb up to Roc'h Toul (the pierced rock) a cave of Mesolithic occupation in a towering outcrop of bright sandstone.

This place is surely touching the sacred. Simple, natural architecture and yet the atmosphere is mesmerising, quite distinct from its surroundings. Here twelve thousand years ago a little group of humans created a place of safety and protection from the elements. It may have provided only seasonal or intermittent occupation, but they left stone tools and charcoal residue for us to find in an unimaginably different world. Inside the cave perhaps nothing has really changed since then. The interior room is backed by a rocky shelf that leads into a second chamber running a long way back into the cliff-face. It's blocked to protect a colony of bats whose ancestors may have enjoyed the very same habitat when itinerant groups of humans roamed the rich countryside establishing shelters and tracking prey. Few visitors here means a purer atmosphere than at some better known sites.

Over the river there's a long, steep ascent through drifts of wood anemones to Luzec, where the gîte complex used to be a conference centre with historical lectures on Sunday afternoons. It was a great stimulation twenty years ago, and the former owner, academic and social historian Anne Guillou, has been a good friend to me and my writing ever since. I pass the unusual Luzec calvaire, perched high on four spindly legs with its back to the road. After the hamlet of Bougès come the first views of the grandiose bell-tower of Saint-Thégonnec far across the fields. It then seems to take an age to reach the outskirts of this expansive village, passing through a modern housing estate before descending to the dominant *enclos*. In contrast to the gentle sweetness of Guimiliau, this one is big, brash and bulbous.

Looking from outside a bulky triumphal entrance, a positive forest of finials pointing upwards drums home the grandeur of this ensemble, which is often regarded as the height of parish close achievement. It's certainly on a monumental scale, with every detail speaking of power and affluence. The calvary has some graphic representation of Christ's humiliation at the hands of bearded thugs in wrinkly leather boots. Inside, apart from the inevitable lavishness of decoration, there's a display relating to the terrible fire in 1998 caused by a neglected votive candle which resulted in extensive damage to the interior and a long period of restoration.

Saint Thégonnec himself appears here and there in large and miniature, accompanied by the image of a wolf and cart. In legend he forced this wild animal to pull the vehicle full of building materials after the wolf killed the stag he was using. The story is symbolic: many Breton saints carry tales of taming wolves, the wild free spirits of ancient paganism, now in captivity by the greater will of God. The construction site is also a powerful image, because the role of saints as the founders of communities is at the very heart of their abiding presence in Brittany's culture. The monastic settlement of an important saint soon attracted the followers, artisans and traders needed to grow a whole neighbourhood. Not to mention the crowds that sought out a miracle-worker, healer or super preacher.

So many villages today bear the names of saints in one way or another, undisguised like Saint-Malo, or with the addition of prefixes. These commemorate not only the individuals concerned, but also the subsequent flowering of Christianity. Saints were the seeds. Out of many possible examples, *Plou* (meaning parish) gives Plouneour (Saint Eneour), *Gui* (parish) Guimiliau (Saint Miliau), and *Lan* (holy place of, monastery) Lannédern (Saint Edern). *Loc* (hermitage/holy place) as in Locronan for Saint Ronan, was a later usage. The patron then retains his traditions and notoriety through legends, miracles (often performed through the relics of his bones, and the waters of the holy spring or *fontaine*), and the annual day of celebration for each saint known as a Pardon.

At this event the banners portraying the holy man or woman are carried in procession, symbol of the village itself, and followed by the entire community who would share a day of religious ritual, feasting and celebration. Many villages still feel great loyalty and pride in their saints, who provide this opportunity for the expression of collective sentiment that has fewer chances to manifest today. There is also still an element of that personal connection, even affection, in the relationship of saints and individuals that is well preserved in the oral tradition. So intimate was this affinity that it was not unknown for the statues of saints to be 'punished' if they did not come up with the goods. Fishermen on the Île de Sein are said to have turned poor Corentin to face the wall when a prayer for the right wind was not fulfilled!

But enough is enough. I begin to find all the imagery and bombardment of message wearisome after a time at Saint-Thégonnec and it gets hard to isolate the glorious individual touches under such a mass of promulgation. The admiration of art and architecture for its own sake regardless of context is something of an unsatisfactory compromise. The effect must have been (and indeed still be) the reverse for the faithful, affirming and inspiring the Catholic journey, such images firing the imagination of medieval and modern pilgrims. We all need to find our sources of comfort and support, but mine will always be outside under the sky. Suffering from a surfeit of architectural niceties, both weighty and claustrophobic in large doses, I'm relieved to be leaving parish close country for a change of tone, a return to something more elemental, and fortunately the route now tends to glorious natural scenes, historic ruins of a very different ilk, and then the open horizons of the coast.

## 3 Opening out: romantic ruins, a founding saint and finding the right place

On a beautiful day in early May my dog and I set off from Saint-Thégonnec, following Tro Breiz signs out of the village downhill on vibrant woodland paths. It feels like the perfect start, but I soon manage to misremember the directions and find myself crossing the motorway on a rough road bridge and heading out into heavily farmed, forbidding territory. I go back and have the good fortune to meet a young man out walking, swishing a great stick much taller than me and whistling happily. He knows all the local paths, giving me very detailed directions before moving on briskly, fast enough not to see me go wrong again within seconds, soon hitting the main road instead of the quiet sylvan route he had outlined. Full of shame, I return and immediately see the tiny path that did indeed turn into a delightful way. Twenty minutes later my good Samaritan appears again, having completed a whole loop whilst I dithered about in the valley.

After that, all is well, as I enjoy fine long views back over the fields to the church tower of the parish close, dominating its surroundings. Once through a tunnel under the motorway I begin to relax and enjoy the blue sky, full of bubbly little clouds, and grain crops burgeoning beside the path. The busy N12 running parallel is no hindrance to appreciating the sense of openness and adventure in prospect. Where directions are unequivocal and well-signed, there is more mental energy for observation and sheer pleasure in the countryside. The way is a friend not an opponent!

Finally turning into the valley of the Penzé for a long descent, I become totally absorbed in natural beauty as the path snakes down steep slopes to a comely wide river. The very water smells fresh and invigorating, whilst its rippling sound fills this enclosed space within layers of trees. When the path crosses a little foot-bridge over the flow soon after, the secret fluvial world is briefly edged by a huge rock-face showing the depth of the valley. Then after a peaceful stretch through meadows, the path rises into the upper lines of woodland, a stylised black ermine sign on one trunk being the only Tro Breiz indication visible for the rest of today's journey. (This symbol of independent ducal Brittany is used on both new and old waymarking for the pilgrimage.)

Horned red cattle sit lazily in the sunshine as I briefly rest on a rock looking down on their territory. It would be lovely to spend a day like this doing nothing but be silently lost in the landscape of this idyllic valley, but I'm conscious that this is a long stage by my standards and I need to press on northwards. A friendly support car is waiting way up ahead should I need it. Past the shell of an old mill in a hamlet, we edge a long field planted with what look like Indian bean trees, bearing huge oval leaves. The route soon leaves the riverside for a while, taking a loftier line on the wooded hillside above with a couple of breaks into human occupied territory. One hamlet contains a former paper mill, a reminder of the working history of the Penzé valley.

The path seems endless, full of petty ups and down, and without views. At one stage I have to pick up the dog when a cheery line of elderly walkers in bright outdoor gear squeezes past in leisurely fashion. It is a relief finally to get back down to the Penzé, and the last lonely section of this is fabulous, with the sweet stream like a gentle companion, and vegetation so luxurious it gives a decided feel of venturing forward through the jungle. A fantastic oak tree, which must be the king of the woodland in these parts, grows strikingly tall on the very edge, spreading sculptural arms out over the river. Its strength and life force have veritable presence, a salient sense of individual character, more real than many a saint.

A final crossing beside a weir carrying the wide lacy water in a delicate rush, and the hill of the Château de Penhoat is looming ahead. The friend who is meeting me here appears from that direction with his dog and escorts me up the sharp slope to overlook the rather romantic remains of this ruined castle. The name Penhoët or Penhoat means 'the edge of the wood'. Its situation well exemplifies this area full of narrow river valleys separated by bumpy hills, the whole generously covered by a density of trees. One stocky battered tower with masked windows, built in solid blocks of local schist, is the most evocative remnant of the fortifications. There's only the base of another together with a section of the east curtain wall to provide evidence of this high bastion above the river.

But the steep banks and deep ditches surrounding the castle mound give quite a graphic sense of the former defensive structure at the confluence of the Penzé and its tributary the Coatoulzac'h. It was built in 1248 by Guillaume de Penhoat, a crusader on return home from the Holy Land. What can be seen today is mainly 14th century, surviving the final destruction during the Wars of Religion two hundred years later. The Penhoat family were rich and influential, with this valley specifically exempt from the *fouage* (hearth tax imposed on non-nobles), thanks to their services to the Duke of Brittany. Jean de Penhoat was admiral of Brittany from 1401 to 1432, and a loyal supporter of Jean V. He even accompanied the duke on a Tro Breiz journey of their own.

After a rest, I limp on to finish the day in the village of Penzé itself, wanting to complete the planned walk myself without help although I'm very tired, so the dogs are taken on in the car to await my arrival. From the château, the road passes the Moulin de Penhoat, an old paper mill converted to the production of flour later in the 19th century, vital services fuelled by the prolific Penzé and part of the Penhoat economic empire. The nearby hamlet of Noteric has some lovely old houses, including an ancient *manoir*, hiding behind stone walls and flowery landscaped gardens.

I pass between the sounds of the road above and the river beside me. There is not a Tro Breiz marker in sight. (I discover later that I missed a path off up the hillside for a short detour to the tiny chapel of Saint Vizias, a saint quite unknown to me, so go back in the car another time to check it out. It seems a sad little place, perched on the hillside with a forlorn and forgotten air, lit only by one very small window in the east end. Inevitably it is all locked up, but apparently a Pardon is still celebrated in July and it seems that Vizias is probably Saint Thivisiau, as in the town of Landivisiau, after all.)

The weather is changing fast with clouds pressing in, dampening the air. The footpath is muddy underfoot as I labour along a hilly track above the river towards the village. Hawthorn blooms luxuriantly to light the way, with little punctuation marks of varied yellow and pink in the banks below. Through the hamlet of Rumolou, there is a steep path down into one of the main streets which is heavily under siege by roadworks at the time of passing. Penzé was once a thriving port as the tidal river starts here, with boats taking out wood from nearby forests in the 18th century and later bringing in shell sand and marl from the Bay of Morlaix to further enrich the soil of Léon. What seems a tiny harbour now was obviously once bustling and thriving in the interests of the local economy. But with the deteriorating weather and the noisy roadworks, it is not a place to linger today and my walk is over.

Soon after I pick up the route here, with a long tedious road walk taking me on from Penzé to Pont Eon, the Eon being a confluent of the larger river. Here there is a resistance memorial beside the central bridge, commemorating Marcel Rochemulet, who was killed on August 8, 1944, aged just 22. The astonishing courage of locals under threat from occupying forces in WWII is a theme that will develop further on coastal reaches of this pilgrimage. A couple of hardy caravans are parked up overlooking the muddy expanse of low tide. Mud now becomes a recurrent assailant when the route finally leaves tarmac and diverts through farmland to cross the last hill before dropping down to the coast. A large herd of brown and white cows with recent calves mooch on one side, churning up their grassy plot, and newly sown soil speaks further of spring on the other. Across the fields I can see a railway bridge over the ever-widening Penzé, but the water is too low to be visible. There is a strong and welcome sense of the landscape opening out as I move ever closer to the sea.

Tro Breiz markers (at last!) sign the route over the D769 and down a no-through road to the start of what will be an engagingly lovely waterside walk. A small tributary water-course comes in from under the road to lead me back to the Penzé. I pause to step down towards a rough beach behind the last house and sink deep into the succulent mud that lines the bed like the flesh of a skinned monster. The banks of this grey mass are criss-crossed with etching-like patterns, their private life revealed in the daily tidal ritual.

The great columns of the railway viaduct (for the Morlaix/Roscoff line) dominate the near view and I am soon back along the main river, heading for the coast. The trees are not yet in full leaf, but fresh young green pioneers shine out above bluebells and celandines dotted amongst the trees. The path is up and down but well-maintained with wooden steps and handrails where necessary, although protruding heads of large nails make some as hazardous as the gradients. A pretty *lavoir* or washing-place suddenly appears to the left, reached by a path made from stout tree trunk rings, fed by a crystal clear stream that tumbles on down to join the river.

When I finally emerge from the trees there are more signs of the farming year picking up pace sharply, with fields of rapeseed already booming out their yellow presence, in contrast with the fresh chestnut complexion of just-turned soil. Boats are moored in the centre of the channel as the river widens and traffic thunders over the Pont de la Corde on the way up to Roscoff. It is Sunday, and many couples and families are out walking this enticing riverside route. My dog is going through a depressing 'teenage' phase of leaping and barking at anything that comes near and I have to do a lot of apologising and restraining as we near the car-park by the bridge. But it feels like a fine achievement to have reached the coast at last and to know that I'm within striking distance of the first cathedral town of the Tro Breiz, Saint-Pol-de-Léon.

Before any bridges existed over the Penzé here, a ferry crossed the river with the aid of cords stretched across the flow for guidance. Hence the name Pont de la Corde for the current bridge, built in 1967, replacing an earlier version. The coast brings an expansion of views and spirits as all the open highways of the sea point to the widest possibilities of travel out across the Bay of Morlaix into the Channel and beyond. Not to mention saints coming the other way in their little boats so long ago, still so easy to imagine as the eternity of the sea smooths out even deep wrinkles of time. The littoral also accentuates the notion of Brittany as an edge place with the dual personality of a shore that absorbs arrivals and suffers departures with the same detachment.

The coast path north to Roscoff is on small roads initially, passing close to the site of the neolithic dolmen of Kerivin, or rather its somewhat scrunched remains. Presumably the site was carefully chosen by our distant forebears for the monument to be visible from the water (or watery plain then) below. There is also plenty of evidence around here of Léon's status as the prime vegetable-growing area of France. Cauliflowers, cabbages, onions and artichokes are the staples. The 'Johnnies' who went over to Britain from the mid 19th to the mid 20th centuries with their bicycles, berets and strings of onions have immortalised this produce of Roscoff. Brittany Ferries was founded by militant producer Alexis Gourvennec in

1973 to exploit this abundance in cross-Channel markets. Prize specimens were flown to restaurants in Paris and even from there (by Concorde) to New York. There has never been a lack of determined ambition among the agricultural community here. A long tradition of organised action over infrastructure and price wars with retailers have regularly seen many tons of vegetables being dumped on major roads and the centre of Morlaix blocked off by tractors.

My route northwards roughly follows the coast via little roads and footpaths, with excellent views over the Bay of Morlaix. From the Pointe de Saint Jean vistas of the seaside portion of Saint-Pol-de-Léon open up at last, and I stop to visit an unusual little octagonal dovecote beside the sadly neglected chapel of Saint-Charles-Borromée, both hidden in trees just a few steps off the path. The patronage of a 16th century Italian cardinal feels rather out of place in this territory of less historical but far more relevant Breton saints, who are part and parcel of the land itself. Thinking of this connection reminds me that further north in Léon is the territory of Saint Goulven, who is said to have asked for a gift from a neighbour. The man filled the messenger's tunic with earth and sent him back, but in front of the saint, the folds revealed a pile of gold. This symbolic transformation story is a proud expression preserved in the oral tradition of the fecundity of the high plain of Léon, a reality which has maintained the prosperity of this area over the centuries.

Following a causeway across the inlet by the walled bounds of the Château de Kernevez, I arrive at the port of Pempoul, which may or may not have been where Saint Pol landed when seeking his permanent settlement. Here at last I begin to touch on the story of one of the founding saints. Following the road up to the town centre through Gourveau, I pass a small *fontaine* said to have been created by the saint, today feeding a huge *lavoir* once used for bleaching cloth and washing clothes. Here Pol met a swineherd who agreed to lead him to the local lord, who was based on the Île de Batz, via the 'Town of the Dead'. This was the former Roman *castrum* (camp) where the town of Saint-Pol stands today.

Pol found a deserted site of abandoned earthworks and some wild inhabitants: a boar and her litter, a bear, a bull. These symbolic representatives of untamed paganism were soon dealt with. The bear disappeared, the bull obeyed an order to leave and the boar was domesticated. But the saint did incur local anger by having an oak tree, focus of pagan worship (with its Druidic associations) and containing a swarm of bees, cut down. He redistributed the bees to indicate that he came bearing gifts and then had the whole site cleansed and blessed, with salt and holy water sprinkled around the boundary. This is the foundation legend for Saint-Pol-de-Léon.

I am soon approaching the modern town centre, full of ancient splendour, increasingly awed by the spire up ahead, not of the cathedral, but the Chapelle de Kreizker. It is the tallest such pinnacle in Brittany, powering up into the sky, saved from destruction after the French Revolution by a decree of Napoléon who was persuaded of its usefulness to shipping as a daymark. The door is open today so I go in briefly to pay my respects to the Tro Breiz altar of the Seven Founding Saints, a first physical indication of the pilgrimage I've been following. Colourful little statues show Pol, Tugdual, Brieuc, Malo, Samson, Patern and Corentin together with their icons, hinting at legendary achievements. I am not tempted to climb the very narrow tower staircase, having no head for heights, but the views over the coast must be spectacular.

And finally, arrival at the cathedral of Saint-Pol-de-Léon. It's a sombre experience on a dull day, even though recent cleaning has enhanced the grandeur of the west face. It is hard to imagine feeling much further from the wild height in the Monts d'Arrée where I began my journey. Here is all the formality and structure of organised religion. Inside, I wander about looking at the skull boxes and their grisly contents beneath a painting of Saint Pol, somehow shown huge in comparison with his iconic dragon. In the choir, full of richly carved oak stalls, the same two figures are portrayed, and off the north aisle, a Neo-Gothic gilt reliquary containing the relics of the saint (skull, arm bone and finger) is topped by a statue of Pol with another superb dragon at his feet.

This symbol reflects a story of events on the Île de Batz when Pol made acquaintance with the lord of the land, at his villa on this elongated island just off the coast by Roscoff. Withur welcomed the new arrival (they may even have been cousins) and was soon asking for his help in ridding Batz of a marauding dragon which was destroying crops and eating people. The saint obliged, using his stole like a lead to escort this monster to the rocks beside the sea and persuade the beast to hurl itself into the waves. (This feat of order destroying wildness is commonly attributed

to various other saints in other places, a representation of Christianity's triumph over the destructive dangers of paganism.) The dragon is an elemental beast symbolically, with wings (air), scales (water), tail (earth) and, of course, fiery breath. A series of evocative stained glass windows (1920s) in the choir side-chapel illustrates all these events surrounding the arrival of Saint Pol and his subsequent settlement, with the saint ageing in each depiction.

Just as interesting is Saint Pol's back-story. The manuscript of his earliest *Vita* or Life was written down in 884 by a monk named Wrmonoc at the Abbaye de Landévennec, perhaps Brittany's oldest monastery. Other later biographies and local traditions add details. Pol, born about 480CE, was from an eminent Welsh family (his Latin name Paulus Aurelianus suggests a connection with the famous Ambrosius Aurelianus who fought the Anglo-Saxons in the 5th century, and may have been the model for King Arthur). He studied at the monastic school of Llantwit Major under Saint Ildud before his great missionary expedition, firstly to Cornwall, where he was refused a bell to take on his further journey by King Mark. It miraculously later turned up in Brittany in the belly of a salmon, and is claimed to be the one on display in Saint Pol's cathedral today.

Pol's first landfall over the Channel was on the island of Ouessant, before moving to the continent and travelling east in search of settlement. Every time he stopped with his 12 followers and began to build huts and oratories for worship, angelic visitations occurred to drive him onwards. By his choice of vocabulary, Wrmonoc in Pol's *Vita* draws an astonishing parallel with the journey of Trojan hero Aeneas, desperately seeking a home in the Mediterranean after the fall of Troy, and believing he had found it in Carthage. Vergil's *Aeneid* describes how he began a passionate love affair with Queen Dido and started to supervise the building of a new city. That is until Mercury, messenger of the gods, turns up to spoil it all. '*Quid struis?*' he says, contemptuously, what are you building? This is not your destined location.

Wrmonoc takes this classical dilemma word for Latin word in his life of Saint Pol. *Quid hic struis?* What are you building *here*? Meaning in effect, stop wasting your time in isolated locations building little huts and get on with your mission. '*Alia terra .... alius locus*', another land, another place is waiting for you. The angel remonstrates with Pol's premature desire to end his journey and settle down in one spot rather than wrestle with the constant practical demands of travel. Told to go and find the local ruler, he continues eastwards, perhaps on Roman roads, just as pilgrims would do later in honouring him. It was a kind of proto-pilgrimage in itself, the traveller forced to continue his migration until the signs are auspicious for settlement. There are places and then there is the right place.

After the arrival at his destined site and the meeting with Withur on the Île de Batz, Pol's future was again decided for him, with pressure to take the role of bishop in a new mainland town. Withur sent a note to Paris, and the Frankish emperor Childebert declared Pol bishop of a new settlement where Saint-Pol-de-Léon stands today. Pol had little choice but to follow the public path laid down for him. A quiet retreat and a life of prayer on the island where he had hopefully established a monastery were not to be. Sainthood is nothing if not devout, and diligently he fulfilled his role, applying himself to the organisation of Christianity in the region of Léon. Place-names reflect the later spread of his cult – Lampaul-Guimiliau, Lampaul-Ploudalmezeau, Mespaul.

Even eventual retirement did not bring Saint Pol peace and respite from public demands. He was soon recalled from the Île de Batz to resume the episcopal role when his successor died suddenly. A second retreat to Batz did not last long before death, but even then he was not allowed to lie quietly. A dispute ensued between monks on the island and monks in the cathedral town over where the body should be buried. It was left to oxen pulling the corpse in a cart to decide, and they moved across the strait, uncovered at low tide, to choose the cathedral side. This story reflects an important later issue of pilgrimage and its economic power. The body or relics of a saint were often claimed as the source of miracles, which attracted more people and therefore more donations and offerings to a church or chapel. Those of the founding saints like Saint Pol in his cathedral were vital in the pursuit of the Tro Breiz in the medieval period.

This strong sense of journey in Pol's progress is in effect a quest motif. Of finding the right place. Of making a home. Of settling. It is something many of us are familiar with. I have lived in half a dozen different habitations in Finistère, all around the Monts d'Arrée, that land poor in soil and rich in soul. That central compass of my life, a fusion of spirit and topography. I have been driven on from particular spots by racist neighbours, by sundered relationships, by sheer poverty, but nothing can break the cord of my special place, which bound me tight on my very first visit to Brittany. We all make our own maps, saints included, and the Tro Breiz arrival at each of the seven cathedral towns honours this achievement of the founders, who did not necessarily have a straight and easy path to the discovery of destination.

## 4 Meeting bravery: daring escapes, King Arthur's dining table and a mountain vision

Setting out from the cathedral in Saint-Pol-de-Léon, I return to the coast by a slightly different route to take in the Champs de la Rive, a vantage point over the bay. In the foreground is the peninsula of Saint Anne, partly obscured by trees, and beyond, the long strip of Île Callot off Carantec. To the north it is just possible to see the ferry port of Roscoff, with its deep water harbour constructed for Brittany Ferries at Bloscon. It's a grey, windy spring day, not the moment to hang around. Sometimes one just wants to get on the march, so instead of retracing the same route along the shore, I'm getting a lift back to the Pont de la Corde. Still, thoughts of cross-channel exchanges are inevitable in this area, with a long history of conflict, commerce and contraband between England and the Breton shore.

There's another aspect too. Once over the bridge across the Penzé, I head on foot eastwards onto the edge of the estuary. Low tide presents an alternative vision of coastal life, a tableau of grey mud and grey water against the grey sky. The line of stranded small boats lies placid beside a thin channel lightly ruffled in the lull before reactivation with rising water. It is like walking through a still life, bringing human motion into this world of deceptive inactivity. A few steps beyond the Pont de la Corde is a modest monument, dedicated to Jacques Guéguen (1876-1957), a local sailor and fisherman, one of the first to smuggle French and British fighters out of occupied Brittany during WWII. He made trips over the Channel to Jersey and once as far as England in his small boat. It was called *Le Pourquoi Pas* - The Why Not - after a famous ship wrecked in Iceland in 1936. A ship that Gueguen had actually served on, between 1908 and 1910 in Antarctica, part of an exploratory voyage led by Jean-Baptiste Charcot, and only one of three long-haul expeditions Gueguen participated in during the first decade of the 20th century.

*Pourquoi pas?* There were good reasons why not, not least German soldiers, always on the lookout for resistance activity around here. The nearby boatyards of Carantec were a constant target of suspicion, and surreptitious heroic actions could easily lead to internment and death or the endangerment of family members. All this for the sake of often foreign nationals who had already openly taken up arms against the common enemy, but now needed help to get back to England. Gueguen himself was imprisoned for six months in 1941 following his first rescue missions, and he made his own escape a year later, aged 65, after learning he was again under surveillance by the Germans. It could be said those voyages were a form of pilgrimage, a statement of convictions, from uncertainty to safe haven, preserving life in dangerous times. And wasn't the notion of rescue behind the first crusades in the Holy Land?

After the war, this man, who had voyaged so far around the world and so intrepidly closer to home, returned to the peaceful life of a fisherman beside the Pont de la Corde, his selfless contribution acknowledged by awards of the *Légion d'honneur* and *Croix de Guerre*. No-one meeting him by chance in later life would have any idea of the wide human experience of this humble individual. The simple memorial here on the shore in 60s brutalist style, like a large chest freezer, bears a metal cross, a plaque and the main inscription reads simply *Passant, souviens toi* – Passer-by, remember.

The heroism of these men and women in Resistance networks is hard to forget here, even as today we live in a comfortable material world far removed from the demands of war-time stealth and secrecy. How to respond to the call to risk one's own life for unrelated others is not something we are likely to lose sleep over in contemporary rural Brittany. The stream of cars and lorries flashing along the main route over the bridge towards Roscoff, and modern houses with desirable views over the estuary packing the chain of little roads above the wide riverbed are reminders of life moving ever onwards. One hopes not in the direction of obliteration of the memory of men like Jacques Gueguen. Not all heroes die in action.

Sombre thoughts take over as I stand on the shore, mulling over the contrasts, suddenly reluctant to move on. This is a shrine of sorts, as important as that of any early medieval saint. As ever, the emotional tremors of WWII soon conjure up memories of my father, my beloved father, from whom I was estranged for many years. He fought in various theatres of the war, including the siege of Monte Cassino in Italy. A degree of survivor guilt always coloured his reluctant reminiscences: he later wrote a memoir ironically entitled A Good War. I suddenly remember the gap in his hand, the tight, scarred skin where his index finger had been. As a child I had no inkling of what had happened and thought 'lost' meant literally just that. It was hard to imagine the carelessness that could leave a whole digit lying around in some scrubby Italian woodland.

Further along the coast towards Carantec I come to another identical memorial, this time highlighting the name of the honoured deceased, Ernest Sibiril, a more renowned smuggler of human cargo, the boat-builder nicknamed 'The Ferryman' who was at the heart of a network of evacuation for allied forces. The monument has a very low profile, at the end of a no-through road with narrow access to the rocky beach and obscured from view by a thick hedge surround. From the shore, I'm looking directly across to Saint-Pol-de-Léon and the triple spikes of glory that proclaim the Kresiker Chapel and cathedral. A more modest spire on Île Callot is visible in the tree-line on the island. There is a little more activity now, with a few men engaged in *pêche à pied* on a shore resembling fustian patchwork, restrained colours of sand, rock and seaweed.

The outlook is beginning to broaden into the Bay of Morlaix, but even in clear daylight it is difficult to get to grips with the realities involved in clandestine activity on the water at night during the war. Nearly 200 people were saved by the courage and determination of Sibiril's actions. Finally suspected in July 1943, he went into hiding for some months before escaping in his famous little boat Le Requin (The Shark), now in the local maritime museum, and eventually making land at Plymouth. He became a pilot in the American navy before returning home after the war to Carantec. In 1950 General de Gaulle, whose family had stayed in the town before escaping to England, came to visit the shipyards and honour the bravery of Sibiril, whose memorial was erected in 1966. An unfortunate end to such a life, he died by drowning in 1961. The map of his life's journey is full of crossed boundaries.

All these dangerous voyages of evasion and escape are the inverse of the advent of the Breton saints, but they reflect the uncertainty of arrival and departure in adverse circumstances that have characterised these shorelines. Île Callot offers another tale of precarious edge places. I reach the causeway that gives access at low tide to this slim ribbon of an island, such an approach being an irresistible element for pilgrimage – a frisson of risk - which has led to many tide-permitting excursions to the chapel of Notre Dame on the highest point. This foundation is said to have been first created by Rivallon Murmaczon in 513, following his victory over Danish marauders who stashed loot from their raids on the island. He kept a promise to build a chapel in honour of the Virgin Mary on the site of the opposing chief's tent. The current version is from the 17th century. The name Callot comes from the Breton *Itron Varia ar Galloud* (Dame Mary of All Power).

Carantec is a disjointed sort of place, less interesting than what you can see from it. The town sits on a peninsula jutting out into the bay, with an undulating coastal path below reflecting the natural beauty of the site. From a painted daymark on the Pointe de Pen al Lann I feel I can almost reach out and touch little Île Louet with its mini lighthouse and patch of green, and the ominous Château du Taureau, welded to an apparently bull-shaped rock which accounts for the name. The fort was established in 1544 to guard the entrance to the Morlaix river, rather late response to a savage English raid on the town itself in 1522. Louis XIV's engineer Vauban later restored the building when another war with England was expected. It was to become a place of changing identity, with incarceration for political prisoners and feeble-minded relatives of aristocratic families. German occupation brought a return to defensive duties, but more recent incarnations include a wealthy individual's party house and a sailing school, before the current state of tourist venue. An interesting evolution, which has created a weighty on-site atmosphere.

Saint Carantec, whose unlovely 19th century church dominates the high town, came from the royal family of Ceredigion in Wales, a noble background shared by many saints. He rejected political and military ambitions for a religious vocation, creating a foundation at Llangrannog (where there is a bronze statue of him today) before going to Ireland to become a wandering monk in the mid 5th century. This is an eternal form of pilgrimage, an end in itself, the gyrovague in endless exile from monastery or church, with no goal, only a form of separation from accepted structures. The monk walks his self-imposed journey with nothing more than a knapsack, staff and bell, the latter to summon listeners for his preaching. I can't imagine infinite ambling with no goal in view, however distant and unlikely finishing the Tro Breiz seems to me at this moment.

In legend, Carantec did actually found a monastery in Ireland, where in accordance with custom he was entrusted with the upbringing of the young noble Thenenan. They became close friends. One small ancient statuette of the two together is above the high altar in the church here. The latter is portrayed as small as a child, holding his mentor's hand and gazing up at him. It's an unsettling image. Saint Carantec got rid of a dragon in the Bay of Morlaix, splitting the rock now known as Rocher de Carantec when he hurled the beast out to sea, a rather more muscular approach than Saint Pol's effortless spiritual authority. There is no clear tradition of his history in Brittany, although toponyms like Grannog (Île de Batz) and Ranngrannog (Plouguerneau) suggest association. He is not to be confused with Saint Caradoc or Saint Caradec, both much later holy men, but his traditions are indicative of common patterns in the lives of the Breton saints, with vague association in different places on both sides of the Channel.

A strange episode involves Saint Carantec in England, documented by a manuscript in the British Museum. During a stay in Somerset, he threw his portable stone altar into the River Severn, vowing to spread the word of God wherever it landed. This turned out to be the current town of Carhampton, where King Arthur was using the altar as a dining table. He said he would only return it if Carantec got rid of a terrorising dragon. This miracle achieved, Arthur was shown the error of his ways by everything spontaneously falling off the so-called table. A bizarre tale, which has echoes in Arthur's somewhat shady reputation in Brittany, as we shall see in other places on the Tro Breiz route.

From Carantec the path hugs the coast past the golf course and former oyster-farm at Ty Nod, but unfortunately there is no pedestrian route beside the Morlaix river, only a busy road, so I take a long diversion past the inland lighthouse Phare de la Lande, following minor roads into the village of Locquenolé. This little haven has a beautiful church dedicated to Saint Guénolé, one of the most important Breton saints (although not one of the founders). In fact he was a first-generation immigrant, his parents Fragan and Gwenn having arrived from Wales to settle where today Ploufragan stands north of Saint-Brieuc. When Guénolé thought of going to Ireland to honour Saint Patrick, an angelic vision told him to remain in Armorica and found an abbey. This was to be the renowned centre of learning that was the Abbaye de Landévennec. It's still there in medieval ruined state today on the Rade de Brest at the end of the Aulne estuary. The modern Benedictine construction on the hill above contains an important library of Breton history open to researchers, where I have spent many hours over the years.

In Locquénolé Saint Guénolé is said to have established a small monastery and struck the ground with his staff to produce a spring where the pretty *fontaine* remains to this day. Its water became the focus of healing for eye complaints and even blindness. This is a reference to the story that his sister Clervie had her eye plucked out by a goose but the saint retrieved and restored it, in a startling early demonstration of his powers! This important link between source and saint is one of the ways Christianity sought a hold over the land and natural forces. If the holy men were able to produce water, the essence of life, then their god must be the ultimate controller. Later, relics were often dipped in the *fontaines*, a ritual to refresh their miraculous power.

Friends Julia and Phil join me for a visit to the church, which has undergone extensive recent restoration. We admire the superb Romanesque capitals around the transept and climb a meticulously crafted modern turning stair to the tribune, a raised platform at the back of the church offering views from above. It is an interesting change of perspective. Outside the church, the village also has a rare surviving *Arbre de la Liberté*, or Liberation Tree, planted at the time of the Revolution. A few months after we were there, a mighty limb crashed down into the square, raising issues of the tree's safe survival.

A rather tortuous and hilly detour through the Bois de Lannigou follows, before reaching the landmark of the Chapelle de la Salette (1860), with its stations of the cross on the steeply descending path. This elegant construction has, from afar, the striking slender grace of a lone birch tree, dominating the Morlaix river. The name echoes that of a place in the French Alps, where in 1846 a weeping apparition of the Virgin Mary came to two young shepherds on a rocky pinnacle. The children said she told them she was crying for the sins of men, urging repentance and renewal of the Christian faith. She was particularly scathing about the profanation of Sunday's sanctity.

There was much agitated dispute about the authenticity and value of this vision. But the Augustinian order of nuns established at the former Franciscan monastery down at road level here in Finistère, hearing the news of this far-off event, were impressed, and even more so when two of their number were cured of serious illness by a series of novenas, which at last had effect on the anniversary of the vision. A chapel in honour of Our Lady was consecrated on this spot in 1860. The main statue inside shows Mary sitting on a mountain, covering her eyes with her hands. The local priest of the real La Salette in the Alps sent the nuns here a fragment of the hill where the vision appeared, an interesting use of place as relic.

The bones of a mountain, like the bones of a saint. The landscape in Christian tradition becomes sacred as the location of revelation. Divine presence is imposed on the mountain, rather than emerging from it. But all this is a reminder of the appeal of the visionary in Breton culture, in religion and legend. Apparitions, divine appearances, ghosts and mystical messages all strike deep into the heartland of emotional response in Brittany. It will be a recurrent phenomenon along the way of the Tro Breiz, and visionaries often garner more local enthusiasm than those old Breton saints from the Dark Ages. La Salette on the Morlaix river became an important place of Marian pilgrimage, with devotions in 1870 during the disastrous events of the Franco-Prussian War, and its terrible loss of life, especially of Bretons who were sacrificed in the front line without proper equipment.

I stop at river level to have a quick look at the original emplacement of worship. This whole site is a layer-cake of religious history. At the foot of the hill, the Franciscan monastery was founded in 1458, destroyed by fire and rebuilt. It housed a printing press in the late 16th century, and the famous hagiographer Albert Le Grand who wrote the seminal, hugely influential work *La Vie des saincts de la Bretaigne armorique*, (Lives of the Breton Saints) published in 1637, spent time here. The church still stands, but by 1830 the buildings were all in dire straits. The remains were bought by a local noblewoman for the religious order of Augustinian Hospitallers from Quimper, who were in need of a new home and still have one here. Their practical faith established a hospital, school and retirement home, the latter still functioning today. The last glimpse as I move on is of a romantic-looking tiny oratory raised up in the grounds and fast disappearing in the luscious vegetation.

The route soon enters woodland again to come out behind the youth hostel in Morlaix. This medieval town is set deep in the valleys of two rivers, the Queffleuth and the Jarlot, with the historic centre at their confluence where the Town Hall now stands. The old port was here before it gradually retreated downriver, making way for commercial traffic and finally, car-parks. Morlaix thrived on European trade through its harbour, with tobacco an important local commodity, fashioned into products in La Manufacture on the quayside. I pass this great site, which is being slowly developed into a centre of cultural significance: eminent Breton publishers Skol Vreizh are based there now.

But the key economic success for the town was the cloth trade with England. Every stage of fabric production was carried out in the surrounding countryside, providing occupation and income for many, before the bales were transported by cart to Morlaix where hundreds of English merchants could be found in the 17th century. It was lucrative business for everyone in the chain. Nobles gave up their status to indulge in commercial transactions and beautify tall town houses with majestic fireplaces and fine furniture. The life-style of these urban aristocrats is vividly conjured up by one such extraordinary building in Grand'Rue, an example of the unique architecture of the *maison à pondalez*.

The historical relationship of Morlaix with the English is ambivalent. In 1522 a flotilla of English ships broached the estuary and made an attack on the walled city, entering through subterfuge, when the garrison was absent. They also ransacked merchants' houses along the quays, amassing booty including an inordinate quantity of wine. Most re-embarked and got away safely but several hundred stayed to drink and celebrate on the right bank above the port. They were still there when an avenging force of soldiers rode back to the town. The Fontaine aux Anglais on the quay (today in a 1716 version, see over) commemorates the day when this stream ran red with the blood of the slaughtered English.

The construction of the Château du Taureau was a later security measure to prevent a repeat of this disaster and it has indeed successfully protected Morlaix from naval attack up to now. It was no protection for air raids, however, and in 1943 RAF bombers came up that same river to bomb the viaduct, a vital train link to Brest for the occupying forces. One arch was knocked out, but there was terrible collateral damage as the school at the west end of the viaduct was also hit, killing 39 children and their teacher. The Germans restored the train line within days.

Crossing from the left to right bank of the Morlaix river at Place Cornic is to step from the historic district of Léon into the Trégor. It's a symbolic move from the once intensely religious and reputationally dour territory of Léon, often designated the 'Land of Priests', into a softer landscape. I am now shifting into a whole new phase of the Tro Breiz journey.

## 5  Savouring small moments: a singular cosmos, Dark Age murk and mutilation

Rivers will be at the root of most of my journey across the Trégor. This historic territory stretched along the north of Brittany from Morlaix eastward to the Trieux estuary. Guingamp, strategically placed for major routes, was the political capital, Tréguier the religious centre developed around the ancient cathedral of Saint Tugdual. At the time of the Revolution, the new departments decided in 1790 cut a swathe across such traditional connections, splitting the area between Finistère (from the Morlaix river to the Douron) and Côtes du Nord, the original name of what is now Côtes d'Armor.

This is one of the many wounds perceived to have been inflicted on Brittany by the new French Republic in the late 18th century. And before the terrible suppression of the Breton language began, there was another equally profound blow: the rejection of the religious faith so deeply embedded in Breton life. Cathedrals were sacked, statues of the saints burnt in the new Republican zeal to stamp out Catholicism. Temples to the Goddess Reason were the order of the day in towns. Many Catholic monarchist rebels, known as Chouans, engaged in rural guerilla warfare for more than a decade after the Revolution in defence of their traditional beliefs and values.

The granite plateau of inland Tregor is distinctive by its wooded estuaries, dotted with homely manor houses on an intimate scale and villages of warm hue. It's these small self-contained units of beauty, like the idyllic setting of the Château de Tonquedec above the Leguer river, sadly not on my Tro Breiz route, that move me rather than the coast.

The latter is the biggest draw for tourism, particularly the world-famous Pink Granite Coast near Perros-Guirec, which has become Trégor's cliché. Passing through the interior of this land on foot offers a walker the most illuminating aspect of Brittany's landscape, instinctive relationship with a series of separate scenes in beautiful countryside of modest proportions.

I walk out of Morlaix via Ploujean and up through woods around the old Château du Suscinio, today the site of an agricultural college, to the coastal village of Dorduff-en-Mer for a last look at the Bay of Morlaix. Then it's time to move inland, following the estuary along a bumpy path through trees. It wends up and down above the water, although there's very little of this at low tide when I pass, and a wide expanse of deep muddy curves provides a grey foil to the burgeoning vegetation. A short detour takes me up to the unusual chapel of Saint Antoine (1574) in Plouezoc'h, first shown to me by my friend Mado, who lives in the village.

On approach it resembles a brightly painted Swiss chalet, with a wooden grill and outer door in red and light blue, enclosing the old porch. Animal and human faces decorate the finely turned spindles and lower panels between two squat granite pillars. On the exterior northern wall is a fine black and white representation of the ermine, symbol of the duchy of Brittany. Inside, the eponymous patron is accompanied by his traditional symbols of bell and pig, and there's a typical representation of St Yves, patron saint of Brittany, between a rich man and poor man. Yves will become more and more present on this journey as I move towards his home territory at the heart of the Trégor.

He was an historical figure of the late 13th century, known for indefatigable trekking on foot all over the area to spread the word of God, and is still associated with specific rocks, rivers and pathways. Whichever route one chooses today for undertaking the Tro Breiz, there will be the chance for close connection with not only wondrous religious heritage and sites of powerful historical interest, but a real sense of the imprint on the landscape of the saints. From tales of legendary Dark Age miracle workers preaching and healing at specific sites, to the liberal sprinkle of chapels, sacred springs (often said to be 'produced' by saints) and wayside crosses in even thinly populated areas, they have left their mark.

The people often interpreted their rural surroundings in terms of saintly presence (such as caves used for hermitages) and action, especially the hurling of rocks (mostly at the Devil, but occasionally at each other) to explain the phenomenon of huge granite boulders congregating in deep river valleys. When local processions were held to honour their patron saints, every step of the route, every striking tree and stone, every passage over streams became associated in memory with the holy men (and a few women) who had once traversed or settled in the vicinity. This intimacy with nature was the norm right up to the 20th century in Brittany, and walking the incomparable journey of the Tro Breiz now offers the opportunity of reconnection.

From the chapel of Saint Antoine the route drops down towards the Dorduff again, soon following a narrow ribbon of earth through effervescent greenery, with flickers of brightness penetrating the tall trees lining the path. One early lesson of this pilgrimage is that sacred can be surprise. An unprepossessing *fontaine* makes me pause. There is no finesse, no statue, no designation to tell of special patronage or legend, but something draws me to step off the trail and investigate. Something beyond the stony surround with its shawl of ivy. The water from the spring falls into a little pool which oddly glitters a brilliant white. I soon see why: a clutch of shimmering points of quartz are lying on the dull bed, as if someone has deliberately sprinkled moonlight in honour of the spirit of place.

I find out later that this is the Feunteun Jésus, inscribed by the local rector in the late 17th century with the words: *Bibe aquas viator de quibus pueri biberunt* (Traveller, drink the water that future generations will drink). Affirming words for a pilgrim, underlining his place in the timeline of history and movement, but sadly the lettering is almost invisible now. I was momentarily transfixed, however, by the simplicity of the scene, and the sense of a magical combination of earth, air, water and fire, with the sun filtering through the leaves to set the quartz alight, and a fresh breeze stirring. I stood in an instant of peace and happiness, without any religious gloss.

This positive feeling was soon lost as I crossed the river in Dourduff-sur-Terre and immediately experienced one of these annoying 'which way' moments. Turn left between two houses is the instruction in the not very recent guidebook I'm following. There are indeed two houses, but they are on the right and joined firmly together. Almost opposite is a track which I assume must be the way, but at the threshold stand high locked gates. Going back to the road I eventually find a tiny old Tro Breiz symbol on a pole indicating the left turn, so I return, find a spot where the grill by the gate has been pulled back, and squiggle round the side, heading downhill towards the Dorduff again. The sense of security that always follows finding the way comes as a relief now, when I have no energy for deviation.

The valley is lonely and enchanting. Outside of hamlets, I see no-one on the route today, so here nothing disturbs the birds, and they sing their hearts out with the clarity that background silence brings. I go slowly to absorb the uncomplicated giving of nature in spring, helping to suppress any reaction to the painful stab under my toes each time the left foot goes to ground. In Kervec the gable end of a cottage by the road has been planted with three beautiful roses, so rare passers-by can enjoy the sight. Pink, red and yellow, but only the latter is scented. I stop for a sensual moment, the glorious blush of the flowers foretelling summer, a reminder that beauty matters for its own sake. It could symbolise this whole pilgrimage, little bursts of colour and joy amongst what is (inevitably on such a long route) a more neutral palette tinted by discomfort.

I press on towards Lanmeur, with a strong sense of anticipation, following a long track across country past a low civil aviation mast. The square tower of the chapel of Kernitron takes shape on the edge of the village, and soon the nearby church spire in the centre is also visible. Here I am stepping into a very singular cosmos. Above and below, as pagans say. The two buildings are only 300 metres apart and together provide the most Breton of revelations, that junction between mystery and history that layers superstition, faith, legend and fact in a satisfying sandwich of convictions. It tugs me back into an ancient narrative which continues to send out surprisingly far-reaching shoots from its Dark Age sources. Jealous rivalry, child mutilation, the nature of leadership, the reality of power. Life is fragile, stories strong and eternal.

First the church of Saint Mélar in the centre of Lanmeur. His history is graphically told on the carved panels of the pulpit. Mélar was the son of Miliau (patron of Guimiliau, passed earlier on the route), the tragic youngster mutilated in the cause of his uncle's lust for power. At the same time as his father was murdered by Rivod, an attempt was also made on the young boy's life, but he made the sign of the cross over the poisoned cup, which shattered. As he grew up, Mélar was increasingly perceived as a threat to the new régime, and men were hired to sever his right hand and left foot so that he would never be able to perform the kingly feats of wielding a sword and riding a horse. But the innocent young man received the ministrations of an angel who provided him with a silver hand and bronze foot that fused into his body as natural working appendages.

Rivod's determination to be rid of the boy soon revived. Mélar took refuge with his aunt, who was married to Conomor, a powerful ruler, offering him protection at a base near Lanmeur, called Castel Veuzit. Eventually, however, the young prince was visited here by an old mentor Kerialtan and his son, whom he welcomed with open arms. During the night they decapitated him, stuffing the head into a bag as proof for Rivod of their mission accomplished. Kerialtan's son had a fatal fall on escaping the castle, and no good was to come to his father for their wicked deed. He was struck blind and then dead in front of Rivod, who himself died three days later. A macabre or pathetic detail: on his journey Kerialtan was close to death from thirst, but the head of Mélar he was carrying took pity and caused a spring to appear and refresh him, a little vignette contrasting purity and corruption.

To the left of the main altar an atmospheric steep stone staircase leads down into the crypt. This probably dates back to the 10th or 11th century, although many would like it to be older still, reaching damp fingers as far as the very Age of Saints. A statue of young Mélar himself stands in this humid vault, the original location of his tomb. In the low space, fat columns are decorated by strange tendril-like carvings. Are they plants or snakes? Is this an age-old serpent cult (like the one said to have operated in neolithic Carnac) or simply ornate Romanesque foliage? A recent spoilsport study has claimed to identify the foliage botanically. How disappointing to be so sure!

And there's another mysterious element. Lanmeur was once called Kerfeunteun, village of the sacred spring, with perhaps a pre-Christian, Druidic association. The crypt, built on marshy ground, has often flooded, despite various improvements to the drainage. Unobtrusively, at the foot of the west wall is the small basin (17th century) of a never-failing source, which has no known origin, nor an obvious path of evacuation. In excavations, coins (two from the 12th century) and religious tokens were found in the channels under the paving slabs, as well as bones that may be relics. But the spring is apocalyptic: legend holds that one day the water will suddenly rise unstoppably and drown the whole area, with the exception of the second religious site a short distance away at Kernitron, which will be a safe refuge when the end of the world arrives. Death and survival, the dark below and the glorious above. Lanmeur is founded on the strata of ages, a place of sacred density even by high Breton standards.

I feel this most strongly in the crypt, a humid space, which seems to wrap its legendary arms around me in a disconcerting manner. Something is here, still here, a past presence that has imprinted itself indelibly on the earth, spreading a touch of otherness into the ancient stones of the fabric. I imagine medieval pilgrims on the Tro Breiz awed by this powerful place and the tomb representing Mélar's tragic tale. If the saints are the flesh of faith, here are the blood and bones. This long shaft of murkiness takes me to a different level of the Tro Breiz, to a clearer realisation that Dark Age Brittany emerged from a land of myth and mystery into, well, the land of myth and mystery it is today. A very Breton equation. I am on a journey way beyond the physical.

Kernitron itself is closed for restoration work when I arrive, so the cavernous Romanesque interior with its ancient carved capitals is off-limits, although I've visited in the past. But the impressive exterior is a reminder of the illustrious history of this 12th century foundation said originally to date right back to Saint Samson, one of the seven founding saints, but a long way from his home in Dol-de-Bretagne. He was given the territory in gratitude for his support against the Breton Bluebeard Conomor, a warlord who operated across the area and is also implicated in the Dark Age stories of Miliau and Mélar, although in more positive light. It is the Samson connection that accounted for the chapel of Kernitron's dependence on the cathedral at Dol-de-Bretagne, whose bishop appointed the priors up to the time of the Revolution.

Conomor had his historical side too and was a major player in the power struggles of proto-Brittany during the Age of Saints. He may have managed the western channel routes on behalf of the emperor of the Franks as *praefectus regis*, prefect of the king, and his name crops up in quite a few hagiographies of the 6<sup>th</sup> century saints, including Mélar. He gets both a good and bad press according to the author and context. Various sites in Brittany are associated with this enigmatic, ruthless figure, like the Castel Veuzit (Beuzit) mentioned above, also giving us more connection between the landscape and Breton saints. A stone bearing the imprint of the *sabot* (clog) of Saint Mélar is in the vicinity.

The name of Kernitron means village (*ker*) of the lady (*itron*), a customary appellation of the Virgin Mary. However, the layers of mystery and intrigue that beset Lanmeur have another story about another woman altogether: Tréphine. Female Breton saints generally present superlative examples of piety, chastity and fidelity, sometimes losing their lives for faith or after false accusations of immorality, playing supporting roles in the tales of male saints, giving birth to saints or, as in this case, being used as pawns in political marriages. Tréphine's father felt that Conomor, despite a fearsome reputation, would be a useful ally and therefore desirable husband material. Encouraged by Saint Gildas, he agreed that his daughter should become Conomor's second wife. Later when she became pregnant, Conomor decapitated her to avoid the birth of a son destined to overthrow his father, a mythological trope of power struggles from the most ancient times of human history. Her head (and life) was restored by Saint Gildas, but she could not save her child Trémeur beyond boyhood from cruel persecution by Conomor and a similar fate.

This is a well-known archetypal Breton tale, with Conomor both the traditional amoral villain of the piece and a genuine historical example of the shifting political sands of Dark Age Brittany. But this is Lanmeur, a place that is nothing if not original. In 1864, eminent folklorist François-Marie Luzel discovered a play in Breton about Saint Tréphine but with King Arthur as her husband rather than Conomor. He produced his own version of this novel tale. Religious plays were common and popular forms of entertainment, often performed in the open air, in fields or even on the moors. Such dramatisations must have done much to keep the personae of the saints alive in people's minds and promulgated legends of origins and foundations, the relevance here. The detail also illustrates the multi-version nature of these stories, with inter-change of character and location common, as well as the repetition of standard motifs.

In the play, Saint Tréphine is married to King Arthur, but the machinations of her evil power-hungry brother Kervoura see her accused of the murder of her baby (whom he has actually hidden away). He also accuses her of plotting the death of her husband. Arthur is convinced and orders Trephine's arrest but she flees and remains hidden for years, working as a servant. Finally discovered, she is brought back, but Arthur accepts her innocence and they are reunited. Kervoura's hostility continues, however, and he has her accused of adultery by false witness. Tréphine is condemned to execution, but just as she is about to lose her head, her son Trémeur returns from captivity (not dying in childhood in this version), challenges Kervoura to a duel and kills him. Once again husband and wife reunite, although I don't think I'd have had much confidence in

Arthur's future constancy after all that. The story has obvious echoes of the more famous infidelity of Guinevere with Lancelot in the Arthurian canon.

So the Lanmeur connection is an alternative foundation version in which Tréphine is said to have constructed a sanctuary in gratitude for her happy ending on the site of Kernitron. Whatever the origins of this sacred spot, it became a centre of pilgrimage, and a symbol of the complex mystical thinking that informs the legendary background of Breton saints, mythical heroes and semi-historical figures. A luscious jam of fact and fantasy brought to life by the unfailing imagination of Breton culture and spiritual life.

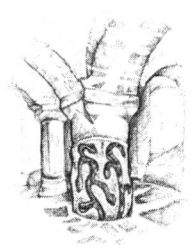

## 6 Crossing a new world: liminal space, the Virgin's bedroom and a farce

My friend David accompanies me on the next stage from Lanmeur to the chapel of Sainte Barbe, nobly taking charge of the dog so I can concentrate on the work in hand. It's a cool, overcast day, good for walking, and I had hoped to get as far as Saint-Efflam further along the coast, but we go wrong a couple of times, using old directions which have been superseded by a housing estate, and the extra distance provokes my feet into painful protest. Reluctantly, after an agonising hobble across the bridge of Toul an Héry, I have to wait with my feet up on a stone bench inside the porch of the chapel of Barbara, the patron saint of fire-fighters amongst others, whilst David rapidly covers the final kilometres and comes back for me in the car.

The curiously shaped porch is a good place to contemplate pilgrims' refuges. I am heartily glad to sit within the shaded sacred precinct, which is protected by a large slab to keep animals out. There is an exterior stone *tronc* or box for offerings on what has always been a popular pilgrim route, the faithful making for the coast and the long trek across the bay of Saint-Michel-en-Grève on the way to the most famous Saint Michael site of all, Mont-Saint-Michel, now technically in Normandy. The position of the box meant they could donate whether the chapel was open or not, something I am beginning to realise is going to be a frustrating lottery on my journey.

Inside is a statue of Sainte Barbe herself, a tragic 3rd century martyr from the Lebanon, so not a Breton saint (they rarely got the chance of martyrdom and mostly died in their beds in old age) but extremely popular in Brittany. She holds as icon an enormous tower, reflecting the story that she was imprisoned by her father after refusing to marry a pagan. As she remained obdurate in her faith, he finally beheaded her before being struck dead by lightning himself. This led to Barbara's patronage of fire-fighters, artillery men and miners, as well as coastguards apparently. The chapel was built in 1609 and dedicated to her as the patron of those who defended the little port here against English attack.

Picking up the route next day I pass along an idyllically spring-decorated defile beside a little stream, making a short detour to see the charming *fontaine* that belongs to Sainte Barbe's chapel. This has a very Breton sense of sacred space embedded in the countryside, blurring the distinction between natural and man-made, the water and stone blending into the rising vegetation. It is tended (wooden supports have been laid over marshy bits) but not manicured. The taste of early May is in the air in this tiny enclave, the sort of place where spiritual uplift, into something both simpler and more rarefied, can be found.

Back on track I am soon descending to the coastal Chapelle de Saint Efflam, set in a corner of the great bay of Saint-Michel-en-Grève. The building (1888) is set in a grassy space and has a little statue of Efflam himself and his 'wife' Enora on the chapel façade. The saint came from a royal family in Ireland, where he ran away on his wedding day rather than betray his vows of chastity and the religious life. He came to Brittany and set up a hermitage where the chapel is now. Enora was to follow him and show her own quiet allegiance by remaining a short distance away in solitary devotion to God. Each day she rang a bell, which was their only communication for the rest of her life.

Efflam was to have a strange encounter with King Arthur here. The legendary hero was exhausted from fighting a dragon without success and urged Efflam to have a go in his place. The saint first struck the ground with his baton (remarkably like the use of a magic wand) for a source of fresh water to appear to revive the warrior. This is the *fontaine* now sited below the chapel. The next morning he went to the beast's lair on the hill Grand Rocher nearby and calmly made the sign of the cross to tame the monster and persuade it to take a suicidal leap onto the rocks below. This story offers an unusual twist on the heroic Christian knight trope. The relationship between faith and might is different in Brittany, land of saints, with the holy man as conduit of divine will, working rather more efficaciously than mere brawn. And let's remember, for all the hype, there is no cult of saint Arthur.

So I go down an old flight of steps leading to the ornate *fontaine* with its upturned-hull roof of neat slates that now covers the spring. There's another stone collection box for pilgrims' offerings, as this chapel was an important stop for those making their way along the north coast to Mont-Saint -Michel before turning south for the route to Compostela in Spain. Many Tro Breiz pilgrims would also have used this well-worn coastal route, once part of the Roman road from Morlaix to Lannion, as the densely wooded interior with deep valleys presented greater problems for travellers. Apparently it passed across the bay from Saint-Efflam to Saint-Michel-en-Grève by the cross of Mi-Lieu, exactly the route I'm about to embark on.

But before leaving the sacred spring, I spare a thought for the rituals once practised here, as the water was also in popular tradition a predicative source for locals. So young girls assessing their marital prospects, jealous husbands questioning their wives' fidelity and victims of theft looking for culprits could seek clarity here. Pieces of bread assigned identities were thrown into the holy water. The one that sank to the bottom was the guilty party or the one that floated apart indicated failed romance. Marital suspicions required three bits named for husband, wife and the saint. If the latter moved towards the other two, all was well. If not... These rites of divination were practised at many *fontaines*, and generally tolerated by the church, despite their superstitious character. It was a typically Breton practical method to get answers to daily problems from the all-knowing saints, with whom they felt a close personal relationship.

Landscape here determines pilgrims' passage. I'm now facing the huge shallow bay of Saint-Michel-en-Grève, with one of the longest tide recoils in Brittany, the sea disappearing onto the horizon for hours at a time, leaving a glistening marine tapestry to coat the enormous space between arms of land. (It also has a rampant problem inshore with a thick band of toxic algae which has marred the beach's daily life for years and resulted in the death of animals and sickness for humans.) Going straight across the bay from the chapel of Saint Efflam to the chapel of Saint-Michel-en-Grève is the most direct route, about four kilometres, but the timing of low tide would be crucial to take advantage of this. Hugging the coast line was a longer way, bringing travellers under the looming height of Grand Rocher, in legend the dragon's lair, and in reality a haunt of robbers who lay in wait for vulnerable pilgrims. There was no real road here above the shore until the early 20th century.

Safer to be out in the open, as long as the tide played ball. A stone cross was placed out on the sea-bed at the mid-point for orientation and a touchstone of the tidal progress. If it was already coming in visibly at this point, it was time to hurry... In fact I was late starting my walk that day and was aware that the sea would soon be on the turn as I made my way out into no man's land in my short blue wellingtons. Soon the shore was a distant blur, people on the beach like ants, the noise of traffic faded away, and I was alone in a great welling silence. Separate from the familiar, completely free, on neither shore nor sea. The sand feels like a magic carpet, transporting me through a new world. Moving away from the norm, losing that sense of the littoral that usually binds beach walks firmly to the land. It is a transient world of infinite space, out here in the bay.

For a long time I feel I've made little progress. Turning back to look at the chapel of Saint Efflam in its raised position, it seems not very far behind. Far ahead, islands loom out to sea, like pale ghosts of earlier living lands. On the shore side, the green mass of Grand Rocher rears up from the bay, holding an ancient frisson of fear and danger. As the sun heats up, the views are sharper behind and blurred in the glare ahead. It is steadily getting hotter, blue sky contrasting with the dark aquamarine strip of sea on the horizon. Light rays bounce off the endless ridges of the sand. But it's a deceptive zone. Time fades away. I am starting to wander, not keeping to a line, sometimes moving out still further. The bodily experience is a novelty, ridged sand beneath my feet lending a certain buoyancy, my eyes constantly adjusting to the sharp sun and the shifting landmarks which seem so very far away. I am overwhelmed by a sense of excitement and liberation.

Progress is taking longer than I imagined and minutes are slipping by. A glance at my watch shows that the tide must already be creeping towards me. I'm not in danger, but there's a slight alert of trepidation. Even if I had to make a direct run to the nearest shore, it would take quite a time to reach it. But the sensations of this great void, a secret world existing between the land and the deep, are so agreeable it seems a shame to hurry. I turn round and round, holding out my arms, feeling light and happily unencumbered by human things. A couple of gulls swoop in for a look but I'm not of any special interest. I'm just there, and I have rarely felt so *there* as I do in that moment. Elementally, there was balance and harmony, although this relentless exposure to the sun would soon start to bother me on a bodily level.

The sand is virtually flat and strangely rock-free, but heavily furrowed and harbouring pools of sea water. I've been looking for the stone cross for a while now, feeling the need to note that marker for my bearings, but it was strangely elusive to the eye, just as it is from a moving car along the coast road. Looking back I can just see the chapel of Saint Efflam and far ahead the village of Saint-Michel-en-Grève, so keeping to that line should be good enough. It feels a very long way, as the heat is now rapidly draining my energy. Suddenly the cross appears up ahead, like a miraculous happening, as I'm sure it wasn't there a minute ago. Surrounded by deep wells of sea water, its shaft is grey and barnacled. Strands of seagrass like thinning hair float gently in the water. I can imagine the relief with which medieval pilgrims touched this landmark. Today it is not the original cross, which disappeared during WWII, but a fairly recent replica, yet it looks old and characterful.

After the cross I am fixed on destination, drawn forward towards Saint-Michel-en-Grève. The little church is hard to pick out in the sun's glare but the large white building of a former hotel is a landmark from this marine perspective. Many inns and hostelries must once have served the needs of pilgrims, as the tides would often have resulted in some delay to journeys. There's a fast flowing river pouring out to sea to be crossed and I wade carefully, enjoying the sensation of contrary movement against my legs. When I finally come within range of the sea-wall where the church and its tiny cemetery are wedged into a corner, it is midday and the bells start as I approach, to give fitting sense of ceremonial arrival.

I have survived the crossing, what felt like a real pilgrim experience of walking the off-shore line between two chapels with an old stone cross midway as a guide. In times with no watches and tide time booklets, that race against the tide must have added a considerable element of uncertainty and anxiety, especially as many pilgrims were probably non-swimmers. I wonder how many have drowned in this bay over the years. From the beach it's a scramble over boulders and onto high steps. I have to resort to going on my knees to breach the gap, in a very pilgrim-like stance. It feels wonderful to enter the soothing dim light of Saint Michael's church. It may even have been constructed in the mid 15th century thanks to pilgrim traffic. Open and welcoming, what a difference that makes to the quality of experience!

After a good rest in the cool, it's time to brave the cliff path. The cliffs of Trédrez are vertiginous, the path very narrow and exposed, to the extent there is an alternative for those who suffer from vertigo. When Saint Yves was the local priest in the 13th century, he is said to have sat up here in prayerful meditation, the open world of the ocean before him, and to have slept out in the field with a stone for a pillow. When it was moved later, this stone returned to the spot. Now it is well-cemented to the entrance wall of the church. I'm out of breath and stop on the way up to look back on my trek, with the bay spread below. What strikes me, just taking in the immensity of the view, is that the Tro Breiz may be a connective thread of many places, monuments and differing landscapes, as I've experienced already, but that this physical dimension is backed by a great treasure-store of legend and folklore, a vertical path into Brittany's past to complement the actual journey on the face of a map. Efflam, Enora and King Arthur – a tiny drop in the bottomless well of oral tradition, faith and fantasy seamlessly blended.

One could follow the coast path from here all the way to Lannion, but my chosen route winds up onto the headland and to the village of Trédrez, where Saint Yves was based for a time in his early career. I want to walk the pavé, an ancient stone path linking church and presbytery. It is a real step into the past. I can easily imagine myself following the swishing cloak of Yves as he hurried off in typically energetic fashion, to his clerical duties. He really should be the patron saint of walkers, not lawyers, as he often travelled the countryside on foot from morning to night. I'll be struggling to reach the next stop on my route, despite his inspiration.

Overland tracks take me on past the Château Porz-ar-C'hoat-Huellan and finally by road with a last almost perpendicular climb to Le Yaudet, one of my favourite places in Brittany. This rocky spur marks the mouth of the Léguer river. The different physical layers of the landscape all fold together here into an exceptional record of human activity over many centuries. There's a fine natural wonder of a hanging rock, neolithic and Bronze Age traces, evidence of Iron Age occupation as an *eperon barré*, a fortified peninsula. Coins of the Osismes and Coriosolites Celtic tribes have been found here, and a more exotic Carthaginian example. Roman stonework remains in the walls above the port. This was an important place of passage before its coastal vulnerability in the unstable post-Roman world led to the rise of Lannion, upstream on the Léguer. Le Yaudet was destroyed by Vikings in the early 9th century.

The legend of Enora, abandoned wife of Efflam, has a scene here. She followed him from Ireland, and landed in this bay after her little boat foundered. Pursued by a local lord with ill intent, she was saved by Efflam himself, who came to her rescue and paralysed her aggressor. I always assumed the Baie de la Vierge was called after her, but apparently it's the Virgin Mary, patroness of the church, built on the site of much earlier places of worship. Inside is the unusual display above the altar of Mary in a double bed with the baby, whilst Joseph sits pensively at the foot. Some identify him as God the Father given the crown and sceptre he sports, but these may have been added later. He looks too ordinary to be God. The whole is a curiously domestic scene, not unique in Brittany, but an unexpected and striking portrayal of the Nativity. The lacy bedlinen looks well cared for.

From here my route follows the river all the way into Lannion, passing below the impressive Flamboyant Gothic church and *fontaine* of Loguivy-les-Lannion, but with direct access to a second waterside sacred spring complete with ancient statue of Saint Ivy himself. This Scottish monk was perhaps the last of the Breton saints to arrive in Brittany, in the late 7th century, from the abbey of Lindisfarne according to one tradition. A healing ritual for children was once common here, or at least a predicative rite. A shirt belonging to the infant would be thrown into the water of the basin. If the sleeves floated on the surface, it was thought the child would recover. It must have been bleak for parents who saw the garment saturate and sink, but sometimes people wanted resolution at any cost.

I like this isolated spot very much and stop to rest my throbbing foot for a while, perched on the stone surround above the wide Léguer. Suddenly, two police-cars arrive noisily in the vast open parking area below. I wonder momentarily if I could have unwittingly broken some strange rule, and hurriedly prepare a little 'I am but a humble pilgrim' speech in my head. But of course they are after worthier targets and leave just as fast, without any obvious communication, sending up clouds of dust as they accelerate away. It's then that I notice some disgusting toilet paper in the saint's enclosure and resolve to remove it out of respect for the genius loci.

A farce follows. Climbing down to the strip of pebbly beach revealed by low tide, I find a long stick and return to capture the offending article and throw it down from the *fontaine*. My over-zealous effort leaves the hideous souvenir flapping like a flag from the branch of an overhanging tree. More stick searches, a spell of trunk-shaking, quite a lot of jumping and bashing finally gets it down. What a fool I am sometimes, unable to leave reality behind in what is a profoundly sacred spot. I would probably have been arrested if the police had lingered.

## 7  Climbing steps: the goddess Athena, travel by winged horse and laying a curse

Coming into Lannion after miles of silent walking, there is an immediate sense of a lively, prosperous conglomeration, rising up the hillsides from the river. It is a place in a hurry. After the decline of Le Yaudet, this town at the first crossing point of the Léguer soon evolved into a major centre and busy port, handling cargoes of wine, cider, salt, grain, cloth and wood after the 18th century expansion of the quays. Today it is a sizeable place and an important centre of the telecommunications industry. The historic half-timbered houses of the old centre are matched by modern development providing for the needs of employees engaged in this 'mini Silicon Valley', as it has been called.

It is a religious site, however, that dominates the skyline. Opposite the monastery of Saint Anne, I leave the river for another 'real' pilgrim experience: Brélévenez or the Hill of Joy provides an ascent of 142 old stone steps to reach the imposing landmark of the Église de la Trinité. The way is lined atmospherically by bijou stone houses and old-fashioned metal lamp-posts. I take my time, pausing quite frequently to look over the valley at the roofs of the main town while my heart rate eases. Above, the church spire looms, a lofty aspiration.

Once at the top, I'm amazed (and grateful) to find the church open. The foundation dates back to the 12th century and may have been established by the Knights Templar - this at least is the local tradition - but it's the overall experience of the climb, the effort required, and the sense of rising upwards that gives a notion of heightened spiritual practice on entering the precinct. Two striking features of the exterior survive from the original Romanesque building, constructed in pink granite from Le Yaudet. The fine chevet (eastern end) and unusual south porch contrast in colour with later use of a greenish schist. This was quarried from the actual hillside for later renovations and extensions, but the excavations also threatened to undermine existing structures. The porch is embraced by three rather odd pillars (1639) poking up into the air. Whilst some see a (bizarre) echo of the Trinity, their purpose seems structural, lending weight to stabilise the flank of the building.

Inside, I enjoy a lovely little 13th century sculpted group of the Ascension over the sacristy door. It shows Mary and six disciples looking up into the sky with expressions of awe and wonder. Something in their profiles reminds me of Noggin the Nog, and I say that as a compliment. The columns of the nave and the *déambulatoire* show their age in the spiral and vegetal decoration of the capitals, lending an ancient backdrop to the customary statuary and paintings from a later era. One darkly tinted altar is ornamented by a fine skull and crossbones. Death is unusually quite a vibrant theme in Brittany, where the line between the two worlds is regarded as thin, hence an easy popular acceptance of the presence of spirits, ghosts and departed souls.

The whole varied encounter is well worth the climb, but I'm not hanging about in Lannion, which is a familiar place, and soon set off to enjoy the atmospheric descent. On the way back to the river I glance in at the parish church of Saint-Jean-du-Baly with its square tower, on the site of the former château's chapel. The interior feels heavy and morose in comparison to Brélévenez, but Art-Deco style windows are small spots of brightness, and there are stylised ermines painted on some pillars. My overwhelming impression is of hideous statuary, but Saint Roch is accompanied by a frisky little dog in an unusual pose. The prancing terrier is an area where I have expertise.

The river walk out of the town is a long, peaceful interlude, although there are plenty of locals about, strolling or exercising their pets. It ends at the chapel of Saint Thècle, an early Christian martyr, in a private garden. Then I take a short-cut via Rospez, which involves a long burst of road walking, but eventually yields the welcome surprise of an ancient slab bridge, some say Roman, set in lovely water meadows rife with bright flowers and that intangible scent of growth bursting from the earth. This tiny dilapidated relic of old journeys is a high point and it has stuck in my mind vividly to this day. The ingredients of simplicity, longevity and sense of passage through the ages, plus that irresistible green/grey combination of stone against verdure all say Brittany very distinctly.

The Roman bridge is in striking distance of Tréguier and the second cathedral of the pilgrimage. David joins me another day for a walk I was eagerly anticipating, one which begins so well. All would probably have continued in that vein if I hadn't made a terrible error of judgment and left

the route we were intending to follow along the lakes outside Langoat: temptation came in the form of a beautifully verdant wide path sporting a shiny new black and white Mon Tro Breizh marker. We had just eaten our picnic lunch in a restful spot and were feeling positive and keen, so I was foolishly optimistic about changing strategy.

It really was a most attractive alternative, a *chemin creux* or hollow way, with high banks and a tunnel of fresh May-green trees, and if the markers held up all the way to Tréguier, we thought we'd be fine. The new route was mostly footpaths, some very beautiful, packed with late spring blooms, and no sign of any other walkers. It was encouraging also to see the yellow waymark with a black monk-like figure, which I assumed was an indication of one of the paths of Saint Yves, as these two colours are those of his flag which flies everywhere on the occasion of the great Pardon, now only a few days away in our destination of Tréguier.

In some places the untended grass was high, but we plunged through, joking about the herd of black and white cows being suitable symbols for the Tro Breiz. I stopped to take photos on a narrow path glowing with bluebells, high above a river valley edged by willows and lush meadows. But I was growing uneasy, increasingly aware that we were not at all heading in the right direction for my first goal of Minihy-Tréguier, the birthplace of Saint Yves. In fact I feared that the river below us was the Guindy, right on the other side of the promontory where Tréguier stands. With this disquiet came jabbing spikes of pain, a reminder of my very limited capacity for taking on extra kilometres.

We were well off the original route by now, but I had no map of this particular version of the pilgrimage, only the growing realisation that Mon Tro Breizh in their waymarking had a totally different approach from the one I'd planned, a much longer, skirting trail to enter the town from an almost opposite point. It would be a delightfully scenic route, just the wrong one for my plans. To cut a frustrating and exhausting story short, inevitably the extra distance was simply too much for my cursed left foot and the anticipated triumphant arrival at the cathedral was totally trumped by a basic longing to sit down and never get up again.

Eventually we decided to abandon those deceptive markers when they led downhill into a steep valley, and stayed up on the spur, walking on roads all the way to the town. Just on the edge, I was cheered by the sight of a most impressive ancient fortified house, with double tower and high walls. The Manoir de Kermein was built in the turbulent times of the 16th century, and later transmogrified into a farm enterprise. There was something about the pleasing quality of the building, the material, the proportions that gave me a spurt of energy to get to the end of the day's trek.

As the road began to rise gently we were finally rewarded by closer views of the cathedral spire. My wonderful plan to come in through Minihy-Tréguier and take the traditional processional route into Tréguier to the cathedral entrance was now impossible, and we had to drive out to this very special village later in the day as an afterthought to see the chapel Yves himself had built. This is a very common phenomenon in walking with challenges, at least in my experience: the overriding memory becomes that of a disappointing slog, whereas in fact we saw many lovely things and enjoyed our conversations. Health problems have limited very many things for me over the years, and it sometimes take a while to remember that, broken down into moments, life is so often rich. And few things are richer than the cathedral of Tréguier, both impressive and intimate for pilgrims arriving in the context of the Place du Martray.

This is the only one in Brittany to retain within the precinct church, cemetery, cloister and bishop's palace as a unit. The Gothic cathedral (13-15th centuries) is glorious, embracing the relic of an earlier Romanesque structure mysteriously called the Hastings Tower, probably after Hasteinn, a Viking chieftain, although his specific connection with Tréguier is unclear. Albert Le Grand in *Vies des saints de Bretagne Armorique* (1636) says he caused the bishop to flee and leave the town without religious leadership for 90 years. A documented reference to this leader in the 9th century raids on the Loire hardly fits with stone construction in the Trégor at least two hundred years later. It's a mystery, and not the only one.

Sitting at last in the peaceful cathedral square watching students eating fast food, tourists taking photos, local dog-walkers strolling by and the seated statue of Tréguier-born rationalist Ernest Renan slumbering on his plinth, it's hard to believe that this was once the scene of an armed stand-off, the guns of 600 soldiers glinting strangely amongst a sea of umbrellas. This was the clash of faith and laicism, against the background of tricky times leading up to the formal separation of church and state in France at the beginning of the 20th century. The eminent local writer, philosopher and historian was at the heart of the conflict, even after his death.

Here in 1903, quiet Tréguier saw the installation of a commemorative statue of Renan (1823-1892), whose *Life of Jesus* had offended Christendom. Worse, it was backed by a huge figure of Athena, classical Goddess of Reason. The placement just outside the sacred precinct of the cathedral was seen by the faithful as an act of gross provocation. It seemed that the French state delighted in this strike against traditional Catholicism, as the event was attended by President of the French Republic, Emile Coombes, and many luminaries of the cultural establishment. A municipal decree forbade the ringing of the church bells during the many speeches that marked the occasion.

The irony is that Renan himself was by native instinct a believer, steeped in the depths of Breton spirituality by his mother (half-Breton, half-Gascon). Even though his illustrious academic career and the scepticism of study took him far from these roots, they stretched behind him, elastic and unbreakable. He was, however, to lose a teaching job over his description of Jesus as 'an incredible man' rather than the son of God. His book, which took the same line, led to the Pope branding Renan a traitor. But memories of his childhood Tréguier, expressed in *Souvenirs d'enfance et de jeunesse*, demonstrate the hold of the place and the religious establishment on his life and thought, despite the later diversity.

Tréguier perches above the confluence of the Guindy and Jaudy rivers, although entering from the land side gives no immediate indication of the remarkable situation of the town. That lure of a spire draws the pilgrim straight towards the cathedral. Its large square is surrounded by solid ranks of shops and houses, from half-timbered to modern, a picture of architectural development over the years. This solidity is an important element of the town's aura, a repository of lofty sentiments and arresting constructions which I find compelling. It has drawn me back many times over the years.

The setting witnesses an uneasy relationship between faith and reason, manifestation in a living urban setting of the profound sense of ancestry in this heart of the Trégor. Even though the clash over Renan's statue was symbolic of the separation of Church and State, formalised in France in 1905, the strong spirit of place is resonant of religion, saints and priests, convents and seminaries, a quiet pulse of active faith even today when many of the ecclesiastical buildings have long lost their original function. The port below is almost an afterthought, somehow separate from the purposeful identity of the upper town around the cathedral. Renan described Tréguier as a 'vast monastery', the nest of priests and monks. In the 21st century, it's still easy to see what he meant.

The town's most famous son is Yves, patron saint of Brittany, who was born in Minihy-Tréguier c1253. We have already made his acquaintance at Trédrez, in the earliest stage of his career, but Yves Hélory was closely associated throughout his life as a priest and ecclesiastical judge with the cathedral which is now dedicated to him. His reputation is largely founded on devotion to the poor and needy, often favouring them against the wealthy in giving legal judgements. One of the most renowned of Breton pardons takes place in his honour on May 19 each year, when thousands converge to follow the grisly skull relic in procession from his tomb in the cathedral to his native village only a couple of kilometres away. At the boundary, the huge gilt crosses of the cathedral and those of the chapel meet and 'bow' to each other. With the crowds, music and banners, it is a memorable occasion, but somewhat bizarre to witness the religious establishment fleshed out by prosperous-looking lawyers, come from around the world to honour the saint who is their patron.

It is Saint Yves (Erwan) who has lent the air of sanctity to Tréguier. His fervour and humility, his energy and compassion set an incredibly high bar for the later religious life of the town. He was an indefatigable walker, covering as many as seven parishes a day on foot, fasting and preaching. He gave what money he had and all his possessions in service of the poor, establishing a refuge for the needy in his own property in Minihy-Tréguier. The name *minihy* indicates the territory of the original monastery (and maybe a notion of asylum), hence that of the cathedral. The chapel he had built in the village there is a major focus for pilgrims. A stone altar in the churchyard represents his tomb and people queue up to crawl through the arch as a ritual gesture of reverence during the Pardon.

The canticle of the saint with its haunting melody is sung by the faithful who march, and then all day rings out on a loop from loud speakers along the route:

*Nann, n'eus ket e Breiz, nann n'eus ket unan,*
*Nann, n'eus ket eur zant evel saint Erwan*

No, there is none in Brittany, not even one,
No, there is no saint at all like Saint Erwan

By the end, the tune and the words are engraved somewhere deep inside even the most un-Christian attendees. I sometimes find myself humming or singing it beneath my breath without consciously choosing to do so, now years after I first participated in the celebration.

But behind the illustrious characters of Yves and Renan lurks a more shadowy figure, important for the Tro Breiz, Tudwal or Tudgual, one of the seven founding saints of Brittany, who is said to have established a monastery here around 535, the origin of the settlement of Tréguier. This monk from Great Britain is something of an enigma, a man of many names and little history, a confusing sort of chap. The islands of Saint Tudwal, where his first priory allegedly stood, are off the coast of Wales near Abersoch. In Brittany, Tudgual (the people's hero) turned into Tugdual at some unspecified point, thanks to a scribal copying error.

He is also known as Pabu with its connotations of a revered Father (the French word *pape* for pope comes from it). His progress from first landfall in Armorica can be read in toponyms from Trebabu near Le Conquet to Saint-Pabu on the Aber Benoit in Finistère, where he is said to have founded a hermitage. Moving eastwards, leaving religious settlements on the route, he was finally offered land by Deroch, king of Domnonée (who may have been his cousin), where Tréguier now stands. In c1050 the site was known as *monasterium Sancti Tutuali Pabut.*

The epithet *pabu* is specifically associated with Tugdual, either deriving from or giving rise to the story that he went to Rome on a visit, arrived at the very moment of the death of a pope, and was surprisingly declared his successor when a white dove landed on his head during the new election process. Hence his title Leo V Papa Britigenus, the Breton pope, and his iconic bird. A magical element is added to enhance the story: he spent two years in Rome before returning to Brittany overnight on a winged horse. This is Tugdual's most original tale and his moment of individual glory: otherwise he is associated with the traditional miracles of Breton saints, healing, resurrection and bossing large animals.

On the other hand, he may have been Saint Tudy all along. Or Tugal or Tual. The first known reference from the year 833 names him Tutuual. There is not even agreement that he was the first bishop of Tréguier, as technically that office began in the 9th century. In fact, Tugdual is not at all conspicuous in the cathedral today, compared with the powerful cult of Saint Yves, despite a grandiose red-robed statue which portrays him as a generic church worthy very far removed from the monk who first set foot on Breton shores in the 6th century.

If the original patron Tugdual was something of a mystery, Saint Yves has one of his own to offer, albeit not a development of his cult he would have approved. Across the river in the commune of Trédarzec are the scant remains of a chapel to Saint Yves de la Verité (Saint Yves of the Truth). It was a place with the macabre association of cursing one's enemies by a specific and elaborate ritual. Because of the saint's reputation as a fair and all-knowing judge, he became in popular tradition the arbiter for individuals looking for revenge on their enemies. If their cause was just, their opponent would be struck down within the year. But if the vow was falsely made, it would rebound on the perpetrator.

Local people speak freely of the process at Trédarzec and describe the participation of their relatives in the first half of the 20th century. I was shown the site by a man whose grandmother had been familiar with the ritual. He told me about it in a matter-of-fact way. It was just something they did in the old days, superstitious, but a practical action against injustice. There is documentary evidence that in the mid-19th century, a woman from Plonevez-Quintin made a pilgrimage to ask Saint-Yves-de-la-Verité to get rid of her husband. She waited a year for the result, but when the saint appeared to have failed her, she murdered the man instead.

To my great surprise I once heard this cult adamantly denied by someone in the St Yves office on the day of the Pardon. A woman asked politely about the location of the chapel and its strange practice. He spoke very sharply to her, a red flush spreading up his face, saying there was no truth in all that. He seemed quite unconscious of the irony. How strange to be protective of the saint, dead for 700 years, who had no direct connection with this malevolent superstition and could hardly be slurred by it. The woman turned away chastened. I was tempted to go after her and give directions to the site of the chapel where I'd been the day before, but it was my turn in the queue to get a new book signed, a *bande dessinée* or cartoon strip, so popular in Brittany with children and adults alike, about the life of Saint Yves. The man behind the desk looked pinched with indignity and satisfied at the same time. He had played his part in defending the reputation of Tréguier's great saint, at the expense of historical fact. Image is all. Faith still incorporates fear of challenge and controversy. I can't help feeling Yves Hélory would have talked it out.

David and I go into the cathedral where they are preparing for the Pardon ceremonies, setting out chairs for the thousands who will come, building a stage for music, and carrying in vast flower arrangements to brighten what is already a luminous space. We are immediately approached by a friendly helper offering information about the event in a very welcoming manner. After a brief chat, we dodge through all the activity to look at Saint Yves' tomb (a post-Revolution replica), where so many miracles were attested after his death. He was canonised forty-four years later following a lengthy papal enquiry, during which many witnesses were called and the Tro Breiz pilgrimage got a mention in the records, from the testimony of ordinary people.

Two women travelling together on pilgrimage to visit the *basiliques des Sept Saints de Bretagne* described how they met Saint Yves on the road between Tréguier and Lannion about thirty years earlier, in the week of Pentecost. They gave evidence of his generosity in their company towards a poor man who had asked for alms. Yves had no money to offer, but gave the beggar his own hood. This reference to basilicas surely indicates the seats of bishops, in other words the seven cathedrals of the founders. Another witness, the elderly Hamon Toulefflam, who had worked in the Hélory household and went on various religious journeys himself, said he had returned home from his last *pèlerinage aux Sept Saints de Bretagne* only to find Yves mortally ill. The reference implies he had done the route more than once.

A monk from the monastery at Bégard, who had known the future saint well, attested that Yves took pious action on hearing there was a poor man on pilgrimage 'either the Saint Jacques or the Seven Saints' (Frère Pierre could not remember which after all this time) staying in the house. The future saint greased the pilgrim's sandals with his own hands. These unexpected little glimpses of the medieval Tro Breiz enmeshed in documents on another subject, must serve to flesh out other scant historical details. The scraps don't exactly make a feast, but each is a piece of the jigsaw that can be said to amount to a significant religious ritual devotion, carried out by many over centuries.

Tréguier is just the place to reflect on this. I love the town and am always sorry to leave it, to tear myself away from the embrace of its distinct identity. Some strong spirit of place dwells in the fabric, some gentle gowned ghosts roam the paved alley ways, and over all hangs a skein of arcane knowledge and devotion. From Pope Tugdual to bona fide saint Yves. Amidst deeply concentrated form and strictures, there is always illumination to be found. Even an old pagan can see that here.

## 8  Sensing the flow: castle on a hill, a murder mystery and paradise abbey

The second stage of the Tro Breiz, from Tréguier to Saint-Brieuc, is a fluid journey with plenty of different options, all never far from water. This sense of flow laps beside me across the Haut Trégor and then the Goëlo, another historic region of medieval Brittany. Crossing rivers that form ancient boundaries, ranging along estuaries, following the ups and downs of the coastal path and touching on traditional fishing ports turned centres of pleasure boats and seaside holidays. My goal is the cathedral in Saint-Brieuc, a town I've never liked particularly, but I'm hoping that in my new pilgrim persona we shall see each other differently this time. It will certainly be a relief if I can get that far before the heat of summer intervenes. It is early June.

Leaving the cathedral in Tréguier with a nod of departure to Renan and the goddess Athena, I descend to the old port area, the entrance flanked by the twin towers of merchants' houses from the days when commerce flourished through the medium of the estuary. But again it is religion that dominates, as the last word of the Renan statue debate stands here near the quay in the form of a monumental *calvaire du protestation*, erected in 1904 (on May 19, St Yves' day) as a riposte to the statue in the cathedral square. It is also called the *calvaire de réparation* in the sense of redressing the 'outrage' inflicted on believers. Statues on pillars forming the enclosure include Saint Tugdual and Saint Brieuc, whilst soldier-saint icons King Louis and Joan of Arc feature behind the traditional crucifixion scene to intensify the militancy of this monument in response to the threat of reason and laicity. Saint Yves is portrayed in key position on the base of the cross. So the saints forged on defiantly into the many challenges of the 20th century.

Across the busy road bridge over the Jaudy, little lanes through quiet hamlets take me to the intriguing enclave of Saint Nicolas, with a large (private) chapel, a couple of *fontaines* and two *routoirs*, large hollows once with living water passing through to ret the stalks of flax and extract the fibres that would eventually be woven into cloth. The production of fabric was important in the Trégor as in Léon in the 16-17th centuries. A walking trail has been developed around these latter monuments of rural industry and the paths offer useful passage for the Tro Breiz in these parts. They also allow cyclists to shoot past us at high speed.

I'm walking with David from here onwards today and we take a wide track south with watery views before a lovely sunken way, greenly cool. The day is heavy and potentially stormy after a long period with no rain. We come down to water, a tributary of the Trieux, at Pouldouran, bucolically nesting beside the wide river, set in mellow countryside of pasture and grain crops framed by trees. The village name meaning 'otter pool' gives the flavour of the place, so far inland, yet conveying the impression of a fishing village, cottages lining the waterside road. Some claim the toponym refers to an obscure saint Douran who must once have had a chapel here. I'm not buying that. Sitting outside the bar over coffee, the scene seems idyllically seductive.

This rapid contrast of environment between the animated lower town of Tréguier and sparsely populated rural tracts is typical of Brittany. There is always space and peace to be found, which is a major factor in the exceptional quality of life here. This has given me the conditions I need to thrive, with silence and solitude so easily accessible at any season. When I used to visit the UK for short visits once a year, the frenetic atmosphere was profoundly upsetting to my natural rhythms, often driving me to tears and headaches in a matter of hours. I can afford to be amused now at the thought that I lived in fairly central London for many years in my 20s and 30s without realising that a simple change of location would transform my mental and emotional well-being to a state where settling was possible at last.

As we move out of the village, criss-crossing a stream and passing a very likeable rustic gate roughly fashioned from branches, there seems to be a fashion for postboxes painted over with the black and white Breton flag. A footpath has noticeboards about the practice of constructing earth banks as field divisions, and dry-stone walling, with a finely executed example to hand. This is also something very Breton, to keep traditions alive and proudly educate the passing public about basic objects that walkers like me see all the time, but too often without any reflection on the skills and dedication contained in what is in effect a simple barrier. Old and new Tro Breiz waymarks festoon metal posts beside the road that then takes us back into woodland. We are looking for the 'stone of Saint Yves', and find it precariously placed on a very steep hillside above the water. It's impossible to make out the alleged imprint of his knees beneath the moss and ivy, but the place is well-chosen for praying of any sort.

As neither of us is capable of resisting interesting diversions, we then follow the sign to a very pretty cascade where a strange, tunic-clad statue with huge pointed ears sits cross-legged above the foamy torrents. He looks not unlike something from Star Trek, and rather remote from any image of Saint Yves. The sight of this elemental figure starts a conversation about sacred nature (and the book of that name by Karen Armstrong), so that soon after, we miss a clearly marked turning and forge on through open country. Of course it is necessary to retrace our steps eventually, labouring back along the edge of a field under a brief burst of hot sunshine. Finding the way again brings relief and relaxation, as well as the shame of having passed a perfectly obvious familiar black and white sign.

We stop for a brief picnic on a wet log in a dense wood, in increasingly hot and humid conditions. Crowds of mosquitoes join us, and I am to suffer severely for their loving greeting later on. The weariness that is never far away washes over me as we plod on between high banks, on a tricky uphill path carpeted with thick mud and slippery stones. I feel a sudden moment of despondency about my chances of completing the Tro Breiz, but David's cheerful company helps to suppress all that. It's a relief to get out of the Bois de Boloï and turn south towards our goal of Roche Jagu. The magnificent Trieux river is now in view, and the scenic railway line that runs up the opposite bank to Paimpol. When we finally reach the parking area of the famous château perched high above the water, our timing is perfect, as the domain opens for the afternoon five minutes later.

From an original basic tower fortification here in the 11th century, the castle of Roche Jagu gradually developed into a major defensive point. We know that Prigent de la Roche Jagu went on the 7th crusade (1248-54) with Pierre Mauclerc, duke of Brittany, under the leadership of King

(Saint) Louis IX. The family sided with Charles de Blois in the Wars of Succession to the duchy of Brittany that blighted the region in the mid 14th century, and as a result the original château was demolished by order of the victorious Montforts. Permission for rebuilding was granted by Duke Jean V in 1405, although a jealous rival in the neighbourhood kidnapped and imprisoned the workmen to put a (temporary) stop to the project.

This later surviving version is essentially an impressive *corps de logis*, a comfortable residence reflecting the prestige of the owners. The façade is studded with windows of differing sizes and levels, the roof topped by nineteen coronated chimney stacks, an indication of the large number of fireplaces deemed necessary for an agreeable standard living for the occupants. Only a skinny round stair turret beside the modest entrance relieves the building's flat rectangular plane. The rear, facing the river valley, has a more sombre and defensive appearance to create a forbidding silhouette on the height for the benefit of potential enemies.

This is the end of our walk together so we have time to visit the castle, where an exhibition of the Nabi artist Maurice Denis is entertaining a large party of young schoolchildren, who fill the gallery spaces. The canvases are restrained, flat zones of muted colour. I don't envy the earnest teacher doing her best to elicit their stories for the Under 11s. The noble rooms of the château are unfurnished, throwing the emphasis onto the bones of the building and its proportions. We go on up to the *chemin du ronde* where there are superb views over the Trieux. The location is stunning, at the apex of a sharp bend with a promontory on the opposite bank. I don't much like heights, but this is worth it.

The Trieux divides the territories of the Trégor and Goëlo. It rises south of Guingamp and forms a *ria*, with sweet water as far as Pontrieux, once known for salmon fisheries. Then it cuts a deep valley, becomes an estuary and flows out into the sea at the Bréhat archipelago. Roche Jagu was just one in a chain of medieval fortified points along the river. Far below the castle there's a jetty giving direct access for supplies and personnel, although the climb up from the water is steep. We look down from a viewing platform in the grounds later, after getting drenched in a sudden violent storm, and briefly touring the gardens, where there is the unusual feature of a huge horse dipping pond.

David is now heading home, whilst I return to pick up the route again and follow small roads the short distance to Pontrieux, where I've booked an overnight stop. Here the Trieux takes a domesticated form with its famous *lavoirs* lining the river through the centre, and little tourist boats scoot back and forward to allow visitors to admire them from the water. Everything looks well-kept and laden with flowers, but there doesn't seem to be any sort of food shop in the centre of the town. In the bar where I stop for coffee, they confirm that quite a walk for supplies is inevitable. A long trek to the big supermarket is the last thing my feet need.

When I finally arrive at the accommodation, there seems to be no way of getting in and exhaustion and frustration overwhelm me very quickly, as so often these days. A text message has gone astray and I cannot open the key-box. Tension highlights the strained relationship between my physical and mental powers. Hindrance also exacerbates the stinging pain in my foot, but eventually the owner responds to a new plea and all is well. The rented studio is comfortable and well-equipped, but unfortunately on the ground floor in one of the main streets. There's no covering for the upper windows, so I am disturbed on and off through the night by the lights and noise of traffic very close by. What little energy I have left is needed to push back against a wave of depression that has been building all day.

The evolution of the day is a great factor in my unfurling pilgrimage. Mornings tend to start well, full of promise and anticipation, but the steady afternoon decline hits morale hard, and evenings are more about recovery from pain than reflection, let alone creative thought. And here in Pontrieux there's a dilemma about the on-going route. Instead of going directly to Saint-Brieuc, the Tro Breiz deviates to the north for important religious sites. I had planned to go across country to Kerfot and then along the Corré valley to the Abbaye de Beauport, an option I've done before when writing about Saint Yves in *Wayfaring in Brittany*. The alternative is a gorgeous route up the Trieux through the forest of Penhoat-Lancerf, with views across to Roche Jagu, and then roads to Paimpol, a longer journey to the abbey which is my destination. This is appealing, but given my morning pain levels, I decide in the end on indulgence and sparing my foot a few kilometres.

I take the train from Pontrieux's little halt, a regular service from Guingamp to Paimpol, which follows the same riverside route, but has better views than walking among the trees. Apart from a totally new perspective on yesterday's castle, with its forest of spiky chimneys dramatically profiled across the water, there's also a good look at the Maison Traou Nez, where the tourist steam train used to stop in the forest for Breton dancing and refreshments. The house, now under renovation, is more interesting for its role in a famous murder mystery. Pierre Quemeneur, the owner, went missing in strange circumstances, having apparently agreed to sell the house to Guillaume Seznec for a ridiculously low price. As Seznec was the last to be seen with his business acquaintance, he was eventually tried and found guilty of his death. Release after many years of hard labour came thanks to the unstinting efforts of his family to prove his innocence. But a new version of events later emerged in which Quemeneur had made unwelcome advances to Seznec's wife... The train trip is well worth it, although very short: within 15 minutes I have arrived in Paimpol, town of sea-shanties and historical cod-fishing.

A famous book and derivative song have given the place a unique status in the annals of Breton sea-faring. From 1852 to 1935, the sailor fishermen undertaking pitiless tours of duty in Iceland to chase vast shoals of cod were regarded as heroes. They were away for many months of the year and their families often struggled to survive in their absence. The uncertainty of return was not the least factor in this grim economic contract. Pierre Loti's incredibly popular novel *Pecheur d'Islande* (1886) about a doomed love affair between the refined merchant's daughter Gaud and Yann, a strong, silent, primitive of a man, inspired the bard Theodore Botrel to pen a rousing song *La Paimpolaise*, the girl from Paimpol, covering the hazardous physical and emotional adventure of the Icelandic enterprise in a few verses of daring and longing.

The ultimate sentimental story of maladroit lovers whose apparent final understanding ends in tragedy drew visiting hordes to the town to see the places mentioned in the book and scan the local talent for pretty girls and hulking supermen. The realities were a good deal less superficial. Many of the crews never came back from these ghastly trips, and those that did were often broken in health after a few tours in incredibly harsh conditions. The ship-owners or *armateurs* exploited these men down to the last ounce of well-being in their drive for securing high profits. There was always plenty of alcohol on board to anaesthetise against the almost inhuman demands of the job. However, at a time when early tourism was starting its triumphant rise in Brittany, the allure of the coast and this valued-added literary fame were irresistible.

Just down the coast in Kerity is one of the best sites in Brittany. I find the Abbaye de Beauport heart-achingly moving. It is not just the romanticism of the ruins, the delicate cloister and lofty church arches, although this certainly contributes to the powerful spirit of place. It's not just the beauty of architectural details from sublime carving on the doorway of the chapter house to the sharp outlined fish on a tiny fragment of tiling. There is something much more than the sum of its parts here. Walking in the cider-apple orchards and walled garden or along the dykes lining the shore gives a sense of the building in its context, a place of ebb and flow over the centuries. It offers a real understanding of what the abbey was like as a working and worshipful place, of the marriage of contemplation and activity at the heart of successful religious communities.

In 1202 Alain de Goëlo, the count of Penthièvre, facilitated the Augustinian foundation in the sheltered bay of Kerity. These White Canons (or Premonstratensians) were to benefit from extensive rights over the surrounding territory including a cut of local fishing, hunting, pasturage and mills. In the 15th century they even sought to profit from the Icelandic cod expeditions of the fishermen of the nearby island of Bréhat, but failed to bring the negotiations to a positive conclusion. The port of Paimpol had to surrender a portion of revenue on salt and wood imports to the abbey, clearly a central player in the economies of Goëlo. Managing their own lands was a more practical occupation, quite apart from the routines of a disciplined spiritual life within the abbey walls.

The exceptional shore location creates a mixed message of the strictures of land and sea, of settlement and movement, of natural flux, of man creating a harmony with raw resources in a spirit of faith and commitment. It was a major stop-off point for pilgrims from across the channel ready to embark on the land-based journey to Spain on the Saint James Way. The enormous Salle au Duc with its two monumental fireplaces may have been a sort of reception area for those disembarking outside or coming from Paimpol. Pilgrims arriving at high tide to the feet of the abbey would have been justified in thinking they were already in Paradise and could forego the risks of travel to

Compostela. A modern marker just outside the abbey helpfully reads 0km – the start of the long route to the edge of Spain.

Here I become aware that my relationship with this pilgrimage is both evolving and settling. The importance of detail, from tiny to grand, sews up the religious seams, particularly here at the abbey. The sense of arrival and departure engrained in the geography of this place evokes responses to both those crucial traveller rites of passage, but despite the unavoidable jerky rhythm of my progress on the map so far, I realise in these inspiring surroundings that internally I am feeling the cumulative effect of my efforts. Physically it may be getting harder, but inside there is a growing satisfaction in the connection of sites and sights, the sense of ancient journeys validated, a focus on human imprint on the sacred nature of the landscape. At the Abbaye de Beauport, I feel not only in the footsteps of pilgrims but also in their spirit of endeavour. My heart is in this, adding a livelier beat to the feeble contribution of my wretched feet.

## 9  Struggling on: coast path blues,
## a saint of many names and pizza not piety

The next stage of my journey gets underway some weeks later. Those positive feelings have somewhat dissipated in the interim as I fear the onset of warmer weather and the exposure of the coast. I've spent the time at home working on the basic Tro Breiz guidebook I've promised to produce for next spring, sitting at my desk with notes and photographs. Nostalgia for the green sunken ways and wooded trails of the Trégor has been a regular indulgence. As summer settles in with temperatures up to 30° I am increasingly afraid of the effects on my health, with energy levels plummeting and my heart feeling the strain of the heat. My enthusiasm for continuing this marathon journey is the only thing that's decidedly lukewarm, yet again, and the knowledge that the highest cliffs in Brittany await only adds to my anxiety.

If I'm this feeble at home, what will happen on the trail? It would be easier, cheaper and more sensible to stay put and lounge in my shady garden, a deckchair pilgrim in the making. Hiding away in the summer months is my usual practice, and the thought of all the solitary effort involved in getting to the end of Stage 2 of the Tro Breiz (only Stage 2!) makes me weaker still. In the event, it will take me four days of slow, challenging and, as it turns out, extremely hot coast path walking to reach Saint-Brieuc. Friends Julia and Phil are spending one of these with me, a much needed bit of back-up and companionship when morale proves low and physical powers are fading.

From the grounds of the Abbaye de Beauport, a causeway crosses the Corré as it trickles into mud flats, before the path rises into woods above the coastline. There are occasional flashes of sea with moored boats and islands off Pointe de Plouezec ahead, but first I make a brief detour to the windmill at Craca and the attractive chapel of Saint Riom before coming back down to the coast at Port Lazo. The tide is well out and tractors pulling flatbed trailers lumber over sands towards the oyster beds. This traditional fishing village has an unusual name. Lazo or the port 'of the massacre' refers in oral tradition to local women setting fire to English ships here in 9th century. A likely story. Perhaps the Viking raids of that period have been mixed up with events of the Hundred Years War, when many an English vessel came to grief on the Breton coast.

If the benefit of the coast-path in general is that there is little chance of missing the way, the drawback of my chosen route is that walkers, let us say those of shorter stature especially, are often short-changed by tunnels of vegetation obscuring all views of the sea. That these are designed to protect the shifting soils of the cliffs, I understand. It doesn't make the obstruction less disappointing. On this particular section, which will later include the cliffs of Plouha, there is going to be a lot of very up and down, steep paths descending and reascending to and from beaches. It is the sort of walking I like least of all: apart from the physical demands, the sea, however mesmerisingly beguiling, always makes me uneasy.

Where the path opens up, the perspective is spectacular, with all the promise of the Bay of Saint-Brieuc, one of the most memorable points in walking the Tro Breiz. In medieval times, I imagine pilgrims would have thought more about security and practicality than pretty views, but scenery has an important role in modern pilgrimage. Even though I'm taking a fairly direct route, the coastal sections do add new significant dimensions, literally and metaphorically. The natural world offers its own eternity, albeit a wild and disturbing one. Elementally, water represents the emotions, and all that welling infinity can quickly add its weight to turbulent thoughts, shaking up the past. On the other hand, the mercurial dynamism is impossible to ignore, but it often ends in emotional over-stimulation for me, the biggest challenge of hyper-sensitivity.

The focus of religious heritage lies mainly inland at this point of my journey, but I take advantage of those kind friends to visit Lanloup and Lanleff by car. At Lanloup the richly decorated Gothic church in its walled precinct, is dedicated to Saint Loup de Sens, who replaced the earlier cult of Saint Loup de Troyes, a 4th century companion of Saint Germain Auxerre. It has a triangle of bells in the campanile, apostles in the 16th century south porch and an 18th century calvary. Inside, the saint is shown in full bishop's garb. I know nothing about him, except an association with the famous Festival de la Saint Loup at Guingamp. One little detail jumps out of the biographical trawl later on: he was a lover of music. What did that amount to in the 6th century? I've no idea, but assume religious chants, pipes and stringed instruments.

The circular pink temple of Lanleff adds an element of mystery to its unusual design. This is another site attributed to the Templars, although there is no evidence to support the claim. It lends an enhancement of status and significance to the exotic glow of the coloured schist. I try to imagine an original roofed version, a more domestic image than the ruined state of today. The double row of

Romanesque arches have richly decorated capitals, geometric, vegetal and human. A naked Adam covering his private parts with enormous long-fingered hands is hard to make out. In 1834 the mayor applied for permission to knock the whole thing down and re-use the stone for building repairs elsewhere. The Prefect of Côtes-du-Nord refused on the grounds of the antiquity of the temple. Some took a gloomy view of the relic: 'this temple is made for Death, and Death for it' said Frédérique Le Guyader in a late 19th century poem.

We finally begin our walk proper in the territory of the Shelburne network, an organisation to facilitate the escape of parachutists and secret agents during WWII. After a look at the site of the Maison Alphonse where radio signals were received, and the house was later destroyed by the Germans, we come down through the tunnel, a modern addition to stabilise the cliff in 1973, to the Plage Bonaparte. People are swimming and sun-bathing on the pebbly beach. Loungers block the slipway. I wonder how many are aware of the daring history of this place. And how many care about such things as valour and taking risks for others nowadays? As German soldiers manned the cliffs above in WWII, a cell of local resistance activists, men and women, led the escapees down an almost vertical path to the beach. In single file, each person holding the back of the coat of the man in front. They then had to wade out to waiting boats en route to safety in England.

A section of cliff looks recently fallen, leaving a dangerous red slash in the rock-face. The coast here might have been gnawed by a giant sea mouse: many chunks are missing, baked and crumbly brown innards eat into the green. I feel the whole place atmospheric, a lingering spirit of the courage of those extraordinary saviours. It's very hard to fully understand the dangers, but the tenacity of the resistants is clear in the saving of so many lives. And never losing a single one. Crew members on the waiting boats said they could see the glowing cigarettes of the German guards above. Imagine living through that tension and palpable danger over and over again. These heroic acts were spoken of after the war by the participants in modest and pragmatic terms. It needed doing and was done.

We pass a more obvious memorial on the cliff top a little further on: the pink granite stele is inscribed *à la gloire de tous les reseaux d'evasions*, to the glory of all the escape networks. These are journeys and movement of the most momentous kind. From fear of death and discovery to safety and a chance to fight again for the values worth the risk of losing one's own life. It was no easy way out. The actions of these groups were so important beyond basic life-saving because they restored trained pilots to active service, when so many others were lost over France. The missions were real journeys of faith in the values of liberty, a pilgrimage from the evil of occupation to hard-won survival. I think fleetingly again of my father, who witnessed horrors and knew the worst of humanity that flourishes in war. Here on the Breton coast today, it is more appropriate to remember the best.

The tide is just going out, the sea a vast flat, blue-grey expanse, sky-merged on the horizon. The morning cloud cover disperses to make way for glaring sun. The way we've come, those gentle green headlands stretch out along the coast towards the unseen abbey. One of the pleasures of coastal walking is looking back on distance covered. But the soft contours are also very crumbly, and the path needs concentration. There's a sharp descent on grey gravel to Port Moguer, where we have our lunch sitting on the tiered pink granite jetty. It's a local swimming spot: a man takes his labrador into the deep and the dog paddles round and round him in circles, having the time of its life. There are other walkers on the path at intervals now, mostly coming the other way and striding out. I see no sign of obvious pilgrims of any kind, but how would you know? Maybe walking poles have replaced the traditional wooden staff.

The route is taking its toll on me as the heat rises. I struggle to manage one long, almost vertical ascent on a rocky, runnelled path, the trees closing in overhead. Julia and Phil (who nobly carries my rucksack, a big difference to me and none at all to him) wait calmly on a stone seat for my sweaty, breathless arrival. But we are still not at the top. With dismay I see the path rising and rising ahead. Below is a lovely little beach of dull sand that looks totally inaccessible. I wish I was there, lying down motionless, looking up at the sky. The rude good health of these great friends makes me even more conscious of my frailty and my unnatural aversion to warm sunshine.

We are approaching the cliffs of Plouha, coastal peak of Brittany at a little over 100 metres high. My legs feel every centimetre of the climb. They are on poor terms with the expression 'rugged'. We stop at the long view of an arresting sight. At Gwin Zegal (which endearingly means 'wine from rye'), small boats are moored to rows of wooden stakes. These are tree trunks, 8-10m tall, planted with their roots. The stones wedged around their bases to stabilise can be seen at low tide. As we get closer the site is more and more impressive but sadly I don't have the energy to go right down to the beach and then up again. I'm happy to wait and rest while the others disappear for a few minutes, soon popping back up as if the gradient is nothing at all. I can't do much more, and after walking only a little further, it's over for the day.

Somehow, I have to go on after a night's rest. Two small coastal towns beyond Plouha sum up the essence of maritime Brittany, and break up the coastal path. The scale returns to humans and their endeavours. Saint-Quay-Portrieux, an amalgam of leisure and fishing ports, is the first. It's a place I've stopped before to swim at a quiet central beach on my way to the Abbaye Saint-Jacut on the north coast. It prides itself on being the scallop capital of France these days. Half the houses are holiday-homes, closed up outside the summer season, a shuttered fate suffered by much of Brittany's coastline now. A hundred years ago it was a thriving sea-bathing venue when the concept of holidays was developing.

The 'Quay' may in fact be Saint Ké, said to have landed here in the early 6th century and been attacked by local women, who took him for a demon. Not surprisingly, as he turned up alone in the bay on a block of stone. Even by Breton standards, Ké is a bit of a broad-brush saint. He may have been Scottish or Welsh or Irish or English. Or Norwegian. His name might be Ké or Kenan or Kay or Kea or Kelly or Kyle. Or Collodoc. A 17th century Breton poem has it:

*E Bro-Saoz e zo be ganet*
*sant ké e kenan anvet*

Saint Kay was born in England
And is also known as Kenan

Or he may be the Arthurian knight Sir Kay after all.
And let's not forget that he is often confused with Clether
or Cléder. Indeed the Finistère village of that name claims
him as their founder and his strongest tradition attaches
this mystery man to that area.

The Saint-Quay-Portrieux tale seems a separate strand,
but no matter. Beaten with broom twigs, he was badly
wounded and left for dead on the shore here. The Virgin
Mary caused a spring to pour forth beside him so his
wounds would heal in the holy water. The *fontaine* still
exists, albeit in rather later form. The women were soon
ashamed and returned to make up for their hostile
welcome, but it would be very surprising if strangers
arriving alone from over the seas were not treated with
suspicion and sometimes perceived as attackers or of
malignant influence. This seems to be increasingly the case
these days. The saints with their new ideas and rejection
of traditional local practices must have had an initial rough
ride in many places along the Armorican shore. They also
needed land and resources, a potential menace to local
equilibrium. Legend gives only hints of such tensions and
we have to pick out those threads of hostility from a blanket
of hagiography.

There is also the notion of identity coming under threat
or receiving a make-over with the influence of incomers.
The saints may have spoken a language sufficiently like the
natives to make communication possible: indeed Breton

would eventually derive from this fusion. Today there is plenty of prejudice against British people who have main or second homes here, a perceived 'invasion' of language and ignorance of local history and culture. The tendency for 'Brits' (I can write this word but cannot bring myself to utter it) to huddle together and patronise British workmen and buy British food only exacerbates this image. Of course it is a stereotype. Anyone who makes an effort to speak French (or Breton) and join in with community events is usually welcomed.

I like to play the Welsh card in circumstances of prejudice and say (with tongue in cheek) that it was my ancestors who founded modern Brittany. The glaring subtext is 'I'm not English, don't blame me'. Attitudes change quickly then: I am a cousin, a fellow-Celt. Vocabulary is enough to change the perception of a human being and all that they are. To hell with individuality, just slap a label on. I lived in England for most of my life before coming to France, but my parents were from Swansea, my father proudly so, and talk at home during my childhood was, pejoratively, of 'the English' as if an alien race, despite the fact we lived in their midst. I found it confusing until I learnt some history and discovered the shifting oasis of portable Celticism. Here in Brittany my roots feel strong, but it is in the landscape (and the weather) that I most reconnect with Wales. Places not people are always my most powerful ties.

Binic is a pretty place if that is not to damn it with faint praise. Once a major cod fishing centre sending men on the accursed Newfoundland and Iceland routes that cost so many lives, it is now a charming pleasure port and family resort. Of course, as this is Brittany an annual festival honours the historic tradition of the cod fishing – La Morue en Fête – so fish have their heritage following as well as saints. It's the same principle. One could argue that fishing has given Bretons on the littoral as much as religion ever did. The name Binic means the 'end of the Ic', the river that flows out here. If it can find any sea to flow into, as the recoil of the Bay of Saint-Brieuc can stretch to seven kilometres at the times of highest tides.

I've been staying overnight in a gîte not too far from the coast path. A mean gîte, where a lot has been spent on interior finish and absolutely nothing extra is provided, in order to recoup the money as quickly as possible. Not a drop of washing-up liquid, no bath mat, no useful seasonings left by previous occupiers. It is a bare, skimpy place despite the faux leather chairs and smart décor. There is no sense of welcome. The owners, who live in the next house, do not put in an appearance. I drop my bag, have a supermarket 'fresh' salad to eat and go to bed early, completely exhausted. I wake in the night to be sick. Repeatedly. I immediately think, what if I collapse with another heart attack and die here in this measly rented apartment? I can't remember telling anyone exactly where I am. This is not a lucky stop-over. I blame the summer. Nothing good ever comes of it for me.

Starting out on the last leg of this journey, I pause at the Pointe de Pordic. It's a beautiful day, not yet insufferably warm and the air feels gently invigorating. A table of orientation stands next to remains of a coastguard hut. Across the Bay of Saint-Brieuc, headlands unfold, Val André, Erquy, and in the far distance, a misty smudge is the famous Cap Fréhel. Nearer at hand I can see the mouth of the Gouët, the river leading up to my final destination on this stage, Saint-Brieuc. Viewed like this, it's a soft, comfortable coastline. I can do it, surely? A white motorboat chugs across the still water below me and then a fishing boat comes the other way, heading out for a day's work. A steady stream of runners pass on the coast path, breathing heavily and making the ground shake with their impact. Just ahead across a vertiginous drop is a remarkable bright green hill, a huge rounded mound, like a giant's burial place.

Just beyond this, Les Rosaires is a purpose-built holiday resort with a huge sandy beach. Gracious villas from the early 20th century abound. I walk along the promenade lined by tamarisks in full pink flower mode. There are not too many people about and it's tempting to imagine spending the day here, eating ice-cream, but I've reached the end of the coastal section of my walk and must now turn inland. A tantalisingly ajar metal gate (unsigned) points the way towards the steep wooded hill behind the beach. Hesitation. Is the gate open or closed? Is this the right way? Stepping through, will it clang shut on my heels? A moment of doubt before I move on decisively, leaving my unquiet companion, the coast path, behind.

Up I go, very slowly on an earth path under trees. A lone scallop shell lies on the ground, maybe dropped by a pilgrim? At the top, it's onto little roads, still rising but with no views, passing a wheat field with poppies thickly mixed in the border. Then a little footpath plunges down steeply, into a bowl of green. At bottom, there's a sign to the Chapelle Argantel (the archangel Gabriel) and I decide to follow this short diversion. Good decision. The building is simple and low, blending into the landscape. And it's open! I admire the beautiful, gentle interior with a wooden barrel-vault ceiling, white-washed walls, exposed stone behind the altar and small oval modern stained glass. The beam ends have traditional 'crocodile' heads. Everything is bright, light and welcoming. A fine restoration. The chapel was abandoned in 1922 and photos on display show ruins in the 1970s, a desolate picture in the snow. At this time the bell-tower was sold to Connecticut, but, incredibly, later returned when the chapel was restored. It seems a very hopeful little place.

After retracing my steps and continuing up out of the valley, I follow interminable tracks through fields in open farmland, where maze and wheat are surging. It is tedious walking. Eventually a long view reveals the Tour de Cesson, a landmark near Saint-Brieuc, peeping out of trees across the invisible Gouët estuary. There's a growing sense of build-up to a city environment with the hum of traffic and houses starting to fill the space all around. The track descends to the large wooden Croix de Lormel, set in a very pink flowerbed beside a busy roundabout. Exhausted, I scoot across between cars and sit down on one of a series of decorative rocks in the middle of the circle. It's very pretty, with cornflowers at my feet, but after a minute, the sensation of sitting in the middle of flowing cars coming from all directions is horridly unnerving. This is edge of big city stuff, heightened energies and tensions, quite jarring after the sort of peaceful walking I've been doing.

I walk down to the port at Le Légué and then alongside the river under the towering motorway bridge. The water is filled with pleasure craft, the banks lined by bars and restaurants. All appears lively and prosperous. Over the bridge, instead of heading directly uphill to the city centre, a devilish impulse sets me to follow the new Tro Breizh signed route along the road and then down a footpath to the cool green raised banks of the Gouët. It looks little walked and quite overgrown in places. I can hear but not see children playing nearby. It's a great relief to be out of the sun.

Finally I come out at a road bridge for a blast of smelly traffic before continuing along a quiet residential strip beside the river. Then it's uphill to the entrance of the Bois Boissel, all the time following reassuring black and white markers. But here they stop. The GR® continues ahead, plunging into the trees, away from the city. I seem to remember the Tro Breizh guidebook map showing a looping entrance to Saint-Brieuc round through this wood and then back towards the built up area. But if there's no sign here, who's to say there'll be another further on? I am annoyingly only about a kilometre from the centre and frankly more than ready to go straight as the crow flies.

There is another small, unsigned path heading in a much more promising direction into the wood. A young man is coming down it towards me with his dog. I ask him the quickest way into the city and he points back the way he's come. *Tout droit, tout droit.* Straight on. I set off optimistically, quite happy to jettison a stroll the long way round. But paths in woodland are rarely straight. After making instinctive decisions at the various junctions, I am deep in the wood and lost. The only occasional waymarks are for mountain bikes. No-one is out walking. I sit on a damp bench, very tired and unsure what to do. My energy is limited by pain now and I can't take risks. My IGN® map has no detail of minor footpaths in this sector. My phone has no signal. The map from my guidebook didn't show this way at all. My own folly has brought me here. Time ticks by in that moist green glade until eventually, I have to face facts. The only option is to try and retrace my steps to get out of the wood.

With physical difficulty and seething frustration, I go back. It seems to take forever, but I emerge at the entrance to pursue the road again and return to the busy main artery which heads into the hub, shooting uphill at an alarmingly steep angle. I trudge up it, trying to keep my rhythm, wincing at every step, but concentrating on the narrow pavement, eyes down, keeping as much distance as I can from the cars and vans flying past. I am nearly blind with pain. At the top, a very long, narrow road leads right into whatever heart Saint-Brieuc is supposed to have. It's a scruffy street, with failed businesses and faded residences. Traffic hurtles along. I can only look forward to the cathedral. Austere and forbidding though I know the exterior to be, and rather admire for its castle-like impression, it represents arrival, the final step of this long stage which has proved so challenging. I will sit inside to recover and quietly reflect on all that has passed, maybe light a candle, fulfil my pilgrim persona. I've earned it this time.

But the wretched cathedral is closed, much of the outside swathed in wrapping to protect the ongoing works of renovation. If I care to return in a few days, the church will be open for a few hours in the afternoon only. What a cold reception! I want to cry, bitterly disappointed that all my endeavour is to be denied any symbolic dimension of satisfaction. But fortunately Catholicism is not the only export of the Roman Empire, and, one might argue, not at all the most important. Nearby I see a vision, a true awakening from the darkness of my suffering. The Italian restaurant La Proue is open, very welcoming, and happy to provide excellent pizza and ice-cream. Really, in the circumstances, I think I got the best deal.

## 10 Swinging moods: an unobtrusive saint, nature's bouncy castle, and a famous cocktail

I wait until September to set out on the Tro Breiz once again. At home I oscillate between wanting to go on and wanting to stop. The dilemma keeps me awake at night and rarely leaves my mind, making life more stressful than is pleasant. For all my efforts, I have only completed two out of seven stages and by far the longest are still to come. Physically, resting for much of August is a help, but I'm feeling my age, struggling with an eye problem and a left hand that is finding holding a pen more and more difficult. Someone tells me I must have something called trigger finger. When I look it up, I think I'd rather stick with the old foot pain in exchange. Defiantly, I book up another pilgrimage trip, pore over maps and get on with writing up my copious notes. Work is always the answer to everything with me.

Finally leaving the centre of Saint-Brieuc is no hardship. The cathedral is still with limited access for visitors, and I don't mind missing it this time round. There is something rough and ready about the interior, perhaps due to its sacking by soldiers in 1589 during the Wars of Religion, and later use as stables at the time of the Revolution. I am again joined by my friend David, and we wiggle through the confusion of streets to the Parc des Promenades, a sparse green space next to the Palais de Justice. After that, an unobtrusive, unsigned footpath off a busy main road leads us down gradually into the deep valley of the Gouédic. It is a revelation. I must have driven on the express way overhead hundreds of times and never felt the least curiosity for this secret space, a poor cousin of the more obvious parallel valley of the Gouët which houses a wide river and contains the pleasure port of the Légué. The contrast of leaving the city centre only a few minutes behind before plunging into a green seclusion leaves the senses struggling to adapt. Brittany has such changes in such short spaces in abundance, a constant stimulus for the traveller.

Saint Brieuc, of a noble Welsh family, himself arrived here in a river valley c480CE with a company of about 80 followers. Looking for a suitable place to settle, he was soon arrested by guards and hauled before the local ruler – who turned out to be his cousin Riwal. One story says Riwal was stricken by paralysis for his instinctive hostility and it was left to Brieuc's miraculous powers to restore him to health. Once land was granted, the monks began to clear the surrounding forest, astonishing locals with the speed of the subsequent construction, a metaphor for the civilising spread of the incomers' Christian message. The process of settlement was in itself a symbolic imposition of something 'better' in real terms, the start of an organised pattern that would one day evolve into village parishes, many surviving into the modern world.

Brieuc is a curiously colourless saint in comparison with the other founders, and not associated with showy miracles involving dragons or exorcism. The first oratory he established by a spring is now attached to the chapel of Notre-Dame de la Fontaine, north-west of the cathedral. His icon is a wolf or pair of wolves after the tradition that he was being carried on a cart in old age when a pack of these wild creatures attacked. His monks fled, but Brieuc was unafraid and made the sign of the cross, at which signal the wolves bowed down in submission. An unsubtle representation of the triumph of the new religion over paganism. A wooden statue of Brieuc and these new crouching companions stands unobtrusively in the choir in the cathedral, where Guillaume Pinchon, bishop 1220-1234, and Brittany's very first official saint, has a much more obvious presence than the traditional founder.

We stroll on along the valley. What is a cultivated city space for exercise and relaxation manages to feel secluded and natural at the same time. There are plenty of people out: groups of school-children, cyclists and walkers predominate, but we soon pass into a wilder section with high rocky boundaries, the vegetation gradually being contoured by super-invasive Japanese knotweed. At the far end is a sewage farm, that only lightly spoils the calm, but here there is a choice of three paths to continue and we make a bad one. It was our intention to walk along the coast path to the Tour Cesson, a ruined tower that is a landmark for any travellers to or through Saint-Brieuc, dominating the promontory across the river from the centre. But this route seems to lead through the industrial port area and we decide to retrace our steps and follow new Tro Breizh markers up onto the hillside behind it. Lessons have clearly not been learnt. After passing through some humdrum residential streets, we are decidedly too far east, on a trajectory cutting out the tower altogether. We go back and get to the closest point possible, but the Tour Cesson is not open to the public at the moment, although it has apparently been bought by the town of Saint-Brieuc with a view to making a feature of it.

There is nothing to see except glimpses of the topmost segment of this broken structure, open to the winds of the bay. What is now a four-storey romantic ruin was

constructed in 1395 by Jean IV, Duke of Brittany. Its chequered history includes strategic importance overseeing commercial and offensive highways in the bay, dismantlement after the Wars of Religion and more modern use as a daymark for shipping. It is probably one of those monuments best seen from a distance. I say good bye to David at the Plage de Valais as he returns to Saint-Brieuc, determined to find in reverse the GR® path we shunned earlier. My route lies on round the Bay of Saint-Brieuc, with an overnight stop in Yffiniac.

The coast path from the Grève des Courses soon picks up the route of an old railway line that ran along the bay in the first half of the 20th century. At first through a cutting with high banks covered in brambles and ivy, the path curves and descends gently past the boundary wall of the Château de Saint Ilan and through tall chestnuts, pregnant with fruit, to open up to views over the bay. The tide is out and vast expanses of salt marsh that pin down this nature reserve are revealed. In the late afternoon sun the colours and patterns are superb, sharply contrasting lines of yellow sandbars and brown mud, swirls of green grass around the spiralling water channels. I sit for a long time watching the horizontal bands shift under the light, immersed in a liminality that fits both the landscape and my pilgrimage thoughts. At the moment it seems to me that

I am walking with a burden, very much on the edge of endurance, but somehow cleaving to this purpose of completing the sacred circuit. Whatever it takes.

At Boutdeville, a memorial space preserves a record of the economic history of the bay, with industry based around the production of salt, tiles and bricks. Traces remain of the railway that once served this coastal line of business, functioning fully in the first half of the 20th century. After this, nature takes over again, with the path closer to the estuary and the opportunity to wander out onto the surface on a strictly marked way. The plants are glaucous under their daily layers of brine. Masses of tiny crab skeletons, bleached shiny white, lie in the marsh grass. As I move out toward the gradually filling main water channel the sense of a discrete world, self-generating and high performing, is more apparent.

Moving down the coast again, the path still hugs the edge but starts to shed any sense of separateness by virtue of running alongside a road lined by houses all the way down to Coquinet. This seems to be prime dog-walking territory for locals and tourists in camping-cars, the late afternoon generating a low-key busyness, so that I'm more than ready to head for the studio I'm renting for the night, less than a kilometre away on the main road into Yffiniac at Les Hauts Chemins. It turns out to be a comfortable place to watch the rugby – France play Uruguay tonight in the World Cup – and rest up before my walk tomorrow.

Staying on the edge of Yffiniac revives memories of a previous visit a few years ago to see the chapel of Saint Laurent and the *fontaine* of the Seven Saints, only to find the little statues in their niches on the façade had all been decapitated. Just one of the traditional founders makes it into this group of seven which comprises Tugdual, Méen, Guénolé and his brother Jacut, Lubin, Armel and Cadoc, all associated with various types of healing. Given this concentration of useful special powers, the place became a centre of pilgrimage for those seeking cures, a sort of medieval doctor's surgery. Without one of them doing a remote number on my foot, there's no chance of a diversion tomorrow to have another look and find out if Saint Gildas has miraculously rejoined their heads.

Despite the constancy of 7 as a sacred number, often thought to symbolise perfection in religious traditions, the actual composition of seven saint groupings in Brittany varies. Here at Yffiniac, the connection is healing, at the village of Vieux-Marché the Seven Sleeping Saints of Ephesus are honoured. Even lists of the *Sept Saints de Bretagne* mentioned in early texts are not necessarily our special Tro Breiz group, the *Peres de la Patrie*, fathers of Breton society. In 1518, Nicolas Coëtanlem of Morlaix left money in his will for honouring the seven saints, but he substitutes Guillaume of Saint-Brieuc and Pierre of Nantes for Patern and Corentin (the two native founders). Interestingly, he says the funds are 'to make the journey as is the custom', a sign that some form of the pilgrimage was well-established and well-known at that time. Such are the little glimpses we get of the Tro Breiz from contemporary sources. No personal accounts of the journey are available to give a fuller, rounded picture.

The next morning is beautiful, early sun streaming a yellow veil over the bay. The water level is much higher than yesterday, so the dark line of blue signifying open water rests nearer. From Les Grèves the coastal path loops round a bulge of land with grazing on one side and the salt marsh, later invisible behind a high bank, on the other. Being at the bottom of the estuary gives a direct view out to the actual sea and the mouth of the bay is surprisingly narrow. Against the green salt-marsh, the blue-grey water makes a striking contrast. It is a curiously intimate space, with a sense of the sea penetrating the most private parts of the land as the estuary squeezes down to nothing but a narrow stream. And of course fertilisation is what it's all about. From the 15th to the mid 19th century, salt was a major commodity cultivated in the innermost folds of the bay, but it yielded later to the more productive market gardening, which still thrives today.

The salt marsh looks like nature's bouncy castle, with plump tussocks of springy grass between the natural and man-made channels of water. There's strong scent like santolina from the unidentified trees lining the path, which is broad and well-made, allowing plenty of room for cyclists and walkers to co-habit more harmoniously than is sometimes the case. I sit for a while by the birders' hide at Pisse-Oison and watch an egret rummaging on the marsh. Across the estuary are the houses of Langeux on the heights, and below the strip of white houses I passed yesterday, while to the north-west is the distant Tour Cesson, a lonely landmark left behind on the dark hill. Outside the bay is the broad sweep of the sea.

It feels sad to be turning inland away from this luminous coastline and its patterns of abstract art. The modern version of the Tro Breiz continues all around the edge of Brittany, but I'm making for Lamballe across country now. The pretty tree-lined path is at least totally free of other people after that busy session on the GR34®, climbing steadily to join a strip of tarmac which leads on to the village of Hillion. The church here has an appealing irregularity of appearance and what looks like a Norman tower with delicate balustrade. But a funeral service is in progress so I can't go in and have to content myself with excellent coffee from a machine in the Havane tabac. Leaving the village, there's more road walking, relieved by the amusement of an unremarkable modern house with palatial, pillared entrance like a Roman villa.

On the way to Les Ponts Neufs the track rises onto high ground again to give views of the bay, but then it's down to this unusual settlement on the Gouessant river, with its feature curving viaduct over the man-made lake. Just a short stretch of the old Côtes du Nord railway system, but impressive, high above the alarmingly acid-green hue of what looks like high voltage water. In the centre of the village is the wall-painted sign of the Lorand Barre, a former 2 star Michelin restaurant opened in 1929. The owner invented the famous Macka cocktail, to a secret recipe. This is still served in the bar to a very select group of guests at limited hours, surrounded by traditional Breton furniture. Once upon a time, the venue was a magnet for the glitterati of Paris - the Aga Khan, Eddy Mitchell, Jacques Prévert – who arrived in their exotic cars to give a jolt of outside oomph to this placid village in the days before mass transport.

Today I have to cross the awful D786 which has no calming measures whatsoever and is dangerous for pedestrians, to continue round the lakeside, back to peace and quiet. The path goes up and down in short bursts snapping at my knee joints and I'm glad to get back on the semi-road running parallel above. Then it's all agricultural land up to

Coëtmieux. This has a rather showy church, reached by a flight of well-flowered steps, set in a large open space with a recent war memorial and rocky water feature by the same sculptor. It's very hot again and I take a rest in the shade. I also take a very dim view of the public toilets being out of bounds behind a grill, presumably because it's not safe to leave them accessible to all the dangers of lunch-time life in these parts. There's something very annoying about being able to actually see the toilet but not to use it. I pee behind a bush in the car-park, and leave the village without regret.

Next day, the last section of this walk to Lamballe across heavily farmed and populated country turns into something of a nightmare. When planning, I was not anticipating a sudden heatwave in September after weeks of relatively cold, wet weather. A forecast temperature over 30° degrees makes me apprehensive from the start, and not far from Coëtmieux, negotiating twists and turns through a string of indistinguishable hamlets, my body heat rises steadily. The only light relief is a sign on one house's gate with the warning *Chien lunatique* (mad dog). The constant road walking soon begins to jar on the feet unpleasantly, and traffic scurries around at a volume that requires endless stopping and starting to stay safe in the absence of pavements.

Every time I turn with relief onto a track, it is only to find vehicles undeterred by its non-road status or just a few hundred metres of calm before it gives up the struggle and rejoins the tarmac. Crossing the motorway on a road bridge I feel the vibration from the streaming traffic below, and cars fly at high speed up and down the access slopes, barely glancing at other road users when passing the inconvenience of a junction. Several kilometres of country road follows with barely a moment free of rushing vehicles. This is probably the worst walking I've had so far on the Tro Breiz, and worse is to follow.

There is a brief lull on passing through a tunnel under the still-functioning railway and turning alongside the line on a track, but the heat is getting unbearable. I sit on a bank under the shade of an oak tree to eat and drink, wondering if I am going to make it or have to call for help. The number of a local taxi company is in my phone just in case, although it is not so easy to call on this service in France without advance booking. Eventually deciding to press on, I move out into the furnace and drag my swollen feet towards the town, past a farm with skinny goats regarding me with high suspicion, before the path swings round to a pedestrian tunnel under the motorway (again!). Emerging once more into hot, heavy air, I find myself in the middle of a huge industrial estate, cylinders rising into the sky and traffic zooming here, there and everywhere.

I lose the waymarks, hardly able to see for the sweat pouring down under my hat. Although there has been a dearth of Tro Breiz markers all the way, the red and yellow GRP® trail would lead me to the town centre and I've been relying on these. The written direction encourages me to plunge into one of the factory sites which is marked on the ground as a dead end. Not wanting to risk a wasted effort when every step is becoming tough, I go on through the urban horror. Parked juggernauts are occupying all the pavement space, so I have to walk in the road despite totally unconcerned drivers who make no concessions to a struggling old pilgrim in their path. Turning downhill to get out of that purgatory, I find a wall to sit on in shade at Le Plessis, wondering if I will ever again manage to cool down.

In the way of pilgrimage, the lowest moment often precipitates a high. I won't admit defeat, and call on my own guardian deities. Eventually shouldering my heavy pack, I go on only a short distance before a wonderful footpath, waymarked, appears like a miracle, cool and sheltered by overhanging trees. At the end, in an estate of recent houses, is a large windmill surrounded by a little park with benches, perfect for a real rest. I stay there until a resurgence of energy encourages me to think I can make it. What would be for most people a downhill stroll into Lamballe seems to me like a last mountain to climb. But beside the windmill, my body gradually calms, and the tension of all the day's pressures relaxes. It is indeed a long, hot slog down into the centre, but I make the station, where what seems the best cup of coffee I'd ever had is waiting, and a long numb pause of recovery until the train home arrives and the ordeal is really over.

## 11  Heading into history: a political saint, megalith hunting and Roman remains

I am soon in Lamballe again. It's a good place to wander and ponder. Best known these days for two things, the art of Mathurin Méheut (1882-1958) and the horses of the Haras or national stud, where stallions of the king of France were reared, it was once an important centre of political power, stronghold of the notorious Penthièvre family. The town today is solid and worthy, full of signs of past consequence in the form of imposing architecture. There is a certain density of detail all around as I stroll through the centre. The medieval Maison du Bourreau, often translated 'the Hangman's House', but actually a corruption of Bourceau, the owner's name, is a bright flowery half-timbered structure in its own little square. For a long time it housed the works of Méheut, who was born in Lamballe, although in a space badly lit and proportioned for such display.

His drawings and paintings of everyday life in Brittany and particularly of working practices are remarkable. Well-travelled and a specialist of the marine world, he produced effortless sketches of a few sharp lines and blocks of colour to re-create the traditional activities of sailors, seaweed collectors, salt-shifters, potato-pickers and women in tall headdresses working in sardine factories. My first visual ideas of communal events like Pardons with men and women in traditional dress celebrating saints' days in procession to countryside chapels came from discovering Méheut's work. All of Breton life and landscape is paraded through his canvases.

He got a better space for display of this vital record of Breton cultural practice in 2022, with a new purpose-built structure in the precinct of the Haras. Abolished at the Revolution in 1790, the stud was re-established in 1825 and played a crucial part in the development of the Breton horse, stalwart of artillery and agricultural work, originally derived from the imported Norfolk Trotter. I can't help thinking Méheut himself would have been pleased by the transfer. He often depicted these magnificent working beasts in characteristic fluid style.

I go up to the Collegiale Notre-Dame on its high hill, dominating the town skyline. It was once the chapel of the château, but the latter is no more, destroyed not once but twice, thanks to the ruthless ambition of the Penthièvres. After admiring exquisite Romanesque carving on the astonishing north face doorway, I look down over the town and reflect on the power-hungry jealousy that fuelled their resolve to snatch the dukedom of Brittany at any cost. The origins of this ambition date back to the early 11th century, when Duke Alain III gave the territory to his younger brother.

Recent religious changes had brought the bishoprics of Saint-Brieuc and Tréguier into the jurisdiction of the new district, putting the future status of the Penthièvres' sphere on a par with traditional areas of power like Léon (St-Pol-de-Léon) and Cornouaille (Quimper). But it was not enough. In the 14th century, they gambled and lost big in the Wars of Succession, a long-lasting, complex and bloody episode of the Hundred Years War. Jean III died in 1341 without heirs. The dukedom of Brittany then had two claimants: his half-brother Jean de Monfort, supported by the English under Edward II, and his niece Jeanne de

Penthièvre, championed by her husband Charles de Blois, backed by the French king, Philippe de Valois. The conflict split any notion of noble unity in Brittany down the middle. The Penthièvre faction were ultimately to lose a very savage contest that raged over the territory for nearly twenty years.

The Wars of Succession give us an interesting example of the potential politics of sainthood. Charles de Blois, the count of Penthièvre by marriage, and regarded by many as the true duke of Brittany, died at the Battle of Auray in 1364, but it was far from the end of his story. Renowned for his piety, charity and religious devotions, he was buried in Guingamp, and it was not long before miracles were attested at the tomb and elsewhere in his name. He became 'Saint' Charles in local parlance, and a process of canonisation was opened in 1371 by Pope Gregory XI, despite the opposition of the new duke, Jean de Montfort, who had little to gain from such veneration of his dead enemy.

Pilgrimages to honour Charles' relics and seek healing increased, evidence for the contemporary popularity of religious journeys, even creating a mass market for little tin statuettes, souvenirs of a 'modern' soldier-saint. The man who made them was eventually forced to flee the town for fear of the duke's wrath. Indeed, Charles de Blois would always remain a representative of the pro-French, anti-English faction in Breton politics. Later, doubt was thrown onto the question of whether he was actually declared a saint in the 14th century. Unlike with the process of Saint Yves a few years earlier, many witnesses were reluctant to travel outside Brittany to Angers, where the enquiry was held, and fearful of reprisals if they did so. Popes came and went, and it was not until 1904 that Charles was formally beatified, a status marked by processions and crowds in Guingamp.

No-one could fault the Penthièvres for persistence. They had another go in 1420, capturing Duke Jean V, after inviting him to a celebration. His wife rallied loyal Breton nobles to besiege the place of imprisonment and force a release. The château at Lamballe was destroyed after this treachery, although the duke did at least found the landmark Collegiale (1435) on the site. The château precinct was rebuilt in 1556, but the Penthièvres were not done with disobedience and revolted in 1626 against the royal power of France. Cardinal Richelieu had the castle definitively truncated. Not surprisingly, it was the end of ambitions for the grand stage.

All those medieval machinations and gruesome conflicts swirl sadly in my head, although ruthless political ambition is not exactly lacking in our own world. How little has really changed since then. The Collegiale chapel, aloof on the hill-top, is an impressive last sight of historic Lamballe as I shake off the past temporarily and descend a footpath to reach the lake formed by the Gouessant. Out of the town, my thoughts soon move quickly ahead, as happens instinctively on a journey like this. I usually try to push aside the What's next? syndrome, which reduces the trail to a series of separate goals, ticked off on a list. But in this case, I really am looking forward to seeing a couple of megaliths that will be new to me, although when I reach higher ground, there's sight and sound of hunters in the area.

Julia and Phil are joining me for this neolithic treat. We pause at the roadside *fontaine* of Saint Antoine, like a stone sentry box, flanked by two mini-lanterns and topped by a cross. A tiny modern statue of the saint holding a child is clearly identified as Saint Antony of the Desert Fathers in Egypt in the 3rd century by the addition of a little pig, his symbol (and not the Saint Antony who finds lost things). This is a reminder of the importance of icons for identification. The best known saints have symbols that often, but not always, provide clear evidence of identity. Holding a grill? It's Saint Laurent. A fish? That's Saint Corentin. A horned cow? Could be Cornely or Saint Herbot, depending which part of Brittany the statue is in. It's a bit like an I-Spy book.

Flowers have been left in Antony's honour. Who has done this, made the effort to come, probably say a prayer, maybe in thanks, and make an offering to the saint? What has Saint Antony ever done for them, I wonder. He is sometimes invoked for the cure of skin diseases, which could be the answer. A couple of hunters with guns are manning the track opposite, and one snorts gruffly when I ask them if it's safe to go on. He seems indignant, as if I've cast aspersions on their care and attention. I smile cheerily at the other, who relents, saying it's lunch time now and they are winding up for the day. We hang around for a few minutes and sure enough, white vans with barking dogs begin to appear from all directions, filling the narrow road and heading for the nearest village. Gunfire still echoes from across the valley in another direction, but I'm confident that the midday meal will soon take precedence. It's every bit as traditional as killing unfortunate wild animals.

A track leads into the wood where the beautifully mossy Roche or Menhir de Guihalan sits in sylvan sanctuary surrounded by lying stones. We are enchanted by the setting. The whole ensemble may be natural but it certainly has the feel of a place of sacred creation. The relation of stones to the earth is deep and remote from human time. Churches and chapels come and go, get modified, expanded, recycled and disappear, but surviving stones endure in a more consistent, simple form despite their chemical complexities. Left alone, their lives are of proportions we cannot truly comprehend. Touching the rocky skin, as I do now, is partly a way of tuning in to some larger, re-assuring existence, life on another scale, listening for ancient music drawn up from the planet's innards. This is truly space where something special has been nurtured. Something that comes out of the land itself.

The menhir is not the only megalithic attraction on our agenda. After passing a lovely 16th century manor house, we can see the alignment and *allée couverte* of Kervès or Saint-André across open fields. There's a line of trees and a series of stones leading to the great heap which marks the original grave constructed here. It is a bit of a mess. At 20m long, the monument must once have been visible from even further afield in times of neolithic forest clearance when it was erected. While Phil is taking lots of photographs, I gaze at the wider surroundings. In the field below is a beagle hot on a scent, still pursuing her hunting dream in a world of her own well after the final whistle. As we leave the site, a truck stops for the driver to ask if we've seen a lost dog from the pack. I can only give him the general direction she was heading. The bitch is long gone.

We go on by car now to have a look at things further afield and I come back on another day to walk through the Forêt de Saint Aubin, dense with the crossing points of many trails and sometimes tricky to negotiate. It was once even wilder. A newspaper article of 1887 documents the demise of wolves here: eight killed by one hunter, the last a pregnant female carrying 11 pups. The event came at a time when the government offered rewards for culling wolves, and the journalist congratulates this 'disciple of Saint Hubert', patron of the hunt, for his achievement. This place really retains the feel of a traditional forest, often dense and disorientating, in which it is not so difficult to get lost. Fallen trees from the great storm have blocked many of the smaller paths and marshy bogs make detours into the unknown necessary from time to time.

Towards the end of the trees I suddenly manage to squelch mud up over my boot, take a diversion, twist and turn in an effort to regain the path and find myself in a no-man's land of strong young whippy branches, spiky holly and evidence of a series of little sorties that soon come to nothing, as if something recently tried and failed to get out. In the end I decide on a general direction and plough straight through the undergrowth, humbly accepting the scratches and whacks in the eyes as punishment for my incompetence. A final leap over a bank into muddy tractor tracks lands me miraculously on the right path. I think.

Fifteen minutes later I am passing the Ferme d'Antan (farm of yesteryear) to reach the Chapelle Saint-Epirit-des-Bois. Only one of these two attractions is open and for once I'm in luck, if being confronted by a painting in the tradition of the 'Good Death' is lucky. A man lies dying surrounded by his grieving family, a thwarted devil, and an angel waiting to lead him up to Heaven where the Virgin Mary is waiting. Did people feel inspired by this death-bed scene? Did they long to re-enact it themselves and believe that the upward path would be open to them? I sit in this pleasant chapel for a while and think about dying. My pagan notion is that I'll be recycled one way or another and it doesn't seem anything to worry about. Eternal life holds no charms for me.

With the neolithic behind me, I skip forward once again into medieval Brittany. A highlight of this stage of the walk is the Château de la Hunaudaye. An impressive five-towered, moated ruin, it was built in 1220, by the Tournemine family. The duke of Brittany, Pierre de Dreux, supported the establishment of this stronghold as a precaution against the expansive eye of the neighbouring territory of Pourdouvre. The castle was built in what must have been a marshy hollow, now forming the lake and moat. I sit by the water at a picnic table to eat my lunch and enjoy the view of this most picturesque of remains. It was destroyed in the Wars of Succession and rebuilt soon after, declaring neutrality in the Wars of Religion (1588-1598) to save the walls from assault by either Catholics or Protestants.

Developments in the 17th century included a fine Renaissance porch and staircase, surviving in part, open to the elements. There are a pleasing number of tower stairs and dark nooks and crannies to fulfil an ideal castle brief. I am fascinated by a curious series of mainly religious themed vignettes carved roughly in the stone walls of one room and round the door arch. Perhaps this was the work of a prisoner, creating another and more beautiful realm beyond the reach of captivity. The castle was destroyed again in the Revolution, this time dismantled to avoid it becoming a stronghold for the Catholic royalist troops or Chouans, and then burnt to its stone bones. The castle has had many admirers over the centuries, including Thomas Edward Lawrence (of Arabia), who visited many fortified sites in Brittany during a stay in the early 20th century.

Here I have to break my journey for a few days, but soon return to take a small road from the castle leading to the hamlet of Saint-Jean, and the start of an inconspicuous footpath before the rather squat bread oven. An unofficial sign points past a patchwork outbuilding to a little walked path overgrown with ferns leading down the valley. It soon turns into a clearer route, but the stream below is invisible under grasses and brambles. This settles into a gorgeous woodland walk, quiet and remote. The trees have not yet turned but the ferns are already browning and there's a distinct whiff of autumn in the air. Chestnuts crunch underfoot at every step.

A proper river appears as if from nowhere and here the path crosses over to continue to an abrupt T junction with the Arguenon, wide and green, flowing serenely through thickly wooded banks. After an energetic bit of up and down along it, passing a feudal *motte* almost lost in tree cover, I reach the bridge carrying the Pleven road across the river. The Arguenon here is effectively a 10km long strip of lake, since the creation in 1972 of the Barrage de Ville-Hatte to create a reserve for drinking-water. Historically, the river formed the boundary between Penthièvre and Pourdouvre territories. I decide to give Pleven a miss as I need to make my rendezvous up ahead, so continue along the opposite bank and past the barrage, heading into the

Bois-Bily, with tantalising glimpses of its private château, and relief to see a waiting friend at the other end.

Next time, I search for a while for a wayside cross at the hamlet of La Guiternais, not surprising really as it's tiny and has lost its top shaft and base, crouching headless deep in the long grass on a bank. It would have been easy to pass without seeing it at all. Such tiny memorials, battered and indistinct, are more moving than all the grand calvaries put together. I start to think how small things are becoming more important on this vast journey when I reach the Chapelle Saint Eugenie, with its slated triangle of bell-tower and small calvary. The door is locked, but I walk round the building and see a lovely window with fleur-de-lys tracery and a pattern of coloured diamonds, blue, green and brown. Inside it is probably quite ordinary, but out here in the middle of farmland there's something special, a muted dignity, about this plain chapel. Such surges of pleasure in a well-proportioned and well-sculpted window is what enlivens the great adventure of the Tro Breiz, and I respond to them more and more on these long walks through what is often pedestrian countryside. I'm getting my eye in for finding the extraordinary in the ordinary.

One could hardly call the Château de Montafilan ordinary, as the impressive walls and ruined towers stand high on the top of a very steep hill. It was built in the 12th century by Roland de Dinan, but there is evidence of much earlier occupation of the site. An inscription to a Celtic goddess was found here on a votive altar stone: *to the glory of Augustus and the goddess Sirona.*

During the Revolution the priest of Corseul, who refused to swear the oath of loyalty to the new Republic, took refuge here and held religious ceremonies in secret.

Finally betrayed, he made a dramatic escape dressed in the local miller's clothes. It's a romantic ruin with these hints of pagan worship and illicit gatherings.

I'd like to linger and will certainly come back, but Corseul beckons across the fields. Once the capital of the Celtic Coriosolites tribe, the town is a repository of Roman history, unusual in Brittany. I know the place well, having written about it specifically in *Wayfaring in Brittany*, but this is a new point of entry on foot, past a water-tower and through a housing estate. Suddenly on the rue de Montafilan I draw level with an extraordinary relic of such powerful energy it almost leaps out and smacks me in the face. This huge monolithic cross is from the 11th century and once had a figure of Christ on the face, presumably erased post-Revolution. It has also been moved from a more prominent position, in the interests of traffic flow. There is speculation that the stone was originally a neolithic monument, later Christianised. It feels as if the material itself is the source of its potency, so that theory seems quite possible to me.

The dearth of large-scale Roman remains in Brittany makes for a patchy overview of this period of history on the Armorican peninsula, so that the stage of development immediately preceding the Age of Saints leaves only a limited impression of legacy. Corseul, however, offers both a wider sense of perspective and some fine individual details: the semblance of a street, the outline of a villa, a touching inscription, domestic finds. Over-restoration is a perennial problem, but there's enough here to see past that and be fleetingly immersed in the settling nature of Roman civilisation.

My background is in Roman history research, and although the intrigues of political propaganda during the Second Triumvirate may be far in time and character from Corseul, the essence is all endearingly familiar to me. On the *Tabula Peutingeriana* (medieval version of an ancient map), the town is referred to as Fanum Martis, the shrine of Mars, although this may only signify the related religious site nearby. The Roman foundation is from the time of Augustus, with significant Claudian growth and developments up to the 3rd century CE. It was the tribal capital of the Coriosolites, Romanised Gauls, until dangerous times as the Empire broke up took them to Alet, near St-Malo, where my Tro Breiz route will follow them.

The settlement in its heyday was an opportunity for Celtic nobles to live the benefits of Roman rule, privately and commercially, as the area of Monterfil in the centre of the modern town of Corseul shows. It must have been a gracious place. I walk slowly along a preserved stretch of Roman street, edged by Tuscan colonnades and orientated along the lie of Roman roads entering and leaving the village. Gutters line the avenue, with a large cistern for collecting rain water at the lower end. It is not lacking the trappings of civilisation.

Corseul was at the centre of a transport network linking east and west (Avranches and Carhaix), and the southern centres of Rieux and Vannes. These routes of communication would have been important to later pilgrims on the Tro Breiz, pressing on along the valley towards Dinan. The lay-out, shaped to the sloping contour of the land, is lined by the foundations of a basilica and shops on one side, with houses behind (including the hint of a hypocaust heating system), and a vast warehouse with a courtyard on the other. Originally most of the buildings would have been two-storey, as the helpful reconstruction drawings around the site indicate. It is not hard to visualise this thriving business centre in the early 1st century CE.

A smattering of column bases and half pillars are grouped together beside the *mairie*, including the so-called Jupiter column. Elsewhere in the village, a former school-house, standing on what was probably the ancient forum, holds a dedicated, well-presented exhibition. It is closed on the day I pass through, but I remember how vividly this collection of finds contributes the fine brush-strokes to an image of life in the capital of the Coriosolites. On the other side of the road, the villa of Clos Muton reveals its layout and evolution over time, including a palaestra, or exercise area, and bath-house.

Two inscriptions from the town record individuals, one a high-ranking religious official, the other revealing a more personal picture through a tombstone complete with faded Latin, now in the church. It was erected by the son (presumably a solider in the Roman army) of Silicia Namgidde, who followed him here from her home in Africa. She died aged 65 years. I'm thinking of her and her incredible journey as I leave Corseul. Here am I, making heavy weather of walking around Brittany, when this woman must have crossed the Mediterranean and made her way all though Europe to the wettest corner of France where her son was stationed. Surely such a journey of devotion, *eximia pieta* (exceptional piety) as the inscription puts it, is pilgrimage in another form.

The site of the Temple of Mars lies nearly two kilometres ahead. This was the religious ritual centre of the Coriosolites' community. The lavish remains of the *cella* are impressive enough now, but once measured 22.5m in height, ensuring a dominant feature in a landscape criss-crossed by several roads facilitating the movement of many types of travellers. The foundations of the main complex enclose a vast open internal sacred space of $5000^2$m, once surrounded by colonnades and all the rooms needed for the paraphernalia of religious worship, sacrifice and festivities. A strong sense of ritual and processional activity still emerges from this elaborate pagan sanctuary on its prominence. I wonder what medieval Tro Breiz pilgrims, used to chapels and cathedrals, made of it as they passed. Was it a place respected or avoided?

From the temple a track leads out of the hamlet of Chanteloup (Wolf Call) through fields to the very busy road down to Dinan. I cross over to pursue a quieter route via Quevert. Looking back, the temple looms large across the fields. What a landmark it must have provided for travellers, long after losing its value as a symbol of ancient gods. Reaching the village, I realise it's late and I won't make my rendezvous in Dinan, so time to resort to a phone call and let that modern form of movement, the car, carry me over the last few kilometres.

## 12  Ranging the river: an ugly warrior, delinquent donkeys and a scene of horror

Dinan is a bit of a shock after solitary country walking. Always thronged with people and cars, it's a good-looking, dynamic place, successfully displaying a wealth of history with all the modern trappings of busy lives. There is something about the hustle and bustle of the town today, plus its architectural casing, that evokes the lively centre it must also have been many hundreds of years ago. Impressive walls, towering over the Rance valley, seal the largest medieval enclosure in Brittany, a defensive conceit backed by the formidable château, built in the late 14th century. When I first visited this stronghold twenty years ago, the gloomy greening effigies of knights in the damp basement of the Tour de Coëtquen sent shivers down my spine. But perhaps the real glory of Dinan is the collection of colourful half-timbered houses lining the central streets. As I'm staying overnight, there is time to enjoy the prosperous ambience.

Dinan consists of two parishes, so there are two splendid central churches. Église Saint-Malo, in Flamboyant Gothic style, with a wonderful magnolia tree just outside, contains classy stained-glass windows from the 1920s, on historical themes including the visit of Duchess Anne de Bretagne as part of her Tro Breiz in 1505. Anne is an iconic figure in herself, daughter of the last independent duke of Brittany, François II, duchess herself and twice queen of France by marriage to Charles VIII, then Louis XII. She is a more nuanced figure than the common 'champion of Brittany' image suggests, but her affection for the Bretons is not in doubt, and her pilgrimage around the region, ostensibly to pray for her ailing husband Louis, brought huge crowds out to witness her progress, an early form of 'the people's princess' syndrome.

The sumptuous Basilica Saint-Sauveur was built in 1112 by Rivallon de Roux, on return from the Crusades, a very different sort of pilgrimage. In fact, Jerusalem and the scenes of Christ's life had been a devout destination for the faithful since the second century CE, and in the calmer times of the 12th century, the Pax de Dieu movement within the Catholic Church encouraged pilgrim journeys to Jerusalem, Rome and Compostela. The influence of experience of eastern lands can be seen in the camels that feature on some carved capitals in the earliest remains of the church here. The *Jardin anglais* or English garden outside, where the cemetery once was, now forms a large terrace overlooking the river valley far below.

The heart of Bertrand du Guesclin, the most vaunted of medieval warriors (born in nearby Broons), is contained in a cenotaph inside the church. He is also honoured by a valiant equestrian statue in the large market square Place du Champ/Place du Guesclin. I take a photo of its dark outline in the evening light, prancing horse, brandished sword, Du Guesclin himself a rather stumpy figure true to the unflattering description of his ugliness in the sources: a big round head, short legs and skin as dark as a wild boar's hide. A plaque nearby records how he fought and won a duel here in 1359 with the English knight, Thomas of Canterbury, who was accused of dishonourable behaviour during a truce. A Breton triumph over the perfidious English.

Du Guesclin fought on the side of Charles de Blois and the Penthièvres in the War of Succession, before taking any opportunity to fight the English in other theatres of the Hundred Years War. Captured and ransomed several times, he acquired a formidable reputation as a soldier, enough to be appointed Connetable de France in 1370 by the French king. Glory for some, restriction for others. One consequence of all this seemingly endless warfare in Europe in the 14th century was a drop in pilgrimage, as travel, precarious at the best of times, became downright dangerous all over the place. (An even more serious setback would come with the Wars of Religion in the late 16th century, when many churches were under attack, and the rise of Protestantism led to stringent criticism and mockery of the notion of pilgrimage. Work not religious holidays!)

Dinan seems to sum up all this contrast of military might and the commercial prosperity that opened up after the worst medieval conflicts were over, and trade could flourish again by land and sea. I descend the steep cobbled rue Jerzual to the ancient port and then follow a familiar path down the Rance, passing Taden, somewhere I used to stay regularly with a friend. We walked this towpath many times up to the Écluse de Châtelier, where the river turns tidal. Here I had my first sight of the famous *cabanes à carrelet*, fishing shacks on stilts, structured to hold the huge square nets. They look a bit run down and neglected this time round.

The peaceful valley of the Rance now unfolds, trees pressing down thickly to the waterline. Steep steps lead up to the road at La Moinerie, a haven of pretty tawny houses, and I divert briefly to the jetty for a clear look at the estuary. Up ahead is the rocky cliff-face of La Falaise, and beyond the strikingly romantic Château de Péhou right at the end of a promontory. On through the woods, I lumber down very steep steps to a stream, with a plainly surrounded, otherwise unmarked spring. Up a wooden stair ladder, there's another source immediately, this time the Fontaine Saint Lunaire, who once had a chapel up on the hill. It's a square plunge-pool of a spring, scene of an ancient miracle of healing.

The saint was on a journey from his monastery on the north coast of Brittany to Paris to inform the emperor of the Franks, Childebert, of Conomor's nefarious activities. He was seeking a ford to cross the Rance when he met two blind men at this spot. On being assured they were Christians, Lunaire used the waters from the spring to wash their eyes, but only one recovered full sight. The other had lied about being fully received into the faith, so Lunaire had to baptise him and re-perform the cure, this time successfully! Today a statue, probably 16th century, possibly of an unknown saint (although the face is very feminine) with mitre, collar and baton, stands beside the spring. It provides a personification of the genius loci, adding a certain mysterious cachet to a simple site. Again it is the connection to the element of water that creates this spirit of place.

Just as the craggy cliff approaches, the path swerves back uphill after a little look-out point for another view of the château. It's the closest I'm going to get to the thing itself. A concessionary path cuts across the promontory through loosely planted woodland to ensure the owners retain their privacy. Red and white Private Property notices everywhere have replaced the old ditch and bank defences of much earlier history. But over the rise, the views of the Rance are spectacular and I try to feel grateful for being allowed to cross some rich person's land. The guidebook I've been using was written before this path existed, so I've not only had a beautiful walk, but also avoided a lot of dull road-walking.

The fundamental characteristics of the Rance are visible in this section of its progress: widening and narrowing, twisting and turning, bulging banks on one side or the other throwing out the perspective and distorting the views. The Port de Plouër is on a deep inlet, waterless at low tide. Coming up the left bank, I pause here on the dry shore to watch kids from the sailing school out learning manoeuvres in little boats and bright kayaks. Splash of oars, yelling instructors and high-pitched calls of the children fill the air against the tranquillity of this spreading expanse of water, more like a lake than a river. Just ahead past the Moulin de Plouër is the Pont Saint-Hubert where all this liquid mass will squeeze itself through a narrow gap to the immensity of the valley of the Rance proper. This is now maritime air I breath in, and the views are prodigious. I feel I could write a hymn to this bewitching waterway.

Opposite on a low hill is the dominant church spire of Église Notre-Dame in Pleudihen-sur-Rance. Looking back, across the water is little port of Mordreuc, where the valley was sometimes crossable on foot at very low tide before the barrage was built up north, allowing passage to the peninsula of Péhou. Today the tower of the château there looks from a distance exactly like an over-sized chess rook jutting up from the trees. If I hadn't passed near it earlier, I might think it was on the other bank, so deceptive are the angles of the Rance basin. As I move up the shore, the kayaks are competing, blue against red, and a lot of good-natured shoving and splashing ensues. By the time I turn to follow the V-shape of the inlet, the sailors are all coming in, each pair carrying their boat. A teenage girl slips and falls heavily on the stone quay, but makes little fuss, limping on, encouraged by her friend.

I eat my lunch at a picnic table above the muddy channel at the port before pressing on to the bridge. Or rather two bridges, because just beyond the Pont Saint-Hubert is the bridge of the N176 express-way, a gentle arc with straight supports, teeming with cars and lorries. From this point I have a lift arranged to the hotel in Saint-Jouand-des-Guérets where I'm spending a few nights and doing extremely complicated-to-organise outs-and-backs to finish the coastal section up to Saint-Malo. Next day it's back to the bridge early, turning down steps in Port Saint-Jean to follow the coast path along above the water.

A sense of the Rance unleashed is already there, as I look ahead to a sprawl of river, widening into bays on either side as far as I can see. What a strong identity and entrancingly mercurial personality the Rance has. The power-house of Breton rivers. Quite literally since the construction of the barrage at Saint-Malo. Arriving out of the trees above the beach at Le Vigneux, I have coffee at the bar Le Cargo, which is indeed in a metal ship container, with a terrace over-looking the Rance. The beach is of rough sand on one side of the quay and rocky underfoot on the other. Little boats are hauled upright in a line waiting for their time to come again with the tide. It's a warm day, and a couple are having a picnic on the beach. It seems an idyllic spot, as I look back to the motorway bridge and then downstream at the expanse opening up beyond the promontory of Mont Garot.

Mont Garot was where Saint Suliac, a Welsh prince turned monk, set up his first small monastery in the 6th century. He had to chase a dragon off first, the conventional symbolic action of change to structured civilisation opposed to paganism. The village where the land drops to almost water-level a little way beyond, and which bears his name, has won the accolade of most beautiful village in France in recent years. I am sure that Suliac was persuaded to settle by the rich yet lonely landscape of this wooded hill. He also saw new possibilities, being traditionally the first to plant the vine here in an area which was to become rife with vineyards, as the name of Le Vigneux mentioned above suggests. There is a contemporary vineyard – Le Clos Garot – on Mont Garot today, producing hundreds of bottles of wine annually. Although the Rance is better known for the quality of its cider, the soft sheltered space of the broad valley made it a thriving source of wine production over centuries.

Regardless of his vines, however, Suliac had a lot of trouble with his vegetable crops, equally crucial to survival, thanks to a bunch of delinquent donkeys from across the water, who liked to wander over at the lowest tide when the Rance dwindled to a small stream, and eat their fill.

No physical barrier withstood their determination, so the saint was driven to sterner action.

In mid chomp, they found their hooves riveted to the ground, fixing their guilt for all to see. A nice finishing touch was to turn the donkeys' heads backwards. Just to show he could. When the owners finally turned up to reclaim their stricken animals and begged for their release, promising an end to the daylight robbery, Suliac relented and freed the beasts to return home. But he was a pragmatic sort of saint who understood the workings of temptation, and so took further precautions. He doubled the width of the river basin at this point. So when we say that the Breton saints shaped the land here, it is sometimes in a literal (or maybe littoral) sense.

The old centre of the village of Saint-Suliac is indeed an attractive jumble of low stone cottages, a few retaining the practice of draping the fronts with large-spread fishing nets, set up to dry out. I go up to the church to see the tomb attributed to the saint, with relics on the altar above. Two graphic stained-glass windows draw the eye. One shows the donkey legend, the other an even more remarkable sight, commemorating a relatively modern reality. A line of men with large moustaches and in their underclothes march across the landscape of the Rance valley, led by a priest. The faces were actually based on family photographs of their descendants. This extraordinary spectacle took place in winter, a procession of thanks vowed after men from the village all returned safely from Newfoundland fishing grounds, in a year when many others were not so lucky. The mini-pilgrimage was a profound expression of community sentiment undertaken in 1910 between the churches of Saint-Suliac and Saint-Jouan-des-Guérets.

I head straight out of the village uphill, soon on a walled footpath to reach the Oratoire de Granfollet, set in a wonderful location up above water line. The statue of the Virgin Mary in her little pillared temple overlooks various inlets and branches of watercourse, to the point where one is not sure which is the main river. A young man is sitting up there sketching, to the frustration of an American couple trying to get a dramatic photograph. Only a few years ago, the statue fell off its pedestal and had to be resurrected. Below in the grotto is another safer statue, hemmed in by flowers and votive offerings. This whole structure is also the result of a sailors' vow in thanks for safe return from long-distance fishing. It was built in 1894 with granite from Mont Garot. The blocks were carried to this point by men and by donkeys, the latter presumably keen to make up for ancestral peccadilloes.

I skip the chance to go right around the bulky headland past the former salt-workings at Les Guettes, and turn back from the oratory to cut across the base and rejoin the coastal path, following round on the main road to the tide mill of Beauchet. This was working right up until 1980, from its mid-16th century origins, and is still encircled by remains of the dyke and enclosed lake. A little further on, the beach at Les Gastines has a line of *bacs a marée*, wooden containers for collecting the flotsam and jetsam brought up on the tide. The contents are those of any domestic rubbish bin: bottles, plastic, food packaging, cigarette packets. They have no marine flavour or smell. Many rocks here are covered in white, cobwebby slime along the high water mark, and lying on a stone in the midst is the sinister sight of a single black latex glove from some huge hand. My first thought is of Ankou, the Grim Reaper. It would suit him.

Without high hopes, I go up from the beach to have a look at a chapel marked on the map. The little road passes a round well with thick stone roofed encasement, and inside a rampant growth of foliage and hedgerow flowers. In the village, the Chapel of Saint Roch is open, miracle in itself, a little shrine with the saint's statue and a big votive offering of a ship hanging above the altar. The popularity of Saint Roch in Brittany reflects the devastation wrought by outbreaks of the plague. Here in the Saint-Malo area there was a fatal bout in 1621. Roch lived in the south of France in the mid 14th century and attempted to help those stricken by the terrible disease that was ravaging Europe. On a journey to Italy, he contracted the plague and went into the woods to die, but was succoured by a spring of fresh water and a little dog that brought him bread each day. His statues show him pointing to a festering boil on his leg, whilst the animal that saved him looks on.

The efficacy of healing saints was vital to popular morale in the days when practical help for illness was non-existent or when medicine and doctors were beyond the reach of ordinary people. Their individual prowess was often thought to emanate from events in their own lives, so Saint Roch, who had survived pestilence, could help others in the same predicament. The naturally therapeutic quality of water known from the earliest times was exploited by the cult of *fontaines*, which were given a Christian saint-patron, often with a chapel constructed nearby. Relics, the bones of saints, were dipped in these holy springs to enhance their own power to cure and alleviate.

These rituals were forceful traditions for local people, although barely tolerated by official Catholicism, where they were regarded as pagan superstitions, just like the veneration of megalithic stones. But this was the world of the Breton saints: Ernest Renan said that they, together with their Irish equivalents, were more like Druids than Saint Peter or Saint Paul, the worthies of the Roman church. That statement seems a fundamental concept in understanding their abiding presence, and I rejoice at this closeness to the old ways and rural landscape, ever more present to me as this Tro Breiz journey evolves.

The effect of accumulated saints' stories, magical places and visual legacies still generates a vital energy, not pushed aside by homologation in the 17th century when, in what one might call a form of cultural appropriation, the Church replaced the patronage of many local saints with Catholic luminaries. But traditions breed loyalty, and the Breton saints remained firmly grasped in the hands of the people. They have continued so, despite the fierce contention of the Virgin Mary, whose veneration spread rapidly from the 12th century, ubiquitous in churches in Brittany. She represents something rather different: the feminine, maternal and loving carer, promising a different path of intercession with God Almighty, and the staunch faith of women.

Turning off the road at last on the coast path at the Grève de Quinard, I pass behind another mill, the largest on the Rance, now in a state of semi-ruin, a gaping hole in what was the gable end. The strand is a like a striated painting at low tide, but this is on the turn and water gently laps the muddy sand. The footpath climbs to the Point de Grouin to give a good view of small islands in the Rance. Round the next promontory and the Ilôt Chevret is close, a single pine tree shooting up above the treeline like a cocktail umbrella. This river is a constant mix of openness and secret places, wide water and inaccessible nuggets of land. It has also been the scene of mysterious events.

Past the boat graveyard, I come into La Passagère, close to where I am meeting my friend Lucy to walk together up to the barrage at Saint-Malo, and once a scene of horror. When I was writing about the Rance many years ago for a cultural history of Brittany, I took several boat trips along the river and the haunting tale I heard then has stayed with me. As the name suggests, this was a place of crossing where a ferryman lived on the shore at the service of travellers. His house is still there by the slipway. In the winter of 1790 it was the scene of a gory murder. One evening the ferryman is said to have seen two men carrying what looked liked a wrapped body, but they vanished in the mist when challenged. The next morning, there was no-one to row passengers across the river. The ferryman, his wife and daughters were found at home with their throats cut. No culprit was ever caught. Today the biggest danger is swimming: apparently the currents are notoriously strong.

The Rance is grey this morning, although as the sky brightens later, the water will respond. It is like a huge lake here, incredibly broad, making me think of Italy. I walk up into the village of Quelmer to meet Lucy and we go across country by road and then overgrown grassy footpath to join up with the coast path again. Here there is a sudden view of the wide, wide river. Soon we can see a long retaining wall stretching along above the strand ahead. It bounds the 18th century manor at La Basse Flourie, a Malouinière, the term used for the 17-18th century country houses of wealthy Saint-Malo ship-owners. We cross a little bridge over an inlet and then skirt the domain. As the tide is low, we are able to cross the shore below the wall with its ornamental tower room. The river bed is striped green and blue as we walk through beds of samphire and an expanse of mud, crossing a stream of clear water where discarded scallop shells gleam up from the bottom.

That is the last bit of pleasant walking for a while as we come up to main roads thrumming with cars and lorries pouring in and out of Saint-Malo. We go under the dual carriageway which carries through traffic. The speed and the noise are a savage contrast with the tranquillity of our morning so far. I feel disorientated and unable to hear as well as physical safety demands, making crossing the slipway junctions an ordeal. Harsh sounds swirl and swat every way I turn. I can't work out right and left lanes without extra concentration. It's a horrible feeling. When we reach residential roads lined by old walls and greenery, I suddenly let out the tense breath that's been unwittingly held under that sense of helplessness in a concrete net of rushing human beings, driven by very different imperatives to my own.

Finally we take a short sharp descent to follow the coast path up in the trees above the access road to the barrage. There's a clear view of this famous crossing and its adjacent electrical plant. The site was constructed in 1966 and for nearly 50 years remained the largest of its kind in the world, using tidal power to generate electricity. A Dutch cycling couple who asked us earlier about getting across on bikes seems to have made it. We watch them weaving away and then our path turns from road, northwards. We soon stop to have lunch on a shady seat with views across to the commanding Tour Solidor (several headlands away) through a gap in the trees. There's also a good view of Dinard opposite, and in the channel of the Rance, I can just see the Rocher de Brieux with its pinnacle crowned by a statue of the Virgin Mary, arms raised to heaven. It is almost the end of today's journey.

When I pick up the route next day, I'm intending to follow roads into Saint-Servan as shown in my out-of-date guidebook. But today a demanding coast path is in operation, following the edge above the water with various optional perilous descents to the rocks below. Certain sections have warnings that it is a strenuous route. I certainly find it so with the constantly changing gradient and steep flights of wooden steps, needing to stop to get my breath back every few minutes. But hardy runners skip past with barely a sweat broken. They make me even more tired. I sit on a bench and watch two couples swimming in a little bay of alluring turquoise water. Nowhere in the Caribbean could hold greater attraction at this moment.

The destination makes the route worthwhile, however, as I finally descend from the tree-line at the covered space of Ar Zenith, the first boat to respond to de Gaulle's call from England in 1940 and cross the Channel. The life story of objects is often as interesting as that of people. It was ordered originally as the post-boat for the remote Île de Sein in the Atlantic, a role it returned to after the war (and refurbishment). In its old age, enthusiasts brought the boat to Saint-Malo for a long rest and public display. It seems a bit tucked away here in a corner of this affluent holiday destination, so far from humble roots in Finistère, reminding me of Pablo Neruda's poem Ode to Things, an amusingly serious hymn to all the great and small practical creations of man.

From the quay here the whole bay of Saint-Servan is before me, culminating at the Tour Solidor, a striking legacy of the 14th century rebellion of Malouins against the duke of Brittany, Jean IV, who decided to erect this stone sentry over the mouth of the Rance, even if he could do little about the recalcitrant inhabitants of the walled city. The bars and restaurants are busy as I stop briefly for coffee and a look at the massive ugly church, which is closed. Apparently there's an English corner in the cemetery a little distance away, reflection of a large ex-pat group settled here in the late 19th century. As at Dinard on the opposite bank of the Rance, where I can clearly see the large villas of another era around the Pointe du Moulinet. These were prosperous places made more so by the wealthy incomers. As well as English burials in Saint-Servan, a Protestant church was built in the rue du Chapitre in 1875. They had to raise their own funds for this non-Catholic initiative.

Once past the ever-impressive slender tower, the coast path sweeps round to Alet(h), where the original cathedral of Saint Malo's settlement stood. A skeleton of remains are still here, but in 1145, bishop Jean Chatillon decided to move the episcopal centre to the developing walled city just across the bay, which is now Saint-Malo. Alet had been an important settlement for the Coriosolites tribe, taking over from Corseul in the troubled times after the fall of the Roman Empire. Evidence that it was once a Roman site is demonstrated by fragments of wall on display beside the path. It later became a defensive fortification, exploited in WWII by the German forces.

The views from the terrace of the fort are sensational on this bright day: across the strait is Dinard, out at sea the off-shore islands, close at hand the pleasure port, Brittany Ferries' terminal and the Gare Maritime, backed by the unforgettable sight of the *ville clos* or walled city, usually designated the Intra-Muros. No matter that I've visited this extraordinary place many times: it is with a real sense of excitement that I anticipate entering Saint-Malo. But today will only be the briefest of visits, as other commitments call me home long before I am ready to go.

## 13 Spiralling downwards: bolshie inhabitants, a miserable saint and a paternal spectre

At last it is winter, my favourite time of year. Everything seems clearer and simpler in this season, a nurturing time for someone like me who often needs silence and space well-sheltered from other people. My default mode from November to February is cheerful, although the Tro Breiz is going to give that a good test in the coming months. Still, challenge lends meaning to the task and my Tro Breiz would not be much of an experience without trials and obstacles. So I tell myself. At least I don't expect to meet many people on the paths, and I hope to give all hunters a wide berth so that I can savour the great emptiness of the countryside in real peace. That has been one of the greatest gifts of this pilgrimage. I don't think I am cut out for a busy route like the Compostela, nor anywhere outside Brittany.

I have been looking forward to returning to Saint-Malo. The Rocher, as locals call it, is a personage as much as a place. Inhabitants self-identify with its protected insularity and forbidding exterior. The town is set in a singular, unforgettable environment, both attractive and intimidating, a challenge to the spirit, a formidable theatre of the elements. First I walk out along the mole and back, which gives the best view of the walled city set in the sea and its changing perspective from far to near. As this is a bit of a slow day, to take easy-going time here, I then go right round the ramparts, their medieval bulk mostly hidden in 17th century remakes and expansions to enlarge the enclosed area. I do it every time I visit, it's like an itch that has to be scratched. A few off-season tourists stagger against the wind and soon retreat down steps to the protection of the walls at ground level. Whatever that is here, where many adjustments have been made to fit development into the sloping terrain.

From my windswept circuit it is easy to see that Saint-Malo is the essence of sea as vehicle. It's been the start point of journeys of extraordinary boldness and vim for corsairs, adventurers and explorers. In 1534 Jacques Cartier set off on a voyage that led to the discovery of Canada. Réné Dougay-Trouin left here bound for Rio de Janeiro, which he captured in 1711. Their statues stand on the promenade in the face of icy blasts and salt sea spray, together with that of Robert Surcouf, the corsair who enriched himself to the tune of a vast fortune by his maritime exploits.

He operated in European waters and the Indian Ocean against ships of the East India Company and Portuguese cargo vessels. Surcouf (1773-1827) was also an *armateur*, financing many ships operated by others, and he owned extensive lands and properties in the area outside the Intra-Muros. He epitomises the energy, expertise and sheer canniness that gave the 'gentlemen of Saint-Malo' such a dangerous reputation.

They also had an expansive vision, which continues today. Every four years the great transatlantic challenge for solo sailors begins from this harbour to ply the Route du Rhum to Guadeloupe. The wider world seems very close in Saint-Malo. It would not be surprising to discover that Odysseus put in here briefly before finding out the natives were a match for him in wiles and bravado.

It's an intense sort of place, bolshie, unapologetic, secure in self, a portal as much as a port. During the Wars of Religion in 1590 the town made the audacious declaration *Ni Français, ni Breton, Malouin suis* (Neither French nor Breton, I'm a Malouin) and declared the city an independent Republic. It only lasted until Henri IV converted to Catholicism four years later, but expressed the same spirit that had fuelled local opposition to Duchess Anne de Bretagne's development of the château when the century was young. One of the towers is called *Qui qu'en groigne*, because it was built 'in spite of complaints'. The sum of all the characters shaped by Saint-Malo adds up to one towering personality.

A different journey, that of life from cradle to grave, began and ended here for French literary lion François Réné de Chateaubriand, the Father of Romanticism. As I gladly take a degree of shelter within the tall buildings of the walled city, I pass along the street that now bears his name, where he was born on September 4th 1768. In his greatest work, *Memoires de l'outre tombe*, he remembers his early years playing with the mischievous local children on the strand between the château and the Fort Royal. 'I grew up the companion of the swells and winds', he says. Despite a career in the marine, politics, and diplomacy at the highest level, quite apart from his literary renown and glitzy life in Paris, Chateaubriand's final resting place is also here, on the island of Grand Bé, accessible at low tide. According to his memoirs, *Saint-Malo n'est qu'un rocher*, is nothing but a rock. In the end, it was just that for him.

Saint Malo himself does not have any great presence here, for good reason. In the late 5th century, he landed on Cézembré, out in the Channel, and found the hermit Aaron already established there. A stained-glass window in the cathedral shows Malo, complete with halo, stepping from his boat into a welcoming embrace. The saint went on to set up in nearby mainland Alet, where he was the first bishop, not far from the islet where Aaron had built a small oratory for solitary prayer. This rock was in the heart of what would become the citadel of Saint-Malo in the 12th century. I go there now to have a sense of the actual spot, for it is still there, in Place Saint Aaron, north of the cathedral, topped by a tiny chapel. Pupils from the nearby lycée stream around me, few probably having any idea that this is where it all began.

So the Intra-Muros, restored in the finest detail after heavy allied bombing in WWII, rests on what was once little more than a craggy foothold, and is even now only tenuously connected to the mainland. From the ramparts it is easy to understand that Saint-Malo has no land side. I watched for a while near Grand'Porte, looking down on all the activity around the four enclosed harbours to the south, which mean the *ville clos* is almost completely surrounded by water. Aaron's rock that became Saint-Malo was brought into permanent connection with the mainland initially by the Sillon, a bank of sand supporting a causeway running east from the château. It seems important to take in these details, for the spirit of place here is all in the geography.

An English map of c1715 shows the Sillon as the only entrance into the city at high water. It also illustrates the ring of island forts: Petit Be, Grand Be and Fort Royal. These were established at the instigation of Vauban, Louis XIV's chief engineer, with a careful calculation of overlapping gun-ranges to ensure a powerful deterrent to invaders. And an effective one: Saint-Malo has never been taken by sea, although the English did their best by launching a boat full of explosives against the walls in 1693. Set alight too soon, the 'Infernal Machine' failed to break open a single wall, although most of the windows in the town shattered. Now the danger is from another source: the town is at an ever greater risk of submersion as climate change intensifies.

I think about Saint Malo the monk and his offbeat story on the way to the cathedral. This structure is much larger than the exterior suggests, with changes in floor level reflecting later development from its Romanesque origins. It is now under the patronage of Saint Vincent of Saragossa, a version of sainthood more acceptable to the Catholic Church than Malo's rather strange career roaming the seas, celebrating mass on the back of a whale he took for an island, and quarrelling with his parishioners. A 9th century *Life of Saint Malo* by Bili, a deacon in Alet, records his Welsh origins and that he was a protégé of Saint Brendan. Forced to flee his ministry by local hostilities, he ended his life in Saintes, far from Brittany, despite a brief return to lift the excommunication he had imposed on his opponents. There is not much sign of Malo in the cathedral beyond a modern wooden statue, the window mentioned above and another dedicated to the Tro Breiz. I spend a long time looking at the latter, and fail to make out all seven founders.

Finally leaving the town by the Porte Saint Thomas, I glance up at Saint-Malo's own flag flying from the castle tower. This derives from corsair banners: blue background quartered by a white cross, the red canton carrying the Breton ermine symbol. The device was adopted after the reconstruction following WWII, a phoenix-like resurrection making a statement of restored identity. I've seen this emblem of the defiant walled city often enough in organised Tro Breiz marches, where representatives of the nine historic districts of Brittany carry their local *drapeaux* with pride. Setting out eastwards, my head is full of the open horizons and explorations that fluttering standard evokes.

I take the sandy route below the Sillon causeway as the tide is out, opening up the space like a limitless golden pleasure-ground. Silky blues fill the sky and warm sunshine paints cheery faces on the very best of a sharp, clear winter day. The two off-shore forts and Chateaubriand's resting-place stand out against the starker lines of an exposed bay. Series of tree-trunks are riveted in the sand, standing against the power of the sea, absorbent guardians diluting the flow of the waves. Apparently an equal length of woody shaft as is visible above ground plunges down below the surface. A bit like menhirs, but here they must need every inch of stability they can get. Stepping in and out of their rows is like a path in a fairy story or a magical gateway where one emerges as something else.

I go up onto the road for a different perspective and in search of coffee. A couple with two laden donkeys have found one access to the sand blocked and seem to be arguing about what to do. I offer, mildly, that there is a way onto the beach under the town walls not far away. The young woman turns angry eyes on me and snaps something I don't catch. Luckily. After my pause for refreshment at the excellent F.A.V.orite café, I see them again on the sands, some way ahead of me but, their body language suggests, still in hostile mode. I'm in dawdling manner myself and soon they have left me far behind.

On and on the beach stretches and I stretch out the time, reluctant to finish what has been a perfect day of gentle movement in beautiful weather. I can't believe I'm so lucky in January. Cold, dry and sunny are the desired conditions for winter walking. Many people and dogs are out on the sands, enjoying life in their respective ways. The humans are more leisurely than the canines, often chatting with such engagement that they fail to notice their pet is half a kilometre away terrorising more timid creatures or knocking over every small child within reach. Only the bawling kids seem to mind any of it. Freedom and independence, Saint-Malo style, is a fine thing.

Finally the dark line of a headland not far away signals the end of the journey for now. Although the light is fast fading on this hibernal day, and my accommodation is only 300m away inland, the temptation to finish out on the Pointe de Varde is too strong. Unfortunately, it's a lot further than it looks. At one point I follow a stone causeway that leads to a dead end and so have to come back, then tough steps cut into the rock tax my weary knees. Dusk is definitely falling as I reach the path out to the point. The little groups of strollers reassuringly exchanging evening greetings fade away and I wonder how good an idea this is on several counts.

Alone on a rocky prominence, am I tired enough to fall, or what if I get an attack of pain so bad I can't retrace my steps? Is wandering on a cliff in the dark ever sensible behaviour? Shapes in the gloaming start to take on a vaguely menacing air. Did that rock just move? Is that someone on the path up ahead? Honour is satisfied as I reach the edge of the ruined fort to find it all blocked off, and there's nothing to be gained by making for the headland beyond in the absence of any view at this hour. Sense prevails. This time at least.

Early the next day I'm slipping and sliding in heavy rain on the coast path around Rothéneuf, peering into poor visibility and almost physically weighed down by the lowering banks of gun-metal clouds. There could not be a greater change from yesterday's inspiring clarity. The route turns inland briefly to skirt the site of the sculpted rocks shaped by a reclusive priest, Abbé Forré, between 1895 and 1907, where the granite below the cliff-top has been transformed into the fantastical world of pirates, animals and weird fantasies. This oddity is closed in winter, but I've seen them before and anyway this is not a day for hanging about or descending without very good cause.

A rather more conspicuous structure lies a little further ahead. There are many surviving small stone coastguard huts on the GR34 around the shores of Brittany – the infamy of the English loomed large in the Breton psyche ‑ but this one has been converted into a compact chapel with a gleaming white statue of Our Lady perched on the gable end. A brave stance in these conditions. Notre-Dame des Flots feels like the desperate statement of people giving up on human security and putting their trust in the Virgin Mary instead. Perhaps with reason, as ex-votive plaques displayed on the walls reflect gratitude for safety at sea or other prayers heard. The door is locked because of conditions, but it is possible to see inside through a grill. The plain tabular altar is raised on slender legs, coloured

by plentiful vases of flowers which surely can't be real at this time of year.

I hope my own gods are keeping an eye on me today because this journey is a real test. I can just make out the Île de Besnard with its old semaphore building, but the weather is deteriorating from unpleasant to downright hostile. My way at foot level is almost lit up like a landing strip by the bright green border grass made shiny in the rain. On and on it goes through a great mass of rusty ferns and withered gorse. Clouds descend on the sea, rain cuts sideways with the wind pressure. I can barely hold the phone camera to take a picture and soon give that up, needing to focus attention on the narrow treacherous path. A series of low headlands, hardly discernible, are ahead. I want to give up, although the day is young. All my energy has been dragged out by the cold, windy wetness. January on the cliffs is no fun, and I feel as weak as young leaves against the teeth of rats. I just want to go home.

With the switch off from the landscape, walking becomes more plodding and painful, head down to keep my footing, and thoughts swim up, unexpected and unwanted. As I battle along this unforgiving trail, I find myself having imaginary conversations with my long dead father, as unsatisfactory now as they were when he was alive. He was not a happy man, but days of lone wandering on the moors of the Brecon Beacons made him so on the rare times when he was allowed to escape family life, braving the taunts of shirking his duties from my mother. My love of nature, walking and the need to be outside comes from him. These days I dwell most often on positive memories, but today bludgeoning negativity is welling out of sea and sky.

Both my parents were sad, bitter people in different ways, disappointed with the hand they felt life dealt them, with the lack of choice they believed was the lot of people like them. The WWII generation, when duty and self-sacrifice, often literally, became issues that lingered into later life. My father also felt the real pain of a Welshman exiled in England. I don't know why they never went back to their native Swansea, as he was steeped in antipathy towards 'the English'. He also resented my ability when a young adult to move about, to change direction when things went wrong, to take control of my life. His own sense of trapped helplessness coloured everything. Perhaps realising the destructive frustration of that influenced my own determination to be the agent of my destiny and take whatever I felt in my heart was the right path for me, however unquiet that appeared on the surface. I have never sought an easy life, but my instincts for what will ultimately make a good one have generally proved sound.

The weather and harsh atmosphere has dragged this up from some stagnant depth. I've long since ceased to agonise consciously over the trauma of my parental relationships. I loved and still love my father deeply despite estrangement later in life and baffling cruelties. He fought at Monte Cassino in the war, pinned down for a month in a hole while Germans on the summit took pot-shots at any allied rabbit that risked a taste of fresh air. When I was 17 we went on a journey there, and all around Italy, which my father loved with great passion, dragging a little caravan behind the old car. I have wonderful memories of all I learnt on that trip, not least that I was a natural European.

It is the mark of pilgrimage to have time to reassess and live with new framing of past wounds. On the length of a journey like this one I generally feel nothing but gratitude for the rich paternal things that still illuminate my life. We played chess and snooker together, watched sport, talked of the ancient world, of classic literature, the poetry of Yeats and Eliot. We walked. We both loved dogs. We laughed at the same things (like the Marx brothers) and competed in ironical one-liners. People say pilgrimage is often about reconciliation, but although I cannot be reconciled to some of the unpleasantnesses of my earlier life, I came to acceptance long ago. That in itself is a deep form of healing, and a more objective understanding of the family dynamic has helped over time.

These reflections are no longer as unsettling as in the past, when the emotional charge was so debilitating. Now it's temporary gloominess, something to shrug off, like the weather. In fact, I cheer up with the sudden realisation that my father, freed from daily constraints, would have been a good companion on this journey. So the wind slackens as I reach the long sands of the Anse du Guesclin with its island fort vaguely visible through the brume ahead. Nearer to hand is a memorial to the Irish Saint Columban by the road above the beach. The saint stands solemnly in his small boat or curragh, holding a dove, referencing his name and the Holy Spirit. (He is not to be confused with Columba of Iona.) But his drawn, stern face is far from peaceful. A sweep of stone surrounds him, with commemorative scenes of his travels and foundations, most famously the Abbey de Luxeuil in the Vosges.

This recent weighty granite monument (2019) is on the site of a much older calvary, with part of an ancient cross of the original bizarrely encased in an open stone box at the entry. It records the legend of the saint's arrival on this spot with twelve followers. The nearest village, Saint-Coulomb, is another reminder of his passage. Columban was not a settling saint, however, as far as Brittany goes, and he seems to have incurred hostility and opposition when he did stop for any length of time elsewhere. He was also renowned for healing, invoked in Brittany for the cure of nervous illnesses and depressions. He looks miserable enough in this statue to be a sufferer himself, that common pattern for curative saints.

Disputes over the dating of Easter (and his rather obdurate character) saw him driven out of Luxeuil, and on a restless curve around Northern France, Germany and Italy for the rest of his life, including an interlude in southern Brittany, in the Carnac area. I think of him as a monk on the move, destined to itineration. A concept of my acquaintance. But he was someone who didn't ever find their forever place in this life, although his journeying has led to a more modern distinction. Thanks to the impetus of the Friends of Columban in Bobbio, Italy, Pope Benoit XVI declared Columban the patron saint of motorcyclists in 2011. There's a Pardon in his honour in this context every year in Camaret on the western edge of Brittany. It's a pleasing thought, the saint on a motorbike, to get me through to the end of this difficult day.

Leaving the coastal path with some relief at another guard-house with a tower, I find the tall, narrow Chapelle Notre-Dame du Verger perched well above the beach. Again there is that sense of the change from human constructed forts for defence and protection to statues and chapels dedicated to the Virgin Mary. A huge painting inside above the west door shows the dramatic scene of sailors close to disaster at sea receiving a vision of Our Lady.

The building is a 19th century construction on the site of an earlier chapel, said to have been vowed if rescue from the waves was granted. This triumph over the elements is a rare contrast to the sad stories of mourning women and unburied men that haunt the coasts of Brittany. I think that unavoidable sense of tragedy connected with the sea is at the heart of my disconnect with the littoral.

Cancale is a few kilometres of road walking away by the direct route, so I opt for a lift as far as the neo-Gothic church in the centre above the famous port, and take a much-needed break from my journey overnight. Physically, this has been a hard slog of a day and mentally miserably in all those blustery gusts. But what has been positive is the look back to the origins of my personality, the things I have loved with zeal all my life and which have brought me here in Brittany to a primarily outdoor existence, with work based on searching and finding. It is impossible to imagine a better way of being for a very solitary someone like me. I go to sleep feeling thankful not only for the Tro Breiz, but also my whole life journey.

## 14 Stepping into magic: a very recent saint, sacred summit and a wounded cathedral

Next day there's time to examine Cancale's massive church that dominates the town from its high plateau. It was built in the late 19th century to cater for increased numbers of worshippers. Inside it forms a towering pale space, blue lit around the main altar. The patron is Saint Méen (or Meven), who came to Brittany with Saint Samson and later established a monastery near Saint-Méen-Le-Grand, which my Tro Breiz route will pass later. He is traditionally invoked for curing scabies (known as the *mal de Saint Méen*) and other skin diseases, but many ex-votives of boats here in Cancale reflect the prime occupation of his parishioners. Similarly, one stained-glass window shows Jesus preaching from a boat on the Sea of Galilee whilst the disciples, designated 'fishers of men' cast their nets in the water.

I am more struck by the evidence of a much more recent saint, honoured with a chapel in the nave. Jeanne Jugan (1792-1879) was born here in the town and later founded the order of the Little Sisters of the Poor, in Saint-Servan. She worked tirelessly to help unfortunates in the community, but was pushed aside from the organisation by a jealous priest who presented himself as the originator of this extensive charitable project. She spent the rest of her life in Saint-Pern, training novices for service. A later enquiry brought the injustice to light and the priest was deposed from office, recalled to Rome for a forced retirement. Jeanne was canonised only recently, by Pope Benoit in 2009, after attested miracles of healing. An American doctor recovered from cancer of the oesophagus in 1989 after being given only months to live. His wife had prayed constantly to Jeanne Jugan for intervention. The criteria of sainthood are little changed over nearly two thousand years.

Leaving the church in light rain, I pass statues of two women wielding their oyster baskets, for Cancale is the oyster capital of Brittany. Usually La Houle, the port down below, is packed with tourists feasting on fresh shellfish, but today there are few people about. Everything is dull and damp, most businesses firmly closed. I quickly leave the line of restaurants behind, pressing on round the bay, below the Moulin du Terte à la Caille, a windmill turned holiday home, and down over a rocky way to the beach in front of the Château du Beauregard. This house is a handsome 18th century Malouinière with extensive grounds, white double gates giving access to the shore. The sand is a crunch of microscopic shell underfoot: it would be a wonderful place to swim in better weather.

Between the 'Karting' circuit and the shellfish farms of Les Nielles, the path switches to a track on the land side of the main road. By the time I get to the first houses of Saint-Benoit-des-Ondes, the sky has brightened, and when I finally cross back to the top of the beach, there are runners and a few cyclists out. The close view is green, brown, and the white of sand; further off, blue, grey and ochre streaks tail off into the distance. The line of houses with coloured shutters, all have the air of substantial structures, solidly built and well-kept. This must have been a prosperous place in the late 19th/early 20th centuries. It may be so now, within striking distance of jobs and services in Dol, Cancale and Saint-Malo. Eastern Brittany is quite obviously still more affluent than the west.

To start a journey along the fringe of the Bay of Mont-Saint-Michel is to enter another world. Like that of Saint-Brieuc, with an astonishing tidal range, it belongs to both land and sea, but here the scale transforms into three separate and merging spaces, with the strand the dominant personality, close to the walker when the water line is far away. It is also a pilgrim's metaphor of transformation. The air carries the mixed scents of marine life here: salt, shellfish, seaweed and an intangible vegetal smell from the dunes mixed with newly cut grass from the public spaces by the road. Past the camping, two channels of water pour through mud banks into the bay, one the Canal des Allemands, part of German defensive works to isolate Saint-Malo in WWII, the other its *bief* or offshoot.

Beyond La Vildé La Marine (from *villa dei*, the house of God) I get back on the shore. Horses pulling little chariots are practising for racing on the exposed strip of sand, their drivers hunched dark silhouettes against the grey expanse of exposed seabed. Far out a line of resonant blue water stretches from the port at Cancale off towards the coast of Normandy, out of my sight. In the haze to the east, the shadowy outline of Mont-Saint-Michel, unmistakable in shape but so lacking in detail as to be nebulous to the point of fantastical. A kingdom hovering on the edge of the imagination. There is no sign of my goal, Mont-Dol, much closer to hand but inland, lying too low to impose on the line of sturdy houses that edges the bay. It is not until reaching Hirel and nearly at the turn-off from the shore to cross the polders that I glimpse its wooded contour, just as distinctive in shape as the other 'mountain' of the bay. Mont-Dol was once a semi-island too, which shows how dramatically the bay has changed with rising and falling sea levels over aeons of time.

There are many people out now, some just standing on the dune to look out over the great vista ahead. Coming up to the road, I see hundreds of fragments of scallop shells stamped into the earth, looking like a designed mosaic. The salt marsh grasses intermesh with samphire, and the weird sight of one individual plant unaccountably covered by hundreds of tiny snails is puzzling. The windmills once so common here – more than 100 along the bay in the 19th century – loom ahead. One on the sea side of the path is for sale, with an estate agent called Blot, which makes me smile. British people of my age may remember Tom Sharpe's crazy novel Blott on the Landscape. The mill opposite, like most other survivors, has been turned into a house.

The land bereaved of sea is grey here. A signpost with Mon Tro Breizh and several other waymarks points off the strand and inland on a single lane road across reclaimed marshes. This is to be my last direct contact with the coast for a very long time: more than two hundred kilometres of walking will separate the north and south coasts of Brittany. The abrupt jutting line of hills around St Broladre and Roz-sur-Coueson form a shadowy curtain far ahead. A last look across the bay at the island abbey of Mont-St-Michel shows it still hazy and unreal. A mirage. Like the story I'm going to meet up with on Mont-Dol, a tale of fierce rivalry between the Archangel himself and the Devil.

After crossing the river Guyoult at Haut Pont, the lane pushes forward across the flats towards Mont-Dol. Evidence of water management is all around from the roadside channels to a water treatment plant. The final ascent, rather unobtrusively turning up between a line of houses, is a very steep one, slippery on the stone in damp conditions, and it seems to emerge into nothing much on the summit, a patch of green between two windmills, one very private and fenced off, the other often open to the public. To the right ahead is the new vineyard of Chardonnay grapes, under the Côte du Moulin label, which I've witnessed since its infancy in 2019, now looking established on the southern slope of the hill.

There is something about Mont-Dol that I have never found elsewhere. It has a peculiar atmosphere drawn from the varied elements of geology, history and religion, something that has touched me personally. Energy has seeped down into the earth here from all the human story on the mound, whether still in evidence or long departed. The bones of exotic animals found in 1872 in the old quarry – lion and bear, mammoth and rhinoceros – indicate a palaeolithic site with well-developed trapping mechanisms for the hunt on which survival was based. The stone bases of what may have been the houses of a neolithic settlement can be seen near the huge cross on the south face looking across to the town of Dol.

As a schoolboy over there, Chateaubriand used to come out this way with his teachers and fellow pupils for an afternoon excursion. He describes the remains on the summit as Gallo-Roman ruins in his memoir of early life in this area. One of his teachers, Marie-François Rever, wrote about *taurobolia* found on Mont-Dol, stone altars designed for the slaughter of bulls and a shower of blood for the recipient underneath. These could suggest a cult of Mithras, popular in Roman times, or maybe of Cybele, the great mother goddess of the East. They were destroyed in

1802, and the models made seem to have disappeared, although reference remains in the records of Rennes museum. And I have an old booklet with a grainy photo.

Saint Samson established a monastery on the hill, but the earliest chapel on the summit was dedicated to Saint Michael. Legend records the latter's struggle with the devil here. The Archangel wanted possession of the island that now bears his name, where the Devil had already established himself. So he built a vast glittering palace on Mont-Dol, which so excited the jealousy of the Devil that a swap was agreed. Saint Michael took up residence in the bay, but the Devil discovered that the shimmering edifice he had accepted in exchange was actually made of ice and soon melted away under the sun's rays. In another version the two fought savagely on the hill-top here until the Archangel managed to hurl his adversary from the summit. Claw marks on the stone near the chapel show how the Devil tried to hang on. Another stone, tucked away in the bushes further along the edge, bears the footprint of the Archangel himself, as he launched his flight to Mont-St-Michel.

Monks from the monastery on Mont-Saint-Michel built a priory here. The building fell into disuse at the time of the Revolution, and its stones were used to build a tower for the Telegraph de Chappe in 1802. This form of communication, travelling between Paris and Brest, did not last long. It was destroyed and the stones put to the

construction of the existing chapel to Notre-Dame de l'Espérance. The octagonal tower with a great statue of Our Lady also dates from this time, inaugurated in 1857. After an outbreak of cholera in Mont-Dol in 1849, the local priest had placed little statues of the Virgin Mary outside houses and the village was saved from the worst ravages of the disease. After this, the cult of Mary intensified and pilgrimages to the hill-top became significant.

Prior Philippe Thoreau, in retirement here in the late 17th century, planted the great gnarled, leathery chestnut trees which survive to this day. I wander between them now, touching each one in marvel. They are just as atmospheric as the religious paraphernalia on the plateau. In the autumn when they are heavy with fruit, I have seen whole families come up to collect their fallen bounty from the earth. There are apple trees too, by the mysterious lake which is fed from an unknown source. According to one story, in the 8th century Saint Thuriau planted apple trees that produced fruit even in the winter. This is a fecund kind of place in many ways. I sense a wealth of deep human experience under my feet, matching the density of granite and dolerite stone which form the mound.

Mont-Dol is a great bowl of historical and religious soup under huge skies, with 360° views over the bay and the marshes, Mont-St-Michel in silhouette far away and the massive cathedral of Dol-de-Bretagne on its bastion to the south. Legend says that whilst he still held Mont-Dol, the Devil watched Saint Samson working on the construction of the first religious building across the plain and was outraged by this provocation. He tore up a great rock and threw it towards the nascent centre of Christianity. Such was the malignant force behind this launch that the top of one rising tower was shorn off and the stone rebounded a further three kilometres to land upright in the earth. Indeed, it is still there, and we shall meet this remarkable monument later on. For the moment, I want to stay up here, relishing the sensation of history from the inside out for a little longer.

Eventually, I go down through the village of Mont-Dol, past the ancient church with its graphic frescoes (featuring the devil again) and through the houses to descend onto the marshes. It's not far across the flat lands cut by drainage channels to the citadel of Dol-de-Bretagne, large and real ahead on its escarpment. The profile of the cathedral with one half-height tower (it was never completed after the Devil's intervention) dominates the view. It looms larger and larger as the little lane meanders towards the railway and express-way. The noise of traffic echoes all around as I pass through the tunnels to come out below the fortifications. Up a steep flight of steps, I'm on the ramparts, looking back across to the sacred hill of Mont-Dol.

Last summer I was here in the town of Dol-de-Bretagne to see the departure of the annual Tro Breiz pilgrimage, organised by the Association Chemins du Tro Breiz, setting out for a week of walking to reach Rennes. These days the inclusion of Brittany's current capital and the older one of Nantes in the Tro Breiz rather changes the nature of the original which celebrated the founding saints and the earliest days of the Breton state and language. I prefer to stick with the sacred seven. The debate still rages about reunification of Brittany to bring the territory of Loire-Atlantique back into the fold, having been separated by the Vichy government in WWII. Nantes is now something of a political hot-potato. But neither Rennes nor Nantes belong to the Breton-speaking area of historical Brittany, founded by Celtic monks. Those places had cathedrals and bishops from the Church of Rome, before the arrival of the Breton saints from across the Channel.

I can't help dwelling on the memories of last year now, locked into my own very different solitary Tro Breiz, as I sit in the rampart park among groups of students from the college just outside the gate. Early in the morning, hundreds of people of all shapes, sizes and ages were gathered in the cathedral for mass before departure. I'd talked to a few the day before, hearing their motives and hopes for the journey. Predictably these were various, some deeply religious, others apparently social, but clearly a highlight of the year for everyone. Pilgrimage can be the living expression of *communitas*, bringing people together in a spirit of faith, people who may have little in common otherwise.

They will share meals, sleep in village halls, participate in religious services, sing as they march, led by priests and processional crosses. I watched the faces in the cathedral carefully. The route will be hard going physically, up to 25 kilometres a day, so way beyond my capacity. Some look built for distance walking at a brisk pace, others may struggle, but the camaraderie will doubtless carry them along. All exude a sense of anticipation, mostly eager. Some have the wild, restless eyes of religious fervour, others just look tired with the early start. For all the shared goals and purpose of this journey, they remain a collection of individuals. Amongst the happy crowd, motivated by new stimulation within a secure context, a few drawn, anxious faces stuck in my mind.

As mass began, the cathedral appeared full, although the many that came after me during the service were somehow absorbed into the throng. Stewards buzzed about whispering and pointing to spaces that would hold a few extra bodies. I had a good place right at the back in a little row of four seats and was able to see every pilgrim who entered and watch their private rituals with water from the stoop and genuflection towards the high altar. Most are clearly religious devotees, participants in all the stages of the mass. It binds them at a deep level which will be given physical and spiritual expression in their pilgrimage.

The marchers were fascinating: all ages, the families with small children tending to be late, how would they manage for pace and distance, and morale in poor weather? Everyone was clothed with waterproofs for the day ahead, many had banners. The medieval regions of Brittany were on show in the presence of historic flags: I could see the lion of Léon and the dragon of the Trégor well represented. Nantes is there too, Saint-Malo and Vannes, the ubiquitous Gwen ha du (white and black, which has become the modern symbol of Brittany), and the older, simpler Kroaz Du (black cross). The latter may date back to the third Crusade in 1188. Group identity, bound by shared faith. Many pilgrims knew each other, perhaps from earlier years. There were many taps on the shoulders, embraces and broad grins of reunion in and outside the church.

The service brought the spirit of place in the cathedral to life, full of voice and music, prayer and praise, swelling up into the vast space above the nave. All the mixed emotions of so many people coming together in a great surge of something... I suppose faith is the word, but I felt it even though I don't share their beliefs. After the ritual responses, sit down, get up, semi-sing, be quiet, I exchanged a handshake with the young woman next to me, who was tense when she arrived but after mass seemed transformed by joy, stepping forward eagerly to queue for communion.

Outside, momentum built towards the off. Groups gathered, sporting banners and yet more flags. Here, en masse, a display of territorial pride and identification! Bretons have long memories and fierce allegiances to their origins. For all the hundreds scattered about outside the cathedral, the whole thing got underway very smartly on the sound of a whistle, with four high-vis jacketed marshals leading the procession briskly up the narrow confines of the rue Ceinte with its fine old houses once inhabited by canons and chaplains. The long file fell in behind and within minutes they were gone, their string of noise buzzing off with them like a bee in flight.

Back inside, the cathedral was empty and yet still full, replete with something I can only describe as spirit. In place of prayer and chant was an annoying obbligato of droning machinery from the works outside. I sat down again at the back of the nave. A lone individual came in to pray. Two little old men like gnomes fidgeted up the aisle towards me, awkwardly carrying a statue between them. It's Notre Dame du Tro Breiz, 'always at the head of the march' who is about to be stuffed into the boot of a car and transported rather un-magically to her rightful place. The cathedral breathed steadily, well-satisfied with the last hour's exchange of energy.

Remembering all this, I'm here again in the same place on a very different path, physically and spiritually. The magnitude of the cathedral, outside and in, is truly impressive, befitting its status as the doyen of Breton religious history. King John's soldiers destroyed an earlier version cathedral in 1203, and (if you don't accept the Devil's role), only one tower was completed in the subsequent restoration through lack of funds, although pilgrims arriving to honour the relics of Saint Samson certainly contributed large sums to the enterprise. Rather more recently the Welsh author Ken Follet has donated royalties from his book *Notre Dame* to the cause, after being impressed not least by the legendary founder, another Welshman, Saint Samson, one of the founding Seven. The unfinished tower lends character to this remarkable building, which is not without its mysteries, like the double well, linked by an underground chamber, with shafts inside and outside the walls.

The soaring height of the long narrow nave is splendid, and enhanced by the oldest stained glass decoration (some from the 13th century) in Brittany. Saint Samson is given his due place here, from arrival in a little boat shaped like a wooden turret to a group vignette where he is surrounded by the other founding saints. The apsidal chapel with a modern statue is dedicated to him, and the extensive ambulatory with ten chapels indicate the footfall of pilgrims over the ages. I wander through these sacred spaces in awe at the skill of medieval builders. The glorious windows throw down their light, deep blues and reds onto the massive yet delicate Gothic columns. It is a space one could almost live in, uplifted and inspired on a daily basis.

Outside the west door stands the Maen Vag (stone boat, see p.208) honed from granite in 2000 by Jean-Yves Menez, in reference to legends of the saints arriving on Armorican shores in this fashion. A beautiful object and yet far from ornamental as it has made numerous short voyages with crews of up to 20 people. The stories probably have quite rational explanations – boat-shaped rocks on the beach, cooking-stones or ballast thrown overboard, a confusion of vocabulary between Breton *koum* (valley shape = stone trough) and Latin *cumba*, a small boat – but the miraculous transportation of saints across the Channel was an important part of their impact and status in the legendary tradition. In fact, navigation across the strait in more practical wooden vessels was commonplace well before the Age of Saints: as early as the Bronze Age, oak plank boats were plying these waters.

Even on this wintry day, the town is busy, a bundle of history in modern wrappings. Dol-de-Bretagne is full of surprise and wonder. The oldest house in Brittany with 12th century hound's tooth carving on the arches stands proud in the main street, which itself is named after the Stuart royal house of Scotland. Their originator, Walter FitzAlan, the High Stewart, was descended from nobility here. The family of Geoffrey of Monmouth, author of the Arthurian industry, he who put the Holy Grail on the map, came from Dol. A representation of that sacred object decorating an early 16th century bishop's tomb in the cathedral is lit by shafts of sunlight at midday on the summer solstice.

Apart from these absorbingly odd strands of connection, the town is architecturally dazzling, with rows of colourful half-timbered houses, glorious stone manors and ecclesiastical dwellings from the heady period when Dol was a distinguished bishopric. It was even once, in the thrilling years of the mid 9th century, the seat of the archbishop of a nascent Brittany, source of a dispute with Rome that lasted for hundreds of years. When Breton leader Nominoë was intent on creating a kind of nation state in solidarity against the Franks, he sought to strengthen Breton institutions, including the church. Up until this time, the bishopric of Dol (and other Breton bishops) had been subject, in the Catholic hierarchy of the Church of Rome, to the Metropolitan bishop of Tours, outside the bounds of Brittany.

Nominoë brought the Breton churches together under the leadership of Dol, hence Samson's anachronistic place as leader in representations of the seven founding saints, often wearing the *pallium*, or white stole denoting a metropolitan archbishop. There is no doubt, however, that Samson in his own time of the 6th century was a figure of prestige, comfortable with great and good, attending the Council of Paris c550, and interceding with Emperor of the Franks, Childebert, for the release from house arrest of Judual, heir to the throne of Domnonée under threat of usurpation by the tyrant Conomor. Not for him the solitary retreat of a rural monastery. Samson was a mover and shaker.

There are also dubious claims that Nominoë was crowned king in the cathedral at Dol at the time of his promotion of the bishop, but the evidence is equivocal and sources usually refer to him as *dux* or leader/duke. The political issue is less important than the religious prestige handed to the town. It caused an outcry in Tours, hardly surprisingly, and appeals were made to various popes by both sides over the next few hundred years, so entrenched were the two sides. The dispute was finally settled against Dol by Pope Innocent III, in the very different political world of 1209.

The town makes much of the Nominoë connection, searching for the unique claim, the ultimate prestige, as if the rest is not enough. Such manipulations aside, Dol is a strong place on every level and one of the most interesting sites I know. I have much preferred my solitary visit now to the shared experience of the Tro Breiz pre-depart a year ago. I lack that capacity for communal celebration, finding the great mass of out-poured feelings, hopes, fears and longings totally overwhelming. I don't envy them, but it is impossible not to respect and be glad for the joy of others.

## 15 Stumbling into grief: Celtic identity, a celebrity stone and an annoying bird

Those old saints are still alive. Moving around Brittany it would be hard not to feel this with all the visible signs of their heritage from the past, as well as modern initiatives like the Valley of the Saints in Côtes d'Armor, a bizarre kind of tourist attraction. My time in Dol has made me think more about the element of survival, the way their memory was kept alive and kicking through centuries of turbulence, through political changes, the Catholic Church's preference for bloody martyrs and the Holy Family, the religious rejection of the French Revolution and many other factors that might have seen the end of our Seven Founders. But they endure, and there are reasons for that in what they represent.

The elevation of the cult of Samson and another forceful action of Nominoë in replacing non-Breton bishops with Breton-speakers in his territory may have consolidated the importance of the seven founding saints, who were clearly holding their own in popular appeal long after their deaths. There was now a physical structure ready and waiting for pilgrimage. The writing of *Vitae* or Lives of saints in the scriptoria of monasteries was well underway in the 9th century, as we have seen with Wrmonoc's *Life of Saint Pol*. The first *Life of Saint Samson* appeared perhaps

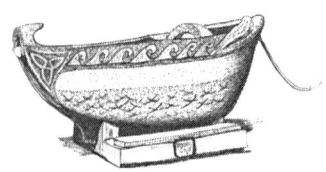

even earlier, in the 8th century (some say the 6th, soon after his death). These texts, hagiographical though they were, presented another key element in the perpetuation of their memories and miracles. They also bound the saints to specific localities, tying their stories into the power of place.

In the 11th and 12th centuries, a time of reconstruction after Viking upheavals, there seems to have been solidification of a cult of the Seven Saints of Brittany. The building of stone abbeys and cathedrals must have been literally awesome to ordinary people and enhanced the profile of the Breton saints. From this period also comes a prayer to the founding saints in the missal of Vougay in Finistère, and a reference in *The Song of Roland*, a famous *chanson de geste*, to a banner with the inscription *VII. Sains de Bretaingne*. What appears to be a *Life of Saint Ronan* includes a numbered list of their names in the form of a cartouche: Brioci, Sanson, Machut (Malo), Patern, Courentin, Paulus, Tuduualus.

Their association with the beginnings of Brittany, the growth of settlements and the development of the Breton language were already looking back to a distant past. When nobles and monks, who had left to escape all the turbulence of the Viking incursions into the vulnerable peninsula of Armorica, returned from an embryonic France, there was a growth in the use of French and consequent decline in Breton. On the other hand, there was also a great return of relics, a tangible reminder of the saints and an inspiration for the affection in which they were held by ordinary people. Tombs and remains attracted pilgrims (and their donations), and were the source of many a miracle cure, which in turn boosted the reputation of these holy men even long after death.

The saints are therefore a link to the Celtic origins of Brittany, a crucial support in the notion of that seminal stage of identity, pre-dating the arrival of Franks (and later French rule). They reflect the importance of ancestors and faith that seems to have lasted right up to this time. And yet, the Tro Breiz pilgrimage really is like a jigsaw puzzle. I feel it in the fragmentary way in which I'm pursuing the journey, and in the nature of the evidence, tantalising references to names and titles with very little specific detail of who and how and in what manner. Tens of thousands of pilgrims followed this route but we know nothing of the experience, the individual response to such a pious undertaking. They honoured the relics at each chapel, church and cathedral, made offerings, sought remissions of sin and perhaps healing for themselves or others. But their voices are almost silent, and it's the sound of the saints we still hear, an ancient music of unquiet memory.

Leaving Dol, I am about to move into country I know well. Not far away is Combourg and its famous château, childhood home of Chateaubriand, sadly not on my route for the Tro Breiz, but my second spiritual home for the last decade. I spent a month there for research in 2013 and made many good friends, not least local historian Christophe Deceneux and his wife Jacqueline, who showed me many places of interest in the area. Places that lie ahead now, as I pass the railway station and descend into the valley of the Guyoult. Across a watery system of basins and channels lies the former Abbaye-sous-Dol, now a retirement home. It was where young François-René de Chateaubriand took his first communion.

The road curves round into the village of Carfantin, past another lake, and through houses of distinctive mauve stonework to a little oasis where the *fontaine* of Saint Samson sits on often saturated ground, riddled by streams. The name Carfantin is from the Breton *ker feunteun*, village of the sacred spring. The structure itself is a relatively recent re-working with a wonderfully human statue of the saint, hand raised in benediction with the air of waving a friendly greeting. It always makes me smile. This is the spot where Samson is said to have arrived via the river and set his first oratory before the miracle of curing local ruler Privatus' wife of leprosy and exorcising his daughter of possession by a demon. The green spirit being pulled out of the top of the girl's head is shown in Samson's stained glass illustrations in Dol cathedral's main window. It looks rather like a magic trick.

This prowess brought him the land for the monastery of Dol and the subsequent cathedral. Here at Carfantin, I feel even closer to the essence of the saints than in the grand building up in the town. Samson became a public figure of standing, but here in the green depth of this humble valley, a small group of monks stopped, looked about and thought of settling. Here nature must have been a big part of their decision with fertile soil and fishing grounds, above all plenty of water, that sustainer of life and community. Spirit of place may also have played its part.

Here connection to the past is close, and the ghosts of those pioneers whisper still.

It's impossible to resist the siren call of the nearby Menhir du Champ Dolent. I walk uphill to the plateau where the neolithic stone sits, astonishing in its bulk and height (9m). The Devil had some force to hurl it from Mont-Dol. But what did those monks make of this ancient statement? Did they even realise it was man-made, in their own age when building was in wood? Did it just provide a useful landmark for giving directions – make for the big stone and then our place is five minutes downhill towards the river? The early church's attitude to 'pagan' monuments wavered about from papal decrees urging destruction to a more pragmatic notion of assimilation, by re-using sites and Christianising standing-stones with crosses.

Here in a Breton landscape littered with megaliths, so many of which survive (although so many are lost), maybe the incoming saints left well alone, and let the people keep their rituals around these ancient landmarks. Or re-spun the origin stories to bring them into their own remit, as with the tale of Saint Pol, claimed to have placed Men Marz (6m) himself, to set a boundary for the sea to respect after flooding at recently established religious settlements in north Finistère. It's like scribbling 'Pol was here' on the stone, Christian oneupmanship.

This section of the Tro Breiz will pass a series of abbeys, once vital facilities for travellers, each forming a sharply controlled contrast with the stark raw power of the Menhir of Champ Dolent. On the way to the first I pass through Baguer-Morvan, an attractive village with a very solid church and an interesting name. The definition is uncertain but a favourite is 'a group' (bagad) of men from the sea (*morvan*)', which could reflect the arrival of those Dark Age incomers from Great Britain, but it seems more likely that *bagar*, recorded in 1181, is a hagionym, reference to an unknown saint. There were a lot of those, reduced to nothing more than a heap of linguistic hints. Unfortunately, I've no time to linger in Baguer and anyway the church, dedicated to those contrastingly high Catholic icons Peter and Paul, is closed.

At the end of a lane through tall trees (some still lying smitten by Storm Ciaran) the view opens up to embrace the well-tended gardens around the harmonious façade of the Abbaye de Beaufort's 18th century version. Today it is the softest of sacred places one could imagine. The sisters are tidying the area around the car-park as I pass through very close by and, although they are speaking among themselves, none looks at me or acknowledges my presence which is understandable, but a little uncomfortable as I feel suddenly invisible. Just a silent smile would have been nice. With my rucksack and walking boots, don't I look like a pilgrim? And pilgrims are welcomed here by long tradition.

This was originally a medieval château under the control of the Comte de Combourg, and after the typical ups and down of Breton châteaux over the centuries, came into religious use in 1950, followed by the arrival in 1963 of four Dominican nuns to build a new community. And to renovate a long neglected building. Today all looks immaculate and the gardens are beautiful. Apparently, apart from the traditional jams and honey in the on-site shop, the enterprising sisters make and embroider liturgical vestments and altar cloths. But the shop is fortunately closed during my visit, although equally fortunately, the chapel is not. I am looking forward to seeing it again.

I am not prepared, however, for the strong feelings that sweep over me on entering. I felt something rather happier on the day many years ago when I first came here with Christophe and Jacqueline. But now the emotion is one of overwhelming sense of loss, recalling that lovely day, so I sit down for a quiet cry. Christophe died very suddenly in 2019. He was only 57. His quiet knowledge and wisdom fill my memories of this area. The work he has left behind reflects a mind piqued by curiosity for megaliths, sacred geometry and all facets of the esoteric. But most of all this fellow-searcher was simply a good companion. I wish I could have had the chance to discuss this journey with him.

The small chapel is comforting, with its unadorned stone walls and barn-like wooden beams. On the west wall, a clear round window with thin black tracery in a sunburst frames the blue sky and an ivy-laden tree skeleton outside. Two large panels replicating this design divide nave and choir, whilst a simple stone table serves as altar, with bright religious icons spontaneously arranged on the walls behind. There is a gentle intimacy here. Unlike so many religious spaces with their weight of grief and sorrow, this has a cheerful atmosphere and a sense of emotional safety, so I stay until it has percolated my sadness, and leave feeling lighter.

Coming out onto the steps I am looking down on the end of the Étang de Beaufort and its wooded surround. The trees are not yet in leaf but the grounds of the abbey feel full of latent growth. Birds are busy, the nuns still gardening as I retrace my steps and set off for another idyllically situated abbey, this time at Le Tronchet, only a little over 4km away. Here there is not the same sense of unity as Beaufort because the impressive former *logis* by the water is now a smart lakeside hotel and I have neither the means nor appearance to check it out. The 17th century church and cloister higher on the hill are still open to the public. The latter unusually has a huge holly in the centre, a tree I'm very fond of and visit when I can. It is said to be three hundred years old. I remember a friend once saying, as we walked through a wood, he didn't know holly could be a tree. Here's the finest example, dazzling when illuminated by copious red berries.

My next goal is closer to my own personal sense of sacred than enclosed religious buildings. Somewhere I really feel inside a place, not looking in as an observer. The Forêt de Mesnil and an *allée couverte* like no other. Mesnil is a corruption of the word *maison* and the whole forest was once managed for the Malouin corsair Robert Surcouf, who bought it to build a hunting lodge and exploit the sporting opportunities. Covering over 600 hectares, it is a rich environment for flora and fauna. Oak and beech dominate, with Scots pine and spruce muscling their way into the mix. The main paths are straight avenues, but plenty of inviting tracks lead into the wilder sections. It provides a glorious walk, twisting and turning, rising and falling until I find, after two attempts, the way through to the Fairies' House, a megalith excavated and 'restored' by Sir Robert Mond in 1931. A small but rather vainglorious pillar beside the monument records this fact. He was helped by suffragette writer Vera Christina Chute Collum, whose name is also inscribed. She was later to write a pamphlet about the excavation, posing her ideas on mother-goddess cosmology.

Even with this modern 'help' and a busy footfall of visitors today, the site retains a depth of numinosity. It is a place of presence. Nothing can change this, not people climbing all over the stones, nor kids screaming as they play inside. The atmosphere is of itself. One factor is the sense of anticipation. There is a five minute walk up from the car-park which builds the prospect nicely and sets my blood tingling. But this time I've approached from quite a different direction on foot right through the forest, a heightening of experience even though I know what's ahead. Perhaps the close acquaintance built over many years only adds to the expectation, as travelling to see an old friend would do in everyday life. The dimension of antiquity, of inevitable mystery is the spice here. It inspires a profound sense of awe, and I have to sit down for a while on the edge of the glade that surrounds the stones. Getting up very close will fizz my energy. The sense of ancient movement and purpose still lingers for me. The honouring of death on the land and effortful send-off for the departed. The importance of memorial, a speciality of Brittany as the Tro Breiz journey has brought home to me.

At 14m long and over 2m wide, it is a substantial construction. More than 40 stones remain, and the chamber at the end has four round spheres carved in a line on the outer face. Except they have been struck off, at the behest of an angry priest, but the empty circles bear witness. On the stone at 90° to it there are four more, untouched by hatred. What are they? The standard version for these orbs that turn up on various Breton megaliths is a representation of goddess' breasts, symbolic of a Great Mother cult. I don't know. Maybe we are missing another explanation that escapes us because we are not of the mindset that created them. Why four in each line, equally spaced? Why no indication of nipples? I don't dwell much on the puzzle here, as the aura of the monument is so strong. It is enough to be in its presence and share the same air. There is plenty of time, as I am not going much further today.

Picking up from Tressé, it's road walking to get past the St Malo/Rennes motorway that slices through the farmland, and then silence falls again on a long track down to the lake at Noë Davy and eventually the village of Coëtquen. This is another place I learnt about from Christophe the first time we met and he was explaining his thesis about Arthurian legends derived from the landscape around Combourg. (It was the closest part of Brittany to troubadours in Normandy where the Arthurian legends were developing in performance in the 11/12th centuries, with traditions easily accessible by visit or word of mouth.)

One theme is the undoubted Breton origins of Lancelot, brought up by the Lady of the Lake (at Combourg?) and destined to be the greatest warrior of the knights of the Round Table. His shield, which stoked fear in the hearts of opponents, bears three red diagonal lines on a white background. An image of this is included in the hall décor at the Château of Combourg. Why? Because the castle was once in the hands of the Coëtquen family, as the Marquis was also count of Combourg in the 16-18th centuries, and they have the same coat of arms as Lancelot. Are they the descendants of an historical knight on whom the hero was based? Their most notorious individual, Malo III Auguste de Coëtquen (1678-1727), lost his leg at the Battle of Malplaquet in 1709, an unfortunate incident at the root of the phantom wooden leg said to haunt the Château of Combourg's turning stair.

The ruins of the 15th century Coëtquen château dominate the eponymous village. Outside the gate is a stepped triangular oratory, where I sit down for a rest. It is dedicated to Our Lady of Coëtquen with two inscriptions on low marble plaques. One in French is a saying attributed to Saint Bernard: *there is more to be learnt from trees than books* (and how true that seems in this area of arboreal paradise), another in Breton *Nothing and no-one will stop me staying the course,* heartening encouragement for pilgrims, but actually the motto of the influential *Seiz breur* (Seven brothers) Breton artistic and cultural movement started in the 1920s. I say it over to myself a few times. I've loved this section of my journey, but physically I'm very tired, swollen of foot, and daunted by the vast distance still to cover.

I walk out of the village towards Saint-Hélen past the lofty curtain wall of the château and another low tower with arrow loop. The path dips then rises. Someone has set up a makeshift camp around an old vehicle in the bushes, with signs of active occupation but no-one in sight. I have no instinct of potential danger here, but keep my awareness sharp as the *landes* open before me, an area of moorland and scrubby trees being developed with state and European money as forest, in the face of the effects of climate change. It feels like open, empty land, but perhaps beyond my lifetime it will be filling a gap between established woodlands, creating a vast carbon sink and rich shelter for a myriad of wildlife. I stop and think about this for a minute. And hope.

Next a quick stop at Saint Hélen to eat my sandwich on a windy picnic table near the church. The village seems completely deserted, until a lone car hurtles through and leaves new silence behind. The eponymous Irish monk

Ellen arrived in Brittany with Saint Samson before getting his own gig here. I almost don't bother to try the door after so many locked entrances, but happily the building is open, cleanly 19th century with plain white-plastered walls, of pleasant proportions, bright stained-glass and a surprising clutch of evocative 16th burial slabs in the transept, echoes of the days when Coëtquen lords were running the show.

A steep little road climbs up to the water-tower above the village and then follows a pretty descent through woodland, where I am driven mad by a woodpecker performing loudly but invisibly very near to the path. I can even isolate the actual tree, but not the smallest flash of wings or flutter of feathers, despite the head-banging never letting up. This frustration sets me up nicely for some lengthy road-walking through a series of unremarkable hamlets back towards the Rance. I've switched off now, forced to concentrate on passings cars and frisky dogs, tired and regretting the wonderful landscape of woods, water and historic sights that have felt somehow secret and special. This is the everyday side of pilgrimage, the inevitable bits between contained in most days' journeys. I'm looking forward to an overnight stop before continuing. From now on the world is going to get considerably busier and the margins for conjuring ancient scenarios that much thinner.

Le Châtellier is where I begin my Rance journey again, this time following the opposite bank down past Dinan. The coastal path is considerably more demanding on this side, as my knees soon bear witness. In places the route climbs up well away from the water to hamlets before dropping down again. To avoid a loop in the river, I pass through the settlement of Landeboulou, which seems to be unaccountably full of exceptional architecture and I have no idea why. Later I find out the manor house was one of the earliest noble holdings in the area, but evidence for the development of the village seems scarce.

Past the flurry of Dinan's port, the river bank quietens a little and passes through wooded hillsides down to the archaic village of Léhon, one of the most visually appealing in Brittany, with a humped back bridge, enviable stone houses enhanced by colourful flowers, a ruined medieval castle and an exceptional abbey. Rather a lot for a population of little over three thousand. I love the wonderful Romanesque doorway on the west face of the Abbaye de Saint Magloire, leading into the long but surprisingly narrow church, where stone effigies of the illustrious Beaumanoir family are housed. It's hard to resist touching the gently stunning 13th century baptismal font, its rim worn into a wavy line, with carvings of faces, vines and oak leaves. Outside, the adjoining cloister is a beautifully proportioned space, austere abbey buildings surrounding a medieval style garden.

The story of Saint Magloire's arrival at the abbey is a famous one, and quite a change from conventional tales of founders. After succeeding Samson as bishop of Dol, he retired to his own monastery on the Isle of Sark, where he later died. In the 9th century, when a group of monks from Wales was seeking land in the Rance valley for a new foundation, they met Nominoë, who was out hunting there. He agree to grant them a place if they could bring the relics of a Breton saint to the new abbey. The monks fasted for three days, waiting for inspiration. When it came, they set off for Sark to steal the relics of Magloire. Fortune favoured their enterprise, affording a sort of divine justification for the dubious actions, even diverting the pursuers by a storm at sea as the thievish clerics tried to get away secretly. So Magloire came to his abbey well and truly dead on arrival in the physical plane. These same relics were harboured in the safety of Paris during Viking raids in Brittany before returning to their 'rightful' place.

I finish this long, demanding day up at Léhon's castle ruins. From the walls not only the abbey and the river are visible, but at only one kilometre away, I can see the flag fluttering from the château of Dinan. Inside the fortifications, a makeshift altar to Saint Joseph niched into one of the dilapidated towers seems incongruous. A different sort of power and might held sway here. The fortress was destroyed in 1169 by Henry Plantagenet, but almost immediately rebuilt. In 1359 the English Duke of Lancaster, in support of Jean de Montfort during the Wars of Succession, besieged Léhon and Dinan. By the 17th century, the castle had fallen into disuse and French king Louis XIII gave the remaining ruins to the abbey.

It's hard to imagine Léhon the centre of such activity and significance, the abbey and castle both enmeshed in the lives and livelihoods of the local population as well as noble rivalries. Those things that once symbolised power, control and possession are shadows of their former selves, and yet compellingly attractive to people who now come from far away to look from the outside in at the penumbrae of past glories. And in doing so, keep the village alive.

## 16  Being in good company: Templar chapel, Holy Grail church and forest deluge

My friend Lucy joins me again for two days walking north and south of Yvignac-la-Tour, with a night of welcome hospitality at her house in between. We enjoy the first part of the action very much, with a verdant, lake strewn landscape and scenic country tracks to follow. One flooded path sends us clambering through undergrowth and jumping rivulets to achieve a detour, and then we have our picnic standing among mossy tree-stumps and rampant banks of ivy. It's a great change to have easy company, smoothing out any difficulties of the way. And, great provider that she is, Lucy produces a flask of coffee to set up the afternoon effort.

The highlight of this is the little Templar chapel at Lannouée, dedicated to John the Baptist, evocative and rather moving in its truncated state with the choir intact and nave demolished. An earlier name for the hamlet was La Nouaye or La Nouée, indicating a humid place. As late as the 17th century, there was a manorial headquarters nearby, but it is now gone. For the interior, with its earth floor and small windows, there are only pictures on a noticeboard to go on. Lanouée was a *commanderie* of the Knights Templar from an early date, on a much firmer historical footing than many other foundations claimed as Templar sites.

Documents show that in 1297 Pierre de Launay was received into the order by Pierre de Villers here. This was shortly before the suppression of the Templars' Order by the Catholic Church (1312), and the redistribution of properties, largely to the Knights Hospitaller (later Knights of St John). Further evidence mentions Nicolas Séguin, the commander of the Temple of Guerch and Lanouée in 1395, a merger of two centres in the new organisation. In the early 18th century there were statues of Saint John and Saint Martin (a Catholic saint regarded as the arch-organiser of early Christianity in Gaul) decorating the altar in the chapel, and a magnificent Romanesque arcade.

Very little is known about the activities and organisation of the Templars or Red Monks in Brittany between their formation in Jerusalem in 1120 and their downfall in the early 14th century. Their original role was to protect pilgrims in the troubled times of the earliest crusades, when travel was even riskier than usual. They also acted as bankers, and large sums of money borrowed from the Order was a factor in their destruction, with accusations of corruption as well as outrage over secret initiation ceremonies. Evidence indicates that various dukes of Brittany made them grants of lands and possessions, but outside the region of Nantes, La Nouée and La Guerche (in Ille-et-Vilaine) are the only certain foundations.

Legend and local stories, however, came to ascribe Templar connection to various interesting buildings of uncertain origin, like Lanleff near the Bay of Saint-Brieuc, and perhaps places in need of greater footfall as tourism

developed. The connotation of mystery, attractive to many, also led to some hostile traditions. In the 19th century, the *Barzaz Breiz* collection of popular songs mentions ghostly apparitions of monks in white robes with large red crosses, riding skeletal horses and seeking to snatch infants, who would never be seen again. Perhaps rumours about secret rituals accounted for such fears.

We go on to Yvignac-la-Tour, where the parish church of Saint Malo with its weird round bell-tower, surprises us with a stunning Romanesque west porch, full of lively carvings, human and animal, which may have connection with the chapel at Lanouée. Despite later remodelling, the church has very early origins. The interior was inaccessible and there was no time to track down a key, even if it had been permitted. I regretted this when I looked up the details later, but generously mixed drinks and an excellent supper at Lucy's brought the day to a very satisfactory conclusion.

The next excursion is a different story. Twice the directions from the old guidebook we are following fail, with obvious changes in tracks across heavily farmed land, so there is plenty of road walking to reschedule a route. We don't help matters either by going right instead of left on a main road with no pavement, leading to some unpleasant stomping along with traffic flowing round bends at a scary speed and making little change in their line to accommodate us. When the mistake becomes clear, and by that time we have climbed a hill and passed through a sodden field with no path, there is no choice but to come back to the road further on and do it all again in reverse.

We finally make the broad Rance valley, me limping and swearing under my breath, Lucy resolutely positive, and see the river in relative infancy in comparison to the great estuary that dominated Stage 3 of the Tro Breiz and the wide channel beyond Dinan. Here it has a domestic air, a thin mud-brown stripe ambling between fields and hamlets. By the time we come up the slope to Bénin and the chapel of Saint Yves, our end point for the day, I am in a very low mood and rapidly succumbing to the pain in my wretched foot, brought on excessively by so much time on hard surfaces.

Just before the chapel is a sign pointing down between houses to the *fontaine*. I hesitate, being in the frame of mind that I've seen quite enough sacred springs and do not need another at this particular time, but thank goodness duty prevails because, down a long uncut grassy track is a beautiful little wooded enclave with a simple stone structure to mark the spring and its pretty stream, containing a statue of Saint Yves surrounded by flowers behind a grill. It feels like a special space, and a few minutes there is restorative. The chapel is closed, however, and, after reaching one car, then going back to fetch the other, and then driving back to Lucy's house in Evran, I am more than ready for a long rest.

It was some weeks before I could return and follow the route around Saint-Méen-le-Grand. My prior knowledge of this town was limited to a brief stop to be ill in the car-park when being driven home from Rennes hospital some years ago, and the fact that it was the home town of Louison Bobet, the famous Breton cyclist who was the first to win the Tour de France in three consecutive years (1953-55). The diminutive 'Louison' was an affectionate mark of his widespread popularity. Indeed I'm sure he is better known

Brittany-wide than the monk Saint Méen, who gives his name to the town.

The centre is dominated by the curiously extravagant bell-tower that tops the 1930s town hall. The epithet 'grand' was added in 1918 to distinguish it from little Saint Méen in Finistère, although the saint himself probably merits the appellation in the religious world. Old houses of different styles with their modern shop-fronts line the main street, and in looking at them all, I manage to miss the sign for the abbey church and wander about a bit before finally coming down to the east front, which immediately lends witness to the age of the original construction. It was built in 1024, 2km away from the saint's original foundation (c600CE), which was destroyed by both Franks and Vikings in their turn. The saint is yet another of Saint Samson's entourage, possibly even his nephew. Méen was granted land for a monastery by a local noble or by the king of Domnonée.

After the saint's death, his relics were kept at the abbey until removed in 919 with the Viking threat and returned in 1074 to the new build nearby, the current abbey, which contains his tomb. This soon became a centre of pilgrimage. In 1850 the church was reorientated with the nave and choir swapping places, and a doorway made in the east facade to facilitate access for worshippers, so it's a curiously back to front structure now. In 1986, 14th century frescoes portraying the life of Saint Méen were discovered in the adjoining chapel of Saint Vincent, also called the Chapel of Paradise. It's an impressively elaborate display, faded madder brown on yellowing cream plaster. Scenes show him striking a new spring from the ground with his staff, blessing his abbey and surrounded by monks on his death-bed.

The town of Saint-Méen grew in proximity to the crossing of two Roman roads, Rennes-Carhaix and Corseul-Rieux, the latter providing a rough line south taking the route I'm following towards a very different location, hamlet to hamlet through prime farming country. The impression is more of a road walk than a Roman road walk in this heavily managed land, but it is the transitory stage from the practicalities of rural life to the magical world of the imagination, for now I am entering 'Arthurian' territory. This is a self-proclaimed feat of coherence generated by local tourism that began in the 17th century, accelerated out of the park in the 19th and now powers the economy of a whole region.

The Château de Comper is an 18th century reincarnation of the medieval château built of characteristic purple schist. It could almost dip its toe in the lake which is transformed by romantic association into one possible home of the Lady of the Lake. I find the estate well barricaded to keep the public out in this off-season. Only a few bits of the ancient structure linger like a folly at the entrance to set the mood for the Centre of Arthurian Imagination which awaits inside. The last time I visited, the exhibition was still trying to toe the line carefully between history and legend, with some encouraging analysis and source criticism. I wonder how long it can hold out against the relentless popularism of tourist boards and visitor demands.

Concoret, the village only a few kilometres away, is just as purple. The *mairie* and the church, staple village buildings, lead the way with the mauve bricks, almost acquiring a menace from the depth of shade. The latter is a mishmash of styles, dating from 1406 but extensively remodelled in 1900, with a little round stair turret more appropriate for a castle. There's an impressively sculptural magnolia tree on the north façade. The patron is St Laurent, but it was once dedicated to Notre-Dame de la Concorde (hence the name of the village) according to the story that claims the church was built on the spot where two feuding nobles were reconciled. There's no access to the interior, but I'm not hanging around as I have accommodation booked for the night quite far ahead and want to get on to the forest of Paimpont (or Brocéliande if you accept the hype).

I remember my first sight of the magnificent oak tree, the Chêne de Guillotin, nearly a quarter of a century ago. It is said to be a thousand years old and was still vibrant and bushy, despite some major limbs being propped up for stability. Today it is almost painful to witness. I imagine the damage is due to the great storm last autumn. Now it resembles an elderly knight, trying to stand tall in an echo of earlier vigour. All except two boughs have been lopped, and the reduced outline is gaunt and grim, a reminder of the loss of dignity of old age. It will doubtless look better when some leaves come out, but right now it's a sad sight.

The walk to Folle Pensée through the pine trees is along a wide track, lined by bright yellow fresh gorse, but thick with mud and water at ground level. A few downed trees look like the mark of Storm Ciaran, but nothing on the scale of the damage I have lived with back home in Finistère. Through the din of busy wood-peckers, I hear a hunter on a higher path bellowing at his unruly pair of dogs, and then catch a glimpse of him, gun in hand. I think he has seen me, so assume it's safe to go on. Later he passes in the traditional little white van. I give the required unsmiling nod of acknowledgement as I balance on the verge to let him go by. He ignores me. The dogs are baying and gnashing their teeth through the back window. I know what they are thinking - all that running about after skinny rabbits and we could have had that feeble old pilgrim easy... Two farmers pass in tractors. My nod is correctly returned.

The only other person on the route is a lone cyclist, splashing effortfully through the red mud. Etiquette here demands a *bonjour*, sometimes even a smile. The awful conditions today merit a shared sympathetic look, and he manages a rueful grin. He is filthy, but he'll get where he's going a lot quicker than me. The forest is very still but feels wary, as if waiting for something. I find the walk repetitive and hard-going under foot, but the silence is so lovely I sit on a fallen pine to listen, surrounded by scaly maroon bark in keeping with the mud.

I am spending the night in Folle Pensée, a hamlet actually called Mad Thoughts. I assume it's a reference to the story of Eon de l'Étoile, a remarkable tale of strange behaviour and enlightened justice from the 12th century. He was a rogue monk, living wild in the forest here with a group of supporters who raided churches and abbeys in the vicinity. Some see him more as a Druid-like figure, converted to the powers of nature against the strictures of the Church. When finally brought to trial, he was spared death on grounds of mental incapacity, dying in prison not long after. This is a memorable piece of reality to balance against some of the Arthurian fantasies associated with this Forêt de Paimpont, and its heavy Brocéliande branding.

Various places make the claim to 'be' this literary forest, product of the creative minds of poets and troubadours. My friend Christophe published research to suggest that the Dol/Combourg area was a worthy possibility, and challenged the idea that Paimpont fits the available evidence from early poems. This is not the place to argue either case here, but the publication of a pot-boiler *La Table Ronde* by Auguste Creuzé de Lesser in Paris in the early 19th century revived the public imagination concerning the Arthurian tales. Two enthusiastic locals later made the rounds of this forest to identify specific sites in the stories which would inevitably entice visitors to seek out scenes of a popular myth. This would enhance the reputation of the area and do no harm to local service providers. The endeavour has grown exponentially over the years, and everything here is, often tediously, Arthurian themed. I wish a most beautiful forest, full of wonderful trees, amazing rock formations and sparkling waters was enough, without having to 'perform' as a theatre for self-referential human tales.

In the hamlet, I find a handsome house with red shutters, and Catherine, my gracious hostess. She came from another area to start afresh here more than a decade ago, and has no regrets. I imagine the traffic in summer on the single track road outside her windows leading to parking for the famous Fontaine de Barenton (claimed as the setting for Chrétien de Troyes 12th century evocation of Yvain, the Lion Knight) must be atrocious, but she seems patient and tolerant, as French people so often are. (When I get home a few days later I find I have accidentally stolen a teaspoon, and write at once to say I'll send it, but she lets me off with a charming message of welcome for another time.)

After a very good night's sleep and even better breakfast chatting to Catherine, I reach the morning rendezvous with my friend Alan. He is an historian of Roman Scotland and super map-reader. I can trust him to think about directions and give myself the liberty of looking around. The weather is grey and almost misty as we climb and look back across the valley, with long views blurred by moisture in the air. It is very cold. We talk about the state of the world as we press on, but it all seems very remote here and we could be the last people in existence even without the nuclear strike. Most of the tracks are of hard red stone, but everywhere is under a miasma of damp. Having over-heated internally and taken off my fleece, I'm walking with bare arms. This is a bad idea. They are soon like frozen sticks, in danger of snapping off when negotiating tricky bank walking, brushing against tough stands of gorse.

As we emerge on the road into the village of Tréhorenteuc, three dogs rush out wildly from a front garden and I can feel Alan's instant anxiety. I don't think there's real danger, just habitual pack behaviour. He takes my advice and stands still, but the Malinois is a mean looking brute and his hefty black labrador mate sets up a terrific barking. It's more noise than evil intent, as I suspect they are just showing off to their owner. He comes to the door and yells angrily, maybe at the dogs, maybe at us for having the temerity to walk along a public road. Who knows? They go in, chastened.

It is lunch-time as we arrive. There are two automatic public toilets, something I hate, in a car-park. Before I can ask Alan to keep guard, he has already gone into the one next door. I lock the door of mine and the red light comes on as expected. Luckily I spend a minute searching for a dry spot to put my bag down because suddenly a woman throws open the door and the flush starts...

We sit at a picnic table to eat our sandwiches, which Alan has kindly provided from a bakery in the historic town of Malestroit, where he has an old house. The bar has opened when we finish and its good to sit in more comfort and have hot coffee. The weather is set to get worse.

The church in the village is often called the Chapel of the Grail as it is, unusually, Arthurian themed. This extraordinary little bubble of esoterica was the 1940s work of Abbé Gillard, a priest with great interest in Celtic mythology and the symbolism of the Holy Grail in particular. His work represents, rather more overtly than is customary, that very Breton intermingling of different spiritual traditions. There is stained-glass showing the Grail and the Round Table, a huge mosaic of a Celtic motif white stag, and the 9th station of the cross shows Jesus at the feet of Morgane Le Fey, half-sister of Arthur and powerful sorceress. Merlin, Lancelot and fighting dragons also feature.

Gillard was removed from his post when episcopal authorities realised the extent of these unconventional activities. Astrology was one of his less acceptable interests. After his death in 'exile' elsewhere in Morbihan, he was

rehabilitated to the extent of burial in his beloved church at Tréhorenteuc. Outside there has long been a bronze statue of the priest beside the path to the church door, but it was stolen recently and we regard the empty plinth rather sadly, given the unique contribution made by an exceptional individual who had no difficulty in merging the Celtic and Christian worlds. A replacement is to be made in less valuable material.

We spend a while in the church, which offers rather a lot for reflection. The actual patron is Saint Onenne, but she can hardly compete with the notoriety of her fellows, although there is much to be said for her own contribution to the sphere of Celtic legend. She was a Breton princess who retired to a solitary religious life beside a spring at Tréhorenteuc, where she tended a flock of geese. They saved her by sounding the alert when she was threatened with rape by a young nobleman. Apart from an echo of the sacred geese of the goddess Juno saving the Roman Capitol from invading Gauls, there is also the connection of geese symbolising the links between life on earth and the Other World, and representing the Holy Spirit, rather less calm and peaceful than the traditional image of a dove. The spiritual fusion here seems very natural and calming.

Next day we endure several hours of driving rain, mostly aiming directly at our faces, for what should have been a journey through beautiful scenery. The landscape here is a stunning spread of forest, punctuated by steep outcrops of red rocks, trailed by watery falls. We pass the Valley of No Return (second choice location, after a factory was built in the first one) and brooding Fairies' Mirror lake before striking onto less frequented paths through the woods. I keep my head down against the onslaught and see little of what I was most looking forward to as we emerge onto the moors called Landes Rennaises. Some recently erected menhirs warrant a brief pause, but photographs are almost impossible in these conditions. Exhausted and dispirited, we finally see the landmark Cross of Saint Anne ahead, sheets of lurid green moss all around it shining through the murk. Even on this awful day, the views are fantastic. I seem destined to walk only boring roads through ugly villages in sunshine. By the time we reach the Abbaye de La-Joie-Notre-Dame, we've had enough for the day. It is a place where spiritual retreats are possible, but for the moment we are fixated on more worldly ambitions, like dry clothes and hot drinks.

## 17 Wanting to give up: a mighty bastion, barking women and the power of memorial

Next time I have a few free days, it's back to the trail. Loyat lies at the tip of the Lac au Duc, an expanse of water generally connected to the town of Ploërmel and its associations with the medieval duchy of Brittany. I've decided to follow the Yvel and take the western bank because there's a detour I'm keen to make. The recently seen photo of an unusual country chapel has caught my imagination and I want to visit it in the flesh. The walk to Quelneuc is worth it, as the structure is a real curiosity, more like a little house than a place of worship, with a long cone-topped chimney that is apparently the bell-tower, the only one in the locality surviving Republican vengeance at the time of the Revolution. It really is off the beaten track, on the edge of a quiet village.

The names and addresses of three keyholders are helpfully noted in the window. None are in when I knock at their doors, so the interior which one imagines would be like a little sitting-room, remains aloof. Inside (as the panel outside shows) are two statues, Saint Mathurin and Saint Gildas, who seems a long way from home in St-Gildas-du-Rhuys on the south coast in Morbihan. But the religious networks driving cult connections are as intricate as spiders' webs. Monks from his monastery had set up a priory in nearby Taupont, so honouring their founder in the vicinity was natural. The noticeboard board explains the chapel is probably the oldest in the commune, dating back in part to the 13th century. The year 1761 is inscribed over the doorway. I'll go back one day to get to know this friendly little building more intimately, rather than just rushing through. Pilgrimage throws up this dilemma over and over, the need to keep moving even when places are tugging at your arm and keen to make more meaningful acquaintance.

Now it's off across country via Guillac to see a very old friend, the Nantes-Brest canal. I walked the 365km length of this massive watery snake in 2006 and wrote a guidebook that still sells well today in updated English and French editions. The stretch between Malestroit and Josselin is one of the best sections, with the wide bucolic Oust flowing down towards Redon and its confluence with the Vilaine. There's only a little bit to do today, upstream to the mighty medieval bastion of Josselin, with a quick deviation across the bridge at Saint-Gobrien to see the notable chapel, which is being intensively renovated and not at its best for a visit, although the ancient flooring of earth and massive stone slabs is still visible.

There can be few more impressive entries than arriving at river level in Josselin, with the towering defensive façade rearing up into the sky. The formidable château was built in the late 14th century by Olivier de Clisson, who became an enemy of the duke of Brittany and was forced to take refuge in this stronghold. Partly destroyed in 1488, it was restored as a more domestic but indulgently luxurious residence by the Rohans, one of the few Protestant noble Breton families, with the permission of duchess Anne de Bretagne. The beautiful logis, full of Renaissance finesse, contrasts mightily with the austerity of the military exterior, but I'm not interested in guided tours today and the church nearby is equally worth the attention.

Our Lady of the Brambles is one of my favourites and I go in to enjoy the carved capitals and stained-glass once again before the long drive home. The last time I was here was for the famous September Pardon when the statue and glorious banners of the cult are carried in torch-lit procession. The foundation story tells how the Virgin's statue was discovered in a thorny patch, and returned to the spot each time it was taken elsewhere. And so that place became the site of a new construction in the 13th century. The original statue, said to have healing powers, was burnt at the time of the Revolution, its charred fragments preserved in a reliquary. One great curiosity was its efficacy in the case of the *Aboyeuses* or Barking Women. It is said that the Virgin Mary visited the town in the guise of an old beggar woman and was roundly abused by the local washer-women. She decreed that they and their descendants would bark like dogs. This affliction is attested in 19th century records, with early portrait photographs of stricken women, but touching the statue was regarded as the best remedy.

These stories of sanctity tied to a specific location are significant. It matters where something is, and the presence of place is a powerful element in numinosity. Spirits of whatever kind may be attached to natural features or to man-made structures. They need somewhere to manifest. The Breton saints forged a rapport with the land through hermitages, little oratories, chapels, rocks for meditation posts and springs they conjured up from the ground. The Virgin Mary and her mother Saint Anne were noted for apparition, creating a bond with local communities through this focused attention. The tale of Mary's moving statue, not unique to Josselin, shows us that not all land is created equal. Earlier Celtic religion saw spirit in trees, rivers, hills and stones, but still some spots held enhanced energies: in distinctive natural sites, the genius loci presided, a force to be honoured and appeased. Such heightened, chosen places, whether churches or caves, offer us the chance to step inside the web of sacred space.

I stay the night in the Hotel du Château, revelling in the glorious setting, and spend the evening exploring the alley-ways of the south bank, ending up outside the Priory of Sainte-Croix. I sit beside an unusual four-sided calvary to look down on the town and think about the journey ahead. Next day I'm to meet up with Alan again to start two walking days together. After the grandeur of Josselin, the route will offer small and simple fare, none the worse for that. Trégranteur, Cruguel, Plumelec... we'll move across the territory of Saint Melec.

This Welsh saint ... or was he a native Armorican or perhaps a Roman (Mellitus), sent to England where he became bishop of London, then Archbishop of Canterbury in the 7th century. He has no apparent connection whatsoever to Brittany, so perhaps his cult was brought over by a later wave of immigrants from Great Britain. His iconography seems to insist on the episcopal status. The prestige of the latter incarnation attracted a priest, Canon Guillemot, in Plumelec in the late 19th century, to breathe new life (and maybe a new persona altogether) into the declining cult of Melec. Whoever he was. The history of the 'Breton' saints is fluid and supple enough to accommodate change of this kind.

Next morning we are soon admiring the beautiful twin entrance doors to the chapel of Trégranteur, where there's a wooden statue of patron Melec with a bishop's crozier. A stained-glass window has Pope Gregory the Great sending him out to evangelise the Anglo-Saxons, the monuments of Rome all jumbled up in the background. In the precinct is an oddity. Bright flowers tumble around a granite column of justice, which in relatively recent times stood in the gateway between the entrance pillars before being moved. These rights of judgment over his tenants belonged to the local lord, whose ancient manor has been replaced by the current château (1750), standing behind fancy metal gates we passed on the way into the village from Josselin. Trégranteur is an exceptionally visually appealing village, a poor man's Rochefort-en-Terre, a pattern book of old architectural styles, where the aroma of past life is strong.

A quiet walk to Cruguel follows, enlivened by nothing more than barking dogs, a bull with menacing eyes and a dead frog. People rarely figure along small roads through arable land. Occasionally a footpath takes us through woods and across valleys, or a brief plateau gives welcome views over the wider world. We become excited by the smallest natural detail: a few rocks in the bed of a tiny stream take on the dimensions of a chaos, despite being left behind with a few paces. Alan is in charge of map-reading, fortunately, as we see very few footpath signs of any kind and not a single old Tro Breiz mark. This is a gentle route between unassuming sights, with no intensity and no obvious goal, apart from distant Vannes.

But the pilgrimage rears its head in Cruguel, where the church, an unlovely 19th century model, is set off by wide, prettily-flowered steps. It was created a few metres from an older church site (now marked by calvary with statues further down the road) to rise above the damp! Rare mention of being part of the Tro Breiz is on the panel by the (locked) door. We are in the footsteps of others, which is an encouraging reminder as today has had the atmosphere of a mild country walk rather than a religious journey. The patron is Saint Brieuc himself, a little off his familiar territory. A modern painted statue stands in the over-restored *fontaine* just below the church.

History is soon to interpose its mark. On the way into Plumelec we come up a curving track from the valley to pass the ancient Cross of Kervigo, commemorating a battle Bretons waged against invaders in 938. A nearby pond is called Mare ar sang (Blood Pool) for obvious reasons. This resistance to Viking violence did not prevent destruction in the area and shows the inland penetration of the raids, even away from main water courses. Suffering was severe, with crops and settlements devastated, inhabitants indiscriminately slaughtered, a pattern repeated in many parts of Brittany in the 9/10th centuries. A bishop of Vannes who fled inland to this area may have been a victim of the Norsemen at this time.

Plumelec is a place of memorial. On the approach, we pass a cross and oak trees planted in 2017 to commemorate local losses in WWI, with each of the 21 trees representing 10 men. Beside these are a re-located ancient standing-stone and dolmen. In the town centre we come face to face with the resistance memorial, a large bulbous menhir. The use of neolithic monuments for recording modern history is interesting. They are often thought to have been originally intended to show connection with ancestors and a sense of continuity in human experience. In conjunction with notions of war-dead in our own annals, they give a new perspective of time's elasticity and ways of preserving memories of what has made us.

This Tro Breiz journey has given me many reflections about ancestors. I will have no direct descendants and I know very little about my past Welsh family, as my parents were rarely responsive to questions. We lived as an isolated family unit without any close sense of relatives. And yet I have a strong sense of my human ancestry, especially neolithic pioneers for their engagement with the land, and the Breton saints (or perhaps more accurately the communities founded by these celibates). Because I relate so deeply to place, the monuments of both these groups speak loudly in my ear as I pass through Brittany, listening attentively to the rhythms of the past. The saints in particular are a vociferous lot, telling their foundation stories, the roots of Celtic Brittany. The chain of existence between ancient origins and contemporary continuation is of enormous historical significance, but it is also important to me personally in grounding my own existence.

The busy Plumelec *bourg* is not a place to linger. There's nowhere open to eat and the bar, packed to the gills with men past their prime, stinks of smoke and body odour. Not an easy entry for strangers, but when we sit outside hoping for coffee, the service is very friendly. We take a quick look in the church, which honours Saint Maurice, a most un-Breton saint, and seems to have ditched old Melec. On the route out of town, the *Allée de la France libre* is the site of another reminder of tragic loss of life in the futility of war, this time for the 77 parachutists of the French SAS killed in action in WWII. On the hill-top beside an old windmill, it is a simple reminder of a humble heroism long faded from our world.

The cumulation of these monuments is powerful. The town makes its mark as standard-bearer for those who can no longer speak for themselves, whose bravery and self-sacrifice ultimately led to freedom from tyranny for western Europe. The function of memorial is to keep alive the endeavours that we seem to be forgetting about too easily today in the slide towards absolute power for rulers once again. There is a role for pilgrims of all kinds to keep walking the paths and adding their positive spirits to these places of intense reminder. Religious heritage stands shoulder to shoulder beside war memorials as another kind of endeavour. These acute stabs of local pride are deeply moving, without all the camouflage of church finery.

I pick up my journey alone in the midst of unseasonably wintry weather. Near Plaudren my route through wooded terrain on the western edge of the Landes de Lanvaux passes the raised stone (6m high) known as the Quenouille de Gargantua, a neolithic placement. It looks pinched and miserable on this very wet day. The legend is as thin as the menhir's profile. Was it a stone in the giant's shoe, carelessly discarded here? Or his wife's distaff, equally carelessly left behind on passing through? The stone deserves better, or nothing at all except for its truly impressive original implantation and survival through the ages. I wonder what the Vikings made of it as they roamed the woods looking for stray bishops to slaughter. They may well have accorded it the respect of pagan monuments in their own country, having as yet resisted the charms of Christianity.

In the village, the church is dedicated to Saint Bily. This may be the very same deacon of Alet who wrote that Life of Saint Malo. Or maybe no more than a confusion of similarly named religious figures, Bili and Bily. It sounds like a comedy double act. His association with this area comes from being bishop of Vannes in the late 9th century. He is a cephalophore saint, one who carries their own decapitated head after martyrdom, at the hands of the Vikings in this case, despite taking refuge far from the city. The late 19th century church is a solid pile of stone in the style called Breton 'neo-Roman', on the site of an earlier edifice. All these religious buildings are memorials of a kind to the lives of saints, however nebulous, a flourishing of individuals united by devotion to a greater cause than self-interest. Spiritual rather than martial remembrance. The atmospheric little chapel, *calvaire* and *fontaine* a few kilometres away in the hamlet called Saint-Bily mark the actual traditional location of his awful death.

This terrible weather will hold me in its clutches all the way down to Vannes. Everything is spoilt by the frequent downpours and cold gusting wind. My spirits are low. Far from feeling that progress is being made and taking encouragement from that, the way seems endless, the logistics impossible and my energy at an all time low. I'm just creeping along, not really taking much in, resentful and almost angry, as if someone is forcing me to do this against my will. I long for the immense skies and open hills of the Monts d'Arrée. I want the Tro Breiz to be over and to get my life back, walking where I choose and spending time with neolithic monuments that are always accessible.

Perhaps the sad realisation that, even if I actually succeed in finishing, I will not make it to the end on the year's anniversary of my departure, is influencing my mood, but the desire to go on is fading fast on this last leg of Stage 5.

I try to remember all those medieval pilgrims on the trails with considerably fewer resources than I can draw on, but they would probably not have endured the long drawn-out agony my feebleness enforces. A month was about the time it took to make the circuit traditionally, and that was probably the limit for many who had work on the land to consider. Although Easter, Pentecost and Michelmas were the three most popular traditional seasons for the Tro Breiz, some did walk in the winter whether from choice or necessity. The lull in economic activity at that time of year may have made it more viable then. Folklorist Anatole le Braz records a 19th century example of 'Nana Tro Breiz', an old woman undertaking the pilgrimage annually in the worst of weathers. She was a real person, Marcharit Fulup or Marguerite Philippe, and actually a professional pilgrim, paid to fulfil the vow of someone else. I really can't imagine doing this incredibly long journey repeatedly for a job: it assumes a hardiness quite beyond my conception.

There was considerable advantage in completing the Tro Breiz rather than a voyage to Jerusalem or Rome or Compostela. It offered a substantial journey, but one that stayed in Brittany, so was less risky, less expensive and without the language barriers. There would be no plunge into the unknown. Honouring the founding saints also tied the experience to the Bretons' own origins and many pilgrims must have had personal links to the individual saints. The circular shape of the route also meant that it could be started at the point closest to home and finished there too, a more convenient and satisfying format than the long, linear paths crossing other countries. A Breton saying indicated that everyone must do the Tro Breiz at least once in their lifetime or face doing the same thing after death at the rate of one coffin length per day! At the moment that feels about my style, unfortunately.

Louis XIV legislated against pilgrimage in France in the 1670s on the grounds that it led to an unacceptable loss of working days, presenting religious journeys as a kind of moral outrage with feckless fun-seekers deserting their workplaces. It has certainly been suggested that pilgrimage was the equivalent of medieval tourism, but now the implication was that some people were apparently just pretending to be pilgrims when they were no better than beggars and vagrants. It was decreed that official attestations were necessary for bona fide travellers on such spiritual missions. In fact, after the Wars of Religion at the end of the 16th century, pilgrimage generally was on the decline and there is little doubt that the Tro Breiz would have been no exception.

The scenery beyond Plaudren is gently bucolic, although much of my walking is on roads at this point. I cross the Arz, tributary of the Oust and traditionally the boundary of Breton and Gallo speaking territories, as it meanders through fields, and eventually reach the rural *bourg* of Monterblanc. The name comes from the French version of Breton *mouster-wenn*, the white monastery. This was a dependence of the Benedictine abbey of Redon, mentioned in their archives in the 9th century, before the Vikings' destructive raids that destroyed so many religious establishments. The parish church today is an unimaginative 18th century pile dedicated to Saint Peter, but the village itself is attractive.

Outside Monterblanc is a large military camp at Meucon, established in the late 19th century and still in use today. A public road runs through the centre of basic accommodation blocks and offices, and I remember driving through it many years ago, feeling as if I had landed on a sinister film-set. That they still hold drills and firing tests is very much in my mind as I pass between the camp and an old aerodrome built in 1926 and used by the Luftwaffe as a base in 1940. I had intended taking the route south in hillier country via an Iron Age hill-fort, evocatively named the Camp de César, as Julius Caesar's forces campaigned in the area against the Vénètes tribe, but decide against it in the depressing conditions. I'm still in giving up mode.

On the alternative, more built-up, route, I am very taken by the commandingly austere Chapelle Saint Michel (1524), on a plateau in the woods, and take endless photographs as rain drips onto the camera and down my neck. It's hard to imagine that more than 5000 pilgrims came here in procession in the 20th century. It feels a deserted and forgotten site on this gloomy day. A sacristy was added in 1831 so that the priest from Saint-Avé could stay overnight and not have to journey back right after services. It looks like a domestic two-storey house extension with a gable roof. Apparently it contains a fireplace and a bedroom. The whole idea suddenly makes me smile. I think of him on foot or horseback suffering the same conditions as me but without the option of well-made roads, and imagine him arguing his case for the extravagant extra building before the church council, trying to make it sound practical and unselfish.

The chapel is in the territory of Saint-Avé, on the outskirts of Vannes, and I get there via a descent into the Bois de Kerozer. This is in essence a public park with many gloomy evergreens (although this may be a rather selectively negative view, as I find out later it has a marked *sentier botanique* and arboretum) and a little windmill converted into a viewpoint. I'd like to sit down but there are no dry places to be found. A few people are mooching about or jogging doggedly, all about as cheerful as me, but this is the most outdoor activity I've seen after a long time on my deserted paths. I know the season is against it, but why are there no fellow-walkers? Not even locals in the last few days.

My soggy passage through Saint-Avé itself leaves dim memories of umbrellas, shimmering hail-stones and dull wet stone. At first I mistake the parish church, which does have a beautiful ancient monolithic cross outside, for the chapel that is 'worth seeing'. The Chapelle Notre-Dame du Loc (= Locmaria), very close by across a large square, was once a stop on the Tro Breiz, with Saint Patern's relics sometimes on display. The proximity to Roman roads heading north from Vannes made it a spot to attract travellers. It's a low two-tone edifice with a spindly spire. The *fontaine* is covered in green pond-weed, the brightest colour I've seen all day.

I don't get a chance to see inside, where later research mentions a statue of the Virgin Mary holding an open book to her infant son. This seems a strange twist on the traditional image of Mary's mother Saint Anne teaching her daughter to read. But by now I'm all out of curiosity. I am not going to search for someone to ask about the key to the building. All I want to do is get to Vannes and put an end to this water-logged journey. At least Saint Patern's church and the cathedral will be open. Won't they?

## 18 Getting on with it: the softest of cities, a cat for the Devil and a pilgrimage mecca

I have only the most pleasant memories of earlier visits to Vannes, a soft, sweet city redolent of history. The cathedral stands in a small centre of ancient houses and cobbled streets, enclosed by substantial surviving sections of medieval walls, towers and gates. Just outside to the south is the harbour, leading to the Gulf of Morbihan, and to the north the quarter of Saint Patern with the church dedicated to the founding saint, where I arrive first and triumphantly enter the open door.

Patern's own original cathedral had been destroyed by the Vikings in 919, and the later stone-built version dedicated to Saint Peter from the 11th century. This physical separation of the two main religious establishments led to fierce competition over pilgrim donations, as the church, on the way into the city from the main pilgrimage routes, had a distinct advantage over the cathedral. The dispute turned nasty in the early 14th century, when the cathedral canons tried to block access to the church and threatened those donating there with ex-communication. Patern's priests locked themselves in and urged that offerings should be thrown in through the window. If ever evidence of the importance of income derived from pilgrims was needed, this is it!

And documents recording donations suggest that in the 14th century 30-40,000 pilgrims per year sought to honour the founding saint here. Whether as part of the Tro Breiz or not, it's impossible to say, but the large numbers are telling. A more direct reference to the pilgrimage can be found in court records in Vannes from c1400. The *circuitus septem sanctorum Britanie* (circuit of the seven sanctuaries of Brittany) is mentioned several times, including in one case with the qualifying words *vulgaliter vocabur Trobreiz* (commonly known as the Tro Breiz), giving the origin of its now established Breton name in the modern revival. Saint Patern would lose even his secondary status in the cathedral when a bigger draw turned up in the following century.

Vannes was the ancient capital of the Vénètes tribe before their savage defeat by Julius Caesar's forces in 56BCE, and the subsequent establishment of the Roman settlement of Darioritum. The hill of Mene developed into the fortified medieval city, where the Gothic cathedral stands, today dedicated to Saint Peter and the Spanish Dominican evangelist Saint Vincent Ferrier (b.1350 in Valencia). The latter's reputation was such that the duke of Brittany invited him to the region in 1418 and he spent a year of intensive journeying to re-ignite the Catholic faith. This took its toll on his health and he wanted to return to Spain by ship from Vannes, but storms drove the vessel back. He died here in the city a few days later. It is thought that he was originally buried in the cathedral crypt.

Made a saint in 1455, his tomb attracted vast hordes of pilgrims, as the need for a large ambulatory indicates. A beautiful round Renaissance chapel in his honour was also added in 1537. The money they donated when visiting his shrine contributed to many large reconstruction projects in the body of the cathedral. Another reference to the theme of pilgrimage appears in a stained glass window in the chapel of Saint Anne, showing the major pilgrimage of Saint-Anne-d'Auray, my next port of call on the Tro Breiz route. Saint Patern figures rather unobtrusively by the entrance in the earliest part of the cathedral, sharing the space and an illustrative window with Saint Meriadec, another early bishop of Vannes, also popular in the locality.

By contrast, Patern's church outside the walls is a large 18th century Baroque version containing his relics in a rather startling portrait bust reliquary, and a Tro Breiz chapel with wooden statues of all the sacred seven saints. The other six rather smaller than Patern himself. The little room is housing a children's service when I arrive, so I wander in the aisles until they've finished. Patern is of uncertain origins, traditionally born in Armorica but with Welsh and Irish connections. He is also sometimes confused with Paterne, bishop of Avranches, and may or may not be the same person as Padarn of Wales. One story says he went in search of his father who had become a hermit in Ireland. Another has him visit Jerusalem and return with a magnificent cloak coveted by King Arthur. He is mentioned rather more historically in a document of the Council of Vannes c465, presumably when he became bishop of the original cathedral.

Later, relations with his parishioners deteriorated and when he was refused land to build a new chapel, Patern decided to leave his post and go to the kingdom of the Franks, where he died in 475CE. It is said that a severe drought then struck the territory of Vannes, and the inhabitants realised that propitiation of Patern was essential. A deputation went to bring back the body of the saint, but the corpse could not be moved from its resting place until a rich man in the group promised to give land for a chapel to house Patern's tomb. Then all was easy, rain fell back home and the saint returned to the site chosen for him outside the walls of Vannes. Because of these events, he was subsequently invoked when precipitation was needed. His relics were the focus of pilgrimage there and became part of the Tro Breiz, to the chagrin of the cathedral.

Later in the year that Vincent Ferrier died, Duke Jean V left his residence in Auray and came to Saint Patern's church in Vannes to start his own Tro Breiz, vowed after an attack of measles had seriously threatened his health. He went with a single companion, the official known as Admiral of Brittany, Jean de Penhoat (whose ruined château I passed much earlier on my journey), heading north via Dinan towards Dol-de-Bretagne. He then passed along the coast, probably via the Bay of Saint-Michel-en-Grève, as he soon after ceded territories around here to the admiral, and reached Saint-Pol-de-Léon on November 15th. Altogether it took two and a half months for the two men to complete the circuit, returning to Vannes in December 1419.

I spend a couple of days in Vannes, enjoying the gracious architecture, narrow old streets of stylish shops and the rampart gardens bordering the river Marle with its ancient lavoirs. The bright half-timbered houses of the 15th and 16th centuries enliven the atmosphere: one bears an old wooden carving of a man and woman called 'Vannes et sa femme', Vannes and his wife. They look to me as if

they are in their nightclothes. The cathedral is magnificent, but that experience is spoilt on the two occasions I try by drunks harassing anyone wanting to go in, as well as letting their dogs race about inside. There's a lot of shouting and gruesome singing which reminds me why I love silence so much when taking in the spirit of a place. Even beautiful religious music can be a distraction, but this cacophony is too intrusive.

Under Duke Jean IV, Vannes was the capital of Brittany for a time in the 14ᵗʰ century and he built the famous Château d'Hermine, which was later destroyed (the current one of that name is from 1785). The first step in the treaty of the decisive Union with France, bringing an end to Brittany's independence, was broached here in 1532. In later times, the Parliament of Brittany was exiled from Rennes and set up in this city instead, bringing a demand for the sort of fine town houses still well in evidence. There's a real sense of walking through history. The whole experience revives my enthusiasm and provides some inspiration for the very long stage to come, over two hundred kilometres to Quimper, an intricate mesh of past and present to be unpicked along the way.

Next morning I am sorry to be leaving this lovely place, the easiest of cities to enjoy, but it's time to move on northwards across the railway and the motorway to the suburb of Menimur and the starting point of a new track that will take me all the way to Saint-Anne-d'Auray. This is indeed a blessing as it replaces a fractured hotch-potch of mainly road walking in my old guidebook. It is in effect a Green Way for walkers and cyclists, although unlike any other *voie verte* I've walked (and there have been many).

These long distance paths based on former railway tracks or canal towpaths are usually fairly straight and flat, not always a boon for walkers especially as they are often enclosed by tall trees or steep banks and lacking views. I find the semi-hard surfaces cruel on the feet and hips after a few kilometres and long for a bit of up and down.

This new path, however, which only opened recently, is a different breed, created from scratch, and one can only admire the effort and goodwill which must have been needed to bring the project to fruition. It wriggles and scriggles along across farmland of large fields divided by rows of tall trees (although when I pass many have lately been lost to the great storm of November 1, 2023) and there is rarely any length of 'straight' to be found. Twists and turns, dips and rises make this a characterful rite of passage over open country, far from habitations and enlivened by busy bird activity.

The track itself is either compacted sand or wide wooden walkways, sometimes raised above marshy land, with metal strips to give grip to boots or tyres in wet weather. There are built-in, well-signed diversions to chapels along the way, and I take the one up to Lézurgan, more to see a huge *menhir* situated beside the chapel than the building itself.

It turns out to be well worth the detour. Past a little lake, I come first to the unobtrusive *fontaine* with a statue I can't make out. The chapel was formerly dedicated to John the Baptist, so maybe it's him. Notre-Dame de Lézurgan is a solid, clean-lined structure of 1455, adorned only by the simplest of mini bell-towers. Closed, of course, so no chance of seeing the sculpted beams inside, although a Pardon is still held each year for public celebration.

The site in the commune of Plescop (which means 'parish of the bishop') was part of territory belonging to the cathedral of Vannes. The chapel was built at the behest of the bishop, who had a summer home, the Manoir de Kerango, nearby, but today it is in the middle of nowhere, restored in recent times by an association of supporters. Rather a lot of concrete and new wooden fencing surrounds the building. The *menhir* (3.5m) is superb, but banalised by a large plaque about the origin of the chapel with the date 1984, perhaps when the stone was brought and raised here. Sticking a sign on a standing-stone always seems crass, reducing the stone to an object without intrinsic value or discrete identity. Even war memorials of this type, as at Plumelec, make me a little uneasy.

Back on track, the way winds on, passing through the village of Mériadec. This is named for the saint who was bishop of Vannes in the mid 7th century, but he is more famously associated with the area around Pontivy and the patronage of the illustrious Rohan family. He is an example of the interesting phenomenon that connects saints to the legitimacy of secular power and the origins of dynasties. The Rohans claimed descent from legendary king Conan Meriadec, with the later saint of the same name also inserted in the family line. A bit of sanctity did no harm in creating an image of serious *gravitas*, lending weight to the political ambitions of this powerful family. Meriadec was established in a hermitage at Stival, near the Rohan base, with a widespread reputation for miracles. The Rohans took a serious interest, and such patronage did the saint no harm since he was soon appointed to the see of Vannes. Here in his eponymous village on the *voie verte*, the medieval chapel has gone, finally replaced by what must be a less attractive version in 1913.

I move on slowly towards the important pilgrim site of Sainte-Anne-d'Auray. This is a real 'destination' in addition to the seven cathedrals of the Tro Breiz, a definite goal for travellers. When I finally make it, it's late afternoon and the usual crowds of tourists and faithful are conspicuous by their absence. There are a few individuals, and a large group of priests in long fluttering cloaks beside the *fontaine* and towering statue of Saint Anne, bravely bearing the blustery wind as they are schooled by a female expert about the site.

And what a site it is! This is a place that has built on its pilgrimage tradition to focus attention on a real terminus, and create a brand. The mystical origins of divine apparitions, a Dark Age chapel and buried statue contribute to the charisma based around the iconography of Saint Anne, mother of Mary, grandmother of Jesus. The traditional images show her, a tall, veiled figure, teaching her little daughter to read. It taps into notions of the Breton *mamie* or granny, the essential heartbeat of the family. The vast 19th century basilica church is a shining statement of maternal values that have eternal appeal. The story of Anne is found in the Apochrypha, but she has been adopted as a Breton in local legends or at the very least a *Breton du cœur* who visited the shores of the Bay of

Douarnenez with her grandson, as we shall see later on the Tro Breiz route.

How did this largesse come to pass here? In 1623 a peasant named Yvon Nicolazic had a vision of Saint Anne, who told him that a chapel in her honour had stood here long ago (traditionally founded in 699) and she wanted it rebuilt. The sightings were repeated over the next couple of years, until Nicolazic and some friends were directed to dig and found an ancient statue of the saint. The church hierarchy, formerly sceptical of the mysterious appearances, took note and a chapel was built on the spot in 1630. The peasant honoured by such an apparition still plays a large part in the shrine, with a statue facing his patroness outside and an actual chapel dedicated to him in the nave of the basilica. Not to mention the cottage where he was born nearby, now open to the public. He is the realistic, everyday conduit by which the mythical could enter earthly presence.

The complex here in Sainte-Anne-d'Auray is huge and overwhelming, but it demonstrates a living faith more overtly than any other place I've seen on this journey. A visit from Pope Jean-Paul II in 1996 has made it the *haut lieu* of Catholicism in Brittany and it retains something of the stage set, a place for performances. It is the only experience on my long exploration of a real sense of pilgrimage on a grand scale, and what catering for that means. The bringing of money into the town and supporting many business through the power of faith is obvious here. Saint Anne's name is equally good for selling sweet treats as religious objects.

The massive success of the shrine led to huge development, with the basilica constructed from 1866.

Everyone wanted to see the original statue, and honour the place that Saint Anne herself had marked out as special. This idea of being chosen, place or person, offers enhancement like no other and sacralisation of the landscape soon followed. The Scala Santa is a ceremonial staircase originally built near the first chapel in 1662, a processional way for pilgrims to ascend on their knees. Later as preparations were made for the new giant basilica, it was moved to the current location across the garden, facing the shrine at a distance. The sheer scale of the Saint-Anne-d'Auray site reflects this transition from the simplicity of the peasant originator to a vast monumental complex, including a sizeable and very moving war memorial. This was conceived to honour the memory of Bretons lost in WWI but now incorporates tribute to victims of all wars, giving a devastating sense of the individual lives lost. So the hope of religion weighs in the balance here against the self-destructive tendencies of mankind.

Many conversions and healings on this site have cemented its reputation from the earliest establishment of the shrine. In the fifty years after the first chapel was built, 130 miracle cures were attested. The waters of the *fontaine* were efficacious in this respect. A *Livre des miracles* or Record of Miracles was kept. To cite just one example: a man from Hennebont whose legs would no longer support him made the journey to Sainte-Anne-d'Auray on his hands. It took six days. He prayed in front of the saint's statue and at once felt heat creeping into his legs. Pains and creaking followed, to the extent that he was carried into the cloister to rest with other pilgrims. In the morning, he was cured. The idea of attention to the individual, the personal touch which saints can give is seminal to the popularity of the Breton saints too. Their function is to listen and respond on the sort of one-to-one basis that is not expected from God the Father in Heaven.

Saint-Anne-d'Auray touches something very deep in Breton culture: the peasant close to the land, deserving the vision for his piety and hard work, and divine revelation to him, not to a church official. The strength of faith in ordinary people is the cement of religion in Brittany, despite all the cathedrals and elaborate Catholic shrines. Nicolazic has become a representative of the best of Bretons, visionary, devout, loyal. And despite having to look harder for the simple here in the face of grandeur, it still exists in the expressions of many visitors. The altar of Saint Anne is ablaze with candles when I'm there in early evening, tiptoeing past four elderly people sitting in awe before it. A fragment of the original statue of Anne, a powerful symbol of revelation which was burnt during the Revolutionary years, is set in the base of the new gilded version shining down on the faithful. Continuity and endurance, the essentials of faith.

The precinct, which includes a welcome office for pilgrims, is bounded by restaurants and shops, including a place to buy religious souvenirs such as a roughly carved circle of the seven founding saints in miniature. Just the thing for a coffee table discussion piece? The opening hours of this commerce are almost as long as those of the sanctuary, but pilgrim souvenirs have a long history of their own. They are both proof and memory, an advertisement of achievement. Badges sewn to rucksacks, tie-pin style brooches, even simple scallop shells on the Compostela trail are all evidence and self-identification, putting oneself into the membership of a large club of travellers of faith. I buy a little statue of Saint Hervé with his wolf that looks very like a few dogs I have known. I'm enjoying my experience here: objective observation may lack the intensity of faith, but appreciation of all that has gone into creating the pervasive atmosphere of Sainte-Anne-d'Auray comes easily enough.

After an overnight stay, it's not far to Auray, where the river crossing at Saint-Goustan is one of the most attractive scenes on the whole route of this pilgrimage. I pass the church of Saint-Sauveur and the neo-gothic chapel of Notre-Dame-de-Lourdes (1879), the latter a reflection of the popularity of another pilgrimage, before descending a steep narrow street divided by a metal handrail, dwarfed by tall houses. At the foot is the harbour, an enclave around the ancient bridge invoking the medieval heyday of busy shipping and prosperity based on maritime trade. In 1419 Duke Jean V passed through here on his Tro Breiz journey, accompanied by his lone companion.

This cold, windy day has diminished the customary clientele for the many waterside restaurants overlooking the little port and the ramparts of the former castle of Auray opposite. This was where Benjamin Franklin, an emissary appointed by Congress, turned up from America in December 1776, bad weather halting his ship in the bay of Quiberon. He took another into the sheltered little harbour of Saint-Goustan before continuing his journey to Nantes by road. His mission was to get the support of Louis XVI against the English in the American War of Independence. The little diversion he made here is one tiny detail of a huge event with lasting ramifications. Small pieces can add up to a large picture. I often get the feeling as I unpack the tradition and heritage of this pilgrimage that the Tro Breiz itself is another sort of Russian doll of history.

Over the ancient bridge with its little 15<sup>th</sup> century toll house, I go by the old walls of the medieval defences and take the rising rue du Château, lined by shops and pretty houses, to the High Town. From here the surroundings become rather more pedestrian, until descent down what was once a Roman road to the priory chapel of Saint Cado. This unobtrusive little shrine has a sculpted cat on the gable corner, reference to the saint's most famous story. He accepted the Devil's offer to build a bridge to his island in a single night in return for the first soul to cross the new structure. Whilst the Devil rubbed his hands in glee for this easy triumph and carried out his part of the bargain, Cado sent over a cat... Tricky lads, these Breton saints.

I'm on my way to the memorial of another character who was no fool. Branching off the road by a little *lavoir*, a woodland footpath heads up to the imposing Mausoleum de Cadoudal. Georges Cadoudal was the local Chouan leader in the aftermath of the Revolution, rising to a position of widespread influence and military success. His monument is a large neo-Gothic rotunda, reflecting the family's importance in the area and the respect which Cadoudal himself commanded. The family manor house is opposite, edging a little cluster of attractive old stone houses. Family burials were in the chapel of Saint Cado, but such remains of his skeleton as existed after being exposed for some years after his death on the scaffold in Paris were finally brought back to this resting place.

Morbihan was one of the main strongholds of Chouan resistance to the Republican ethos, which triumphed at the

Revolution. This included, initially, the imposition of secularity, with priests forced to swear an oath of allegiance to the state or be replaced (or worse). Many churchmen went into hiding, protected by their parishioners, and performed mass secretly, sometimes even blessing the guns of Chouan fighters. For many rural people in Brittany, a whole way of life was at stake. Church and priest were at the heart of local communities in the countryside, manners and customs were traditional, loyalty to the king and the kingdom of God were paramount. The greatest damage to churches and cathedrals was in the towns, where the new rising commercial class and the general populace were the drivers of radical change. Rural chapels often survived unscathed, although the numbers of worshippers fell during the hundred years after the Revolution, until a time of religious resurgence at the end of the 19th century.

It was the persecution of the clergy that swung Cadoudal's opinions against the spirit of the Revolution. He was only 18 when it began in 1789, and it was four years before he took up arms after the anti-religious stance of the Republicans became more extreme. He was the son of a farmer in this very hamlet of Kerleano, where I'm waiting to meet up again with my friend Alan. I look across the grassy surrounds. Here a hero of royalist resistance must have played as a child, just in front of the family house. And here his grandiose tomb still stands. From cradle to grave, attached to the same small piece of land. That's not a bad epitaph.

## 19 Breathing into the pain: living stones, a tricky saint and the sinews of settlement

Alan arrives as a light drizzle falls, but our walk will turn out dry and cool, a heavy carapace of grey clouds managing to contain themselves for the duration of our unambitious progress. We follow the valley of the Reclus on a pleasant verdant path under the trees parallel with the stream. It's a 'domestic' route, with plenty of runners and cyclists in activity. Having crossed the stream and hesitated over a choice of paths in the woodland, we finally reach the edge of a huge commercial estate, then continue along a track beside the motorway and its thundering traffic.

Over a road bridge, we pass through the hamlet of Guervec before taking a wide track across country towards Brégoham, dissected by a disused railway line out in the middle of nowhere. We are suddenly surprised by a little car bumping towards us, as no road or houses are apparent for miles around. The driver takes great care not to splash me from one of the deep pools of pot-hole and opens her window to state this just in case I hadn't realised. We both laughed at the absurdity and she kangarooed onwards. I didn't like to ask where she came from.

Alan and I haven't seen each other for a while (he lives in London and visits his house in eastern Brittany a few times a year), so we talk about many things including funerals, mindfulness and organising material when writing historical books, his latest being on the movements of Roman general Agricola in Scotland. This also involves him heavily, like me, in the logistics of walking, although he is capable of covering far greater distances than I can, even though I think my strength and stamina are improving as this pilgrimage goes on. I am even starting to think this may be my main takeaway from the experience. Certainly more positive feelings about progress are generally illuminating the way now and there is nothing new to face in the inevitable physical pain.

We follow the same easy-walking track for many kilometres through unobtrusive farmland with lines of beautiful trees all around. It's very enjoyable, undemanding scenery, with a sense of being far from what we know is actually nearby - the general busyness of Auray and the pulsating channel of transport of the motorway. We finally reach a housing estate where we left Alan's car earlier, and go on into Erdeven by road. I'll be back to fill in the missing kilometres on the next trip. In the village, we eat and then divert to visit the megalithic site that I prefer to almost any in Brittany (with the possible exception of Saint -Just).

The alignments of Erdeven are cut through at their tip by a main road but this doesn't seem to detract from their imposing presence. They stand in rough rows, maybe placed for ceremonial procession, but certainly presenting a forceful statement in their grey mass. Along a footpath like the entrance to a chambered tomb we are suddenly among the Giants of Kerzeho, a collection of immense stones of odd shapes. It would be no surprise if one of these decided to have a stroll around or a chat with his neighbours. They are living things, and totally accessible to us. Down in the valley are hundreds of further stones in a remote setting, but there's no time for extended exploration today. Sadly. I never understand why people rush along to miserable old Carnac when greater connection with the remote past is sitting here in Erdeven, tapping its fingers, just waiting...

Back to pick up the missing route on the next trip, I am not expecting much more from the country walk than the easy way we experienced last time. The weather is grim, however, and I'm soon decidedly soggy, but pilgrimage from time to time throws up little unexpected nuggets of reward for perseverance. Another chapel of Saint Cado is on the route and this turns out to be a haven that will remain with me as one of the highlights of my Tro Breiz. The low, plain building is wedged into the centre of an ancient hamlet, sturdy houses of large stone blocks hemming in a tiny contained space of *fontaine* and *lavoir* fringed by shrubs, looking like nothing so much as an ornamental garden pond. Beside the water stands a squat grey bullet of an Iron Age stele.

This is an old place and I feel it. It strikes me immediately as sacred space. I can hardly believe my luck when I see the door of the chapel standing open. Inside there is a wheelbarrow in the nave, potted plants overwintering in shelter and an open bag of cement propped against the wall. But it certainly doesn't have the atmosphere of a garden shed. The simplicity of the building and its lovely stained-glass is exquisite: a little round window decorated with a fleur-de-lys, another behind the altar showing Saint Cado in prayer with a gorgeous tiny purple-winged devil shaking his fist at a nonchalant grey cat by the newly built bridge of legend. I stand in what would be the choir in a bigger structure and just drink in the essence of legend and faith coming together. This pilgrimage is a series of small stories that gradually add up to one big narrative of settlement.

A man enters and is startled to see this damp weary pilgrim on the premises. He moves the wheelbarrow and puts on the lights for me to admire a couple of time-worn statues behind the altar. We talk for a few minutes. He lives here and passes much of his free time in the chapel, patching the walls, doing what is necessary to show respect for the building and ancient cult of the saint. I imagine he is the attentive gardener too. This combination of practicality and commitment seems to me the basis of Breton religion. Below the surface is a deep pride in heritage and the sense of continuity that Brittany's culture has held onto so well. A guileless, natural part of people's lives, a story told in stone and decorated with feeling. This small encounter is one of the best moments of my whole journey. This place, and what it represents, is why I'm doing this pilgrimage, feeling the living pulse of Brittany's heritage, an inner clutch of emotion.

Cado needed a bridge to construct a community. Arrival, building, settlement, the substance of so many saints' stories in Brittany, and those of immigrants everywhere. I arrived in Brittany twenty-five years ago, without a clear plan for the future. My first novel Moon Garden had done well and I soon embarked on another, which turned out to be torture to write and full of hints at the uncertainty I was experiencing in a new country. Because there was little information in English at that time, I was soon lured into producing a guide to Finistère, then a book of walks, then an account of my massive journey along the Nantes-Brest Canal. Although the right house to live in was elusive, I was building, in my fashion, by returning to my roots in historical research, seeking well-known ways of being to come to terms with a challenging unfamiliar environment. Nothing was easy.

It is one thing to come and live in a foreign country, quite another to settle. Much is made of the necessity of learning the local language, not so much on the importance of fitting in, and these are not the same things. Having arrived with a partner, after a few years I was living alone and for quite a time the odds seemed stacked against my successful survival here. A woman, a foreigner, a solitary trying to find a place in Brittany's tight-knit, family-oriented society. But as my work developed and I travelled all over the region writing books and articles for publishers, magazines and websites, I began to fall in love with this land, so proudly steeped in the past, and yet fiercely innovative in many ways, always holding on whilst reinventing. A Pardon for camping-cars? Saints invoked for exam results? New form for an ancient pilgrimage like the Tro Breiz?

The next chapel, little more than fifteen minutes walk ahead, is dedicated to Saint Laurent, the martyr from the Spanish Pyrenees who was grilled to death in 258CE, memorably urging his torturers to turn him over as one side was done. The statue of this official Catholic saint can be found in a large number of Breton churches, usually holding the instrument of his torture as if he is on his way to set up a barbecue. Mention of this unfortunate round here now, though, is more likely to produce directions to the golf course that bears his name. (He's not the only saint with that honour, of course.) The chapel building is closed up and rain is falling faster. I stop to attempt a photo as a local glares at me from behind a curtain and a car rushes through the hamlet, much too close, swishing water up at me. There's not much respect for aged travellers in these parts. An old Tro Breiz sign decorates an oddly angled finger-post pointing the way through the woods towards Erdeven.

This time I don't linger for the stones. The next section of the Tro Breiz route will be governed by the need to cross two major watercourses, the Ria d'Etel, a wide estuary, and the Blavet river, as southern Brittany is riven with 'blue roads' forging through the land to discharge into the sea. This will provide quite a change of scenery: it's a long time since I walked along the north coast from Saint-Malo and that is a very different beast from here in the south, where the line of the edge land is soft, with very low headlands and beautiful sandy beaches, backed up by extensive dunes. And while I do not walk at any point beside the open sea, it is always there in the atmosphere.

My first target is the Chapelle des Sept Saints, surely a Tro Breiz highlight, but it is closed, giving nothing away. The chapel, in a rural hamlet, is less impressive than I'd unrealistically expected. It was originally restored in the late 19th century, when statues of the seven saints were introduced, but the most difficult episode in its development came with the actions of a zealous rector in the 1930s, who had it covered in cement to protect the building from storms. This gradually endangered the whole structure with sagging walls and destabilisation of the bell-tower. It was not until the 1990s that an association was formed to save and restore the chapel with major remedial works. The thinnest of spires points up from the west end like a little needle. On this façade a plaque reads *Er seih sant/A vreiz izel* (Breton for 'the seven saints of Basse Bretagne' or Lower Brittany, the western part).

I can see with a back-to-front view from the outside that the small windows portray the founding saints, grouped or individually. In the early 20th century, soon after the first restoration, more than 6000 people attended the Pardon here, which included processing with a Seven Saints banner to the *fontaine* 200m away. I decide to come back for that event at the end of August to do the chapel justice (see Epilogue). Today I just want to get on, covering the route being so often the driving motivation of this lengthy pilgrimage. There must be many things I've missed or disregarded in the pressure of progress, because someone is waiting to collect me or there's a taxi or train with a timetable. I have felt this in Morbihan most of all, largely because of the terrible weather that has plagued me for much of the time.

Soon after the chapel, there's a lovely narrow footpath alive with spring flowers, lined by burgeoning may trees. I make a short diversion where it ends, following a sign to the 'alignment of the seven saints', being unable to resist a call to megaliths and the chance to rest my spirit in the neolithic. It is well worth the effort. On a slight rise, a collection of small dolmens sits in a grassy banked setting, etched into the landscape like hobbit houses, but there is no information about the site. It feels a special space, and is of course accessible at any time, unlike many chapels I could mention. Affinity with stones, and their innovative, energetic use in early society, comes more naturally to me than any real rapport with over-organised religion. I think I am happier with less certainty.

From the road at Pont Queno, the route cuts across open fields towards the Sac'h river. Two cyclists come fast towards me talking loudly, and then suddenly veer off on another track and vanish. Coming up to the main road at Pont Sac'h, I cross and go down to the river in a little backwater where houses stretch across a dyke with a sluice gate for the channel of water to pass through. After this the coast path follows the Sac'h all the way to the Ria d'Etel. There are plenty of locals out for their daily exercise, running or walking. I pass an implausibly twisted tree-trunk right beside the path and feel ridiculously uplifted by the sight. It is a wonder of nature, tactile and eloquent, evocatively suggestive of snake.

The tide is low, but this is pleasant scenery with a sense of anticipation for reaching the broad Etel. The village of that name drifts by on the other side of the river, as I near the confluence and feel the full impact of this stunning *ria* or estuary. The coast path leads round towards the Pont Lorois and I'm taken by surprise on reaching Port Niscop to find the rather low-key Oratoire Notre-Dame on the bank overlooking the great expanse of water. I was expecting something of greater impact, given the amazing

location, but perhaps my reactions are dulled by the deterioration in the weather. This grotto of rough stones topped by a sheltered alcove for the statue of the Virgin Mary, contains a simple slab altar for offerings, but the entrance is barred by railings. Votive plaques of thanks and prayers are attached to the walls of the pseudo-cave. It was built in 1952 by local sailors, in memory of those lost at sea, a visible presence of reassurance for sea-farers departing and relief on return. This panoramic spot would have been a great place for me to rest and try to come to terms with the excruciating burning sensation in my foot, but in such slapping winds and slanting rain, not so much.

I pass under the bridge and then up to double back across it. Pont Lorois offers a superb perspective up and down stream even on this wet and very windy day, where I have to push forward holding onto my hat. I'd been hoping to have coffee at the bar overlooking the bridge but it was closed and I don't have better luck on the other side of the river. The route takes me through old fishing villages of low houses, one beautifully thatched, round the harbour of Vieux Passage and then to a real treat even in these terrible conditions, the Roman site of Mané-Véchen. The foundations of this large villa complex straddle a bulge of coastline, looking down the Etel towards the open sea. More than 20,000 coins were found here on excavation, most from the 3rd century CE, reinforcing the idea that it was a point of import and export exchange with Italy in its heyday. My path goes through the site on the river side, emphasising the sensational location a wealthy Gallo-Roman chose to set up home.

A sense of being at home is the turning point for settling in a new place. When does the ferry across the

Channel to Britain become leaving home rather than going home? I think that because of my background in learning, teaching and searching, the more my knowledge of Brittany in all its aspects grew, the more in my element I felt. Not so lost, in this very different context from my earlier life. The sense of space and peace promoted an inner layer of calm even when daily practical or administrative problems were decidedly unsettling. There was always the antidote of walking in the Monts d'Arrée, and landscape has been for me a more than adequate substitute for the company of others throughout my life. Here in Brittany friendships came very slowly and sparsely, but my bond with the land and its history grew ever tighter. This pilgrimage has only served to remind me of the lifeline that has been. The saints are telling other stories than their own.

Turning inland past the chapel at Locquenin, country tracks take me to the Fontaine Saint Cornely, which is very elaborate, yet feels in the middle of nowhere, far from its chapel across the fields. Cornely, once a bishop in Rome, is the patron saint of horned beasts, most famously associated with Carnac and the story of being chased by Roman soldiers and hiding in a cow's ear. God then obliged by turning his pursuers into stones, hence the alignments there. His cult includes a Pardon here where his favoured animals can still be brought for blessing beside the cross. His name, of course, suggests the nature of his patronage: *cornu* is the Latin for horn.

Behind the chapel of Saint Cornely is the Plage de Maguero, a bracing coastline of beaches and wonderfully lush dunes, restricted paths protecting the exceptional flora and nesting birds in season. But a long section is gated off as military territory and I decide not to follow what looks in the guidebook a circuitous route via coastal lakes, and take small roads towards Plouhinec instead. All in the interests of 'getting on'. My foot is hurting by now and I try to breathe steadily into the pain. In the village there's a monster of a 19th century church, imposing from a distance, ugly close up. Inside I encounter a modern wooden sculpture of a hatchet-faced Anne with little Mary, both wearing uncomfortably heavy crowns, Anne's over her traditional head-covering. In a matter of minutes, I am on my way again.

The imperative of this very lengthy stage of the Tro Breiz dictates my current haste, as there is always a feeling of so much more to do, that lingering or diverting is counter-intuitive. Pilgrimage requires a balance of attention and progress. There will inevitably be bad decisions, given I am not slavishly pursuing a marked route, and some places may not receive the contemplation they deserve. I build a list of re-visits I will make later when the walking is over. It is already April, and although sadly the 7th will pass without any anniversary finale, I want to feel that the last stage is within reach after all this time. Quimper still feels a million miles away.

## 20 Feeling the joy: lively capitals, a mysterious effigy and a lapse in concentration

The cross-country route to Merlevenez on a dry day is unremarkable, never far from roads, but what joy is waiting on arrival! And that's appropriate vocabulary as this is actually another Bre-levenez, as at Lannion, hill of joy in Breton. The name transformed in the 15th century into Meur-levenez and then the present form, but I'm a bit puzzled about the original 'Bre' as the land seems pretty flat round here. It is without doubt a joyous place, however, as I am about to discover. The church is dedicated to Notre-Dame-de-Joie, and the contrast with Plouhinec could not be more striking.

Here there is an alluring witch's hat of a spire, centrally placed, and two lovely doorways on the south side, the main pointed porch decorated with hounds' teeth pattern, and other, worn carving. The church construction is of large plain ashlars, bestowing an air of dignity and sense of endurance combined with rural simplicity. Originally founded in the 11-12th centuries, there has been extensive remodelling in the 15th and 19th. It was also damaged in WWII, when there was heavy allied focus on the entrenched enemy garrison at nearby Lorient, and the Germans used the tower as a look-out post.

Entry is directly into the dark transept where the central altar stands. Above, the dome is lined by stone shaped into petals. The stained-glass ahead is modern but effulgent, and there's just something about this place that draws me in. There is no access to the east end of the church and the nave to my left is even darker, so I have a cursory look round and then reluctantly turn to leave. At the door, tucked away to one side, there's a square electrical switch, unmarked but too tempting to leave untouched. I press it and turn around in one movement and suddenly the whole interior is transformed, glowing with light focused on the stunning glory of a double line of Romanesque carved capitals. The designs are animated and imaginative – hunting, acrobats, weird creatures – a veritable life passing by in the upper air. These ancient decorations of detail and evocation sit well with the simple colours of the windows. I have hardly drawn in a breath of surprise when music bursts out. Is it Albinoni? Something like, anyway, at a volume level bordering on the intrusive. There's enough music and poetry in the carvings: their energy and verve totally revive me from a weary slumping struggler to someone eager for experience.

After that refreshing encounter, I leave the village in a happy frame of mind, past a weird modern *fontaine* in concrete, then through a group of semi-ruined old stone houses, echoing the plain ashlars of the church. Finally the track leads off across country with a lake to the left. Looking back, there's one last glimpse of the witch's hat before the church fades away. A herd of Charolais cattle, white and bouncy, jog up to watch me pass but find it disappointing entertainment. I take a photo and move on. The large farm complex on the hill to my right has huge, ominous animal sheds and a water storage system looking like a big yurt. A tractor comes along the track and throws up dust all over me.

Despite the regulated nature of the land, the scenery is mainly scraps of woodland, with a rich flower meadow close at hand. Through the trees, the track rises and falls.

I meet the same tractor again on a different section of the route and this time cover my face with my sleeve. The driver laughs. At last I turn off into woods on a narrow path through high ferns, causing me to worry about tics. This year they are demons. Eventually a short but soothing *chemin creux* or sunken way finishes this section of walking, which has been tough. I have reached my limits for the day, with a left foot screaming at me to stop immediately. Over such a long journey as the Tro Breiz, this on-going restriction becomes harder and harder to deal with, as it is impossible to plan with confidence of reaching a certain point. I constantly over or under estimate my fluctuating abilities. It is fortunate I know kind people prepared to hang about in cars just in case I flake out.

I do feel there have been significant improvements in my stamina over the last few months, but there is no defence against the savagery of stabbing pain, which usually works its way up into a crescendo after three or four hours of walking. I have lived with this for decades and managed it to the degree that I've covered thousands of kilometres all over Brittany for various writing projects, but the price has often been high, physically leading to months of enforced inactivity, and consequentially a deep dip in spirits bordering on depression. I cannot bear either the restriction on liberty or separation from the landscape, especially the moors, where I draw my sustenance out of the very ground. Being outside and on the move is my natural state, so this affliction has often been hard to endure.

On my next expedition, country tracks over streams mark off the kilometres until it's back to roads to reach the estuary of the Blavet. I arrive at the Pont de Bonne Homme and turn across the bridge over the wide river. Two supports of the old span (1904-1974) remain, each topped by a small figure, man on the east, woman on the west, in Breton clothing. Not the originals, but casts from a mould to replicate them. A bizarre story relates that in 1977 the statues were stolen (how, I wonder, given their lofty perches 50m above the river) and dumped outside a newspaper office. They were then replaced by these copies, inauguration recorded by a plaque on the roadside. The double tower view is impressive, as I take a photo of one through the open section of the other. Heavy traffic is fairly constant on the more recent bridge, just inches away over the crash barrier.

To the left is the busy industrial environment of Lanester, with Lorient beyond, in marked contrast to all the peaceful rurality of river beyond the bridge on the other side. Soft wooded waterside folds give a taste of the scenic walking to come. Once over the crossing, the route turns down steeply on a stepped path through the trees and then back under the bridge to continue up the bank towards Hennebont. I soon reach a wide turning point in the river, and a boats' graveyard. The vessels are in various stages of decomposition, from sad skeletal timbers almost sunken from sight to old battered rusters lingering on the surface.

On the bank is an open-air theatre, with this backdrop of ex-vessels. I recite a few lines from Shakespeare's Julius Caesar and then shut up quickly as a couple of strollers approach, huddled together under an umbrella. Yes, it is raining again. The river soon narrows after that 90° turn, and the path emerges from the trees at the Petit Lavoir, a cool green rectangle of water, before I decide to cut across through the hamlet of Le Resto to avoid a great bulge of land, which sticks out like a (sore) thumb in the guidebook map, to reach the Rocher du Diable. I pause here at this rocky outcrop for views up and downstream, before following the coast path round the mudflats of an inlet and back into the woods.

From here, the coastal path is a bit of a blur with the effort involved to follow the trail up to Hennebont, under the motorway and into the western outskirts of the town. So much for enjoying the scenery! A combination of weariness and pain always make for difficult walking, but when I come to write up notes at the end of the day I realise that there has also been a serious lapse of concentration, a period when my thoughts have turned inwards. And not to any great purpose, it has to be said. I've got a little overwhelmed by too many things happening in my daily life, on top of trying to keep this pilgrimage going, and energy levels are depleted as I turn over various decisions that need to be made, lists of various people I'd like to send on long faraway holidays and various practical problems I have no idea how to solve. Why has everything come together in a great pointless stew of flickering reflections today? No idea, except that the views are mainly masked by trees, and with nothing grabbing at my attention, I let the landscape slip away and fill my head with dreary scenes from my personal narrative instead.

Of course, this is by no means the only time my attention has dipped on this crazily long journey. Just as uninteresting places are part and parcel of the route, so are uninteresting phases in one's own inner world. My commitment is to engage with my surroundings, but pilgrimage is about our stories too, even if these are not heroic or profound. The length of time for reflection, the accumulated effort of the path often heralds change in our futures, decisions subtly made. One purpose of my Tro Breiz was to set all my work into the widest context of territorial width and meaningful depth. Now I begin to see that I may be coming to the end of what has been in effect a twenty-five year project to bring the early history of Brittany to a wider public. A very small example of proselytising, hardly on a par with the Breton saints.

Finally entering the suburbs of Hennebont, there's what seems a long stint through residential roads before I pass along the narrow rue du Vieux Château, which gives glimpses over to the imposing ramparts, followed by a steep descent to the water. I cross the road bridge, bearing in mind that the name Hennebont is from Breton *hen pont*, the old bridge. Mention of the town appears for the first time in 1029 in the *Cartulaire* (document of property ownership and donations) of the Abbaye de Sainte-Croix at Quimperlé. At its height this was an important port and gave the dukes of Brittany control over the passage along the Blavet, a major waterway to the interior. Walking along the top of the ramparts today gives a good sense of this strategic position, and I emerge at the formidable gate, Porte de Bro Erec'h, an indication of the strength of the medieval defences.

The town was the scene of a famous incident in 1342 during the Wars of Succession for the dukedom of Brittany. Besieged by Charles de Blois, it held out thanks to the bravery of Jeanne de Flandre, the wife of opposing leader Jean de Montfort, who had been captured. She rallied the troops here in her husband's absence and for her ardour in adversity earned the epithet Jeanne la Flamme. The town was finally relieved by the arrival of an

English fleet, which sailed up the Blavet. In the church, one stained-glass window imagines Jeanne holding up her little son, the future Duke Jean IV, to inspire the troops. It would be the end of the war in 1364 before this young man came into his power.

I'm heading now to this 16th century shrine of Notre-Dame-de-Paradis, with its narrow west front on the square, a refined example of the Flamboyant Gothic style. Anne de Bretagne passed through the town on her Tro Breiz, saying prayers in a little oratory on the 'hill of paradise'. A local blacksmith decided to build a church in honour of Our Lady on the spot, although he died before it was finished in the 1530s. During a devastating out break of plague in 1699, the inhabitants prayed to the Virgin Mary, promising a silver statue and annual procession if they were spared. This vow has given its name to the Fête du Vœu, still held each September. The original statue of Mary was melted down in the Revolution, and had to be replaced. The church gained the elevated status of a basilica in 1913, in recognition of the numbers of pilgrims coming to pay homage at this venue. The vow is commemorated in another of the beautiful stained-glass windows, which reinforce the strong sense of valued history in Hennebont.

Then it's back down to the river to the ramparts, as I've time to spare with an overnight stay just outside the town. Hennebont is an impressive place to linger, with the defensive river frontage decorated by a line of cannons beside the parking area. While I'm taking photos of the ancient stone defences behind brightly planted flowerbeds, I meet an old lady who is on her way up to the shops. She stops to talk and says she's lived in the area around the church of Saint Caradec all her life. I tell her that's my route out of town tomorrow and she describes the beautiful woodland in store, a special spot she's enjoyed for decades. It's a good place to live, she says, and goes away smiling with memories.

So I'm looking forward to this walk next morning, as I cross the Passerelle des Forges and stroll along the bank, looking back at the spire of the basilica on high. Runners are out noisily on the opposite side, a group of students yelling at each other as they round the curve towards the town. The Église Saint-Caradec is not particularly inspiring, but there's a simple ancient cross in the churchyard and a yew tree that has the lower branches hacked off. Moving slowly and steeply uphill, I enter the Bois du Hingair and delight in the verdant aura around a very wide cambered track between banks and tall trees. All is vibrant and thrumming with growth on this spring morning, the wood a mixture of spruce and deciduous, full of chestnut trees with massive leaves.

The track is stony and rough in places but feels good underfoot as it curves and rises, then falls to a stream. I would be happy to go on walking here for hours, the old lady was right about its beauty. But roads always appear sooner and later. Fortunately I have only to cross this one and re-enter the trees on a much narrower earth footpath, but that too is soon over and I come up at the top of the rise to begin a long slog of tarmac past a huge electricity plant with pylons and power-lines everywhere the eye can see, roundabouts and major roads, relieved by short sections on paths through farmyard. After negotiating a major junction with the raised D769 at Saint-Séverin, I find the route is somewhat calmer, but the day has lost that early joy of the woodland.

The roads continue, however, until one finally runs out beside the Moulin de Guindo in its very well-kept grounds, and a grassy footpath soon turns to mud by a pretty stream. After crossing the little bridge, the way begins to climb gently and I meet a woman coming down the slope with a very large and very enthusiastic dog. She calls out to me that it is friendly. I know those kinds of friends and brace myself. As we come level, it takes a terrific leap in my direction, wrenching the lead from the owner's hands and pulling her over flat on her face in the mud. Once I've repelled the dog's advances, I help her up and commiserate. The dog, by way of apology, leaps about some more and tramples on my left foot. I expect they heard my shriek in Finistère.

I am now close to an interesting goal, the Chapelle of Notre-Dame de Bonne Nouvelle at Le Bas Pont-Scorff. This white-washed chapel is 13th century in origin, but refashioned five hundred years later. It contains a curiosity: a recumbent effigy of a very tall woman, in limestone on a granite base, measuring 2,20m. A reasonable conjecture suggests it may have been intended to be an external vertical decoration. Her identity is unknown, (speculation includes Marie de Limoges who married Arthur, future duke of Brittany in 1275), although in popular tradition the figure is simply called Notre-Dame de Tronchâteau, a

reference to the local seigneury. She has an unusual face, both bland and intriguing. Her hands are clasped between her breasts and some sort of headband trails down to her shoulders. I wonder if she is a distant relative of the Venus of Quinipily statue in not-so-far away Baud. They share an other-worldly quality, indifferent to the changes of time, and a sense of mystery.

I cross the Scorff on the old Pont Saint-Jean (sometimes called the Roman Bridge), a beautiful spot with the ruins of an old hospital chapel on the bank, and enter the attractive town of Pont-Scorff, which deserves its status as a '*petite cité de caractère*'. It's an arty sort of place. I pass a modern wood sculpture of seven prophets by Pierre de Grauw (my initial thought was that they represented the seven founding saints of Brittany) to reach the square of the Église du Sacré-Cœur. This late 19th century structure has no bell-tower, due to insufficient funding, but there's a strange wooden structure at the rear which was used for the same purpose. Near the church, La Maison des Princes is a very handsome early 16th century edifice in Renaissance style, now housing the town hall.

Leaving across country past the Chapelle Saint-Aubin at Lesbin, I stop for a moment to admire the beautiful yew trees in the precinct, before continuing on the road through hamlets and down into the valley of the Scao, descending to the stream in a deep wooded valley. The very pretty scene is somewhat spoilt by forbidding notices and warnings that the main path is closed during hunting season, November to February. A red and white metal barrier stands by to enforce the rule, a symbol of the repression of walking in many places in Brittany for nearly half the year. Luckily there's no problem today and I go straight on up to the edge of the *bourg* of Rédéné, which means I have entered my home department of Finistère at last, something of a milestone psychologically.

## 21 Pressing on: a lonely spring, a healing tomb and a limping saint

Glimpses of the church tower appear over a tall hedge as I pass the sports' fields and a modern housing estate to reach the centre. Rédéné looks a typical rural village, with bars and a crêperie, and signs of activity around the bakery and delicatessen in the central square. Here the 16th century church of Saint Peter and Notre-Dame de Lorette was restored in 1904. It is closed, of course, but there is an interesting little former ossuary or bone-house attached to the south wall, which was later turned inwards to become a chapel of the nave, apparently containing the baptismal font. On the exterior of this dinky structure are two mysterious carved faces, one open-mouthed. Man and woman? Hope and despair, perhaps.

From the centre, I follow the rue de Rosbigot for nearly a kilometre before turning onto a wide track which soon curves to cross a stream. I know I need to keep beside this and confidently go ahead, soon espying an old Tro Breiz symbol on an obliging tree-trunk. A red herring, as it turns out. Before long that slightly uneasy feeling I always get when on the wrong tangent steals up behind me, and I remember the important detail that the water should be on my left. No amount of creative thinking can make it so in reality. I go back to the start of the track again and see a very small unobtrusive path wavering along the opposite bank. That's my little-walked route, through the holly trees, skipping over tiny feeder cascades with stepping-stones to aid the crossing. It is a most beautiful path along the hillside, large boulders scattered above the sparkling stream. The valley gets wilder and more overgrown as it goes on, fallen trees and mounds of ivy filling in the spaces. A lost green world, silent but for the murmuring water. There's a Compostela trail sign on the face of a sliced tree trunk, so it must see other pilgrims from time to time.

Across a little road, I can soon continue on the footpath along the Scaff (or Scave). Then there's another stint of road walking before descending into wooded territory and reaching the lonely Fontaine Saint Adrien. This evocative little stone triangle, with the date 1789, seems to be gradually losing itself to the rise of mire and moss. It feels a place to worship nature rather than God, and something about its aloneness moves me to stay awhile and share time and space with this wilding remnant. A quiet contrast with the next step, following the main road towards Quimperlé before diverting to calmer paths down to the river Ellé. This provides a more appealing entry into this ancient town along the Promenade Glenmor, named after the famous Breton singer and poet, a powerful figure in the cultural revival of the 1970s, who died in the town in 1996.

Quimperlé is obscure and relatively unknown to outsiders, sometimes thought to be Quimper wrongly spelt. In fact, it is a wonderful historical centre. Based on two rivers (*quimper* = confluence), the Ellé and the Isole, which after their union here form the tidal river or *ria* called La Laïta, it has suffered from serious flooding in the past. On the riverside I pass a statue of Théodore Hersart de la Villemarqué (1815-1895), author of the seminal work of Breton oral tradition, the *Barzaz Breiz*, who was born and died here. His book is a collection of popular songs and poems, which has become important in notions of Breton historical identity. Although the authenticity of parts was challenged soon after publication, discovery of La

Villemarque's notebooks in 1964 largely vindicated the author, who had been greatly influenced by Welsh traditions. He himself participated as a bard in the Eisteddfod at Abergavenny in 1938, a comparatively recent example of the cultural exchanges deriving at least from the Age of Saints.

Over the bridge, a narrow road leads right up to the Abbaye Sainte-Croix. There is almost no-one about as I approach this majestic structure. The exterior of the complex is sombre but with exquisite detail on the absidal chapel exterior. Founded in the 11<sup>th</sup> century, it is the only example in Brittany of a circular design based on Saint Sepulcre in Jerusalem (not counting the mysterious Lanleff), with an impressive rotunda, and a dim crypt with carved capitals, containing the tomb of Saint Urlou. He specialised in healing headaches and there's a hole for pilgrims to insert their head in hope of a cure. A space underneath provides for larger body parts in need of treatment, indeed a whole person might almost squeeze in and curl up there if everything hurt, pulling painful limbs tight into the sacred spot. It's tempting.

In 1862 a lantern tower, added to the rotunda in the 17<sup>th</sup> century, collapsed, causing massive damage to the church, but sparing the crypt. The distinctive raised choir is a feature of the restoration work. Beneath is a very fine example of the *Mise en tombeau* theme, a representation of

the placing of Jesus' body in the tomb, featuring ten figures of tufa with remarkably rendered headgear, hairstyles and costumes. I feel there's something not quite right with this particular version of a common sculptural group, and finally realise that Christ's body is laid head to the right rather than the conventional reverse.

When I come out of the abbey, the town seems to have filled up considerably. My initial impression was that, like Tréguier, this old religious centre is muted and restrained in atmosphere, but now many people are milling about, groups of young people especially, with nothing much to do. Noise levels rise as a quarrel simmers, a sign for older shoppers and sightseers to hurry by with lowered gaze. It will probably all fizzle out to nothing, but there's not much incentive to hang around admiringly among the wide-ranging displays of historical architecture, with some striking doorways and fabulous houses. Time to cross the Isole, and climb a steep street up to the High Town.

This is my route out of Quimperlé, where the worthy-looking church of Notre-Dame-de-l'Assomption is set in a great oasis of a square, and then past a former 16th century hospital where the figure of a pilgrim on the gable end seems to mark the way ahead beyond all the religiosity. But getting right away from the town takes time, and the noise of the motorway and industrial complexes soon replaces the presence of houses. Just over the whizzing traffic lanes is the chapel of Saint Madeleine, an undesirable location, and the building has an air of holding itself tightly closed against the din. Above the west door is a small, sharply etched portrait of Mary Magadelene herself, holding her iconic anointing bottle. A facility for lepers, outside the boundaries of the town, is thought to have existed on the site.

From here to Le Trevoux, there is little peace to be had beyond pockets of footpath in a spell of road walking near the express way. The countryside shifts from unremarkable to unpleasant, with evidence of intensive farming all around. After passing the ruins of a hospitaller chapel to Saint John at Pont Men, it's back over the dual carriageway, past the grounds of a Franciscan monastery and finally into the village, which proves to be a calm antidote to traffic sickness. Centrally situated is the strikingly shaped church of Saint Peter and Saint Paul, with a thin bell-tower and low, wide body. Its origins lie in the early 16th century. It's closed, but I get the key from a charming young woman in the *mairie*, in exchange for my French identity card.

The setting is very agreeable, with park and lakes directly behind the church, perfect for my lunch break. A statue of Saint Christopher on his knees carrying the Christ child is rather arbitrarily placed beside the path. Inside, the bright nave houses conventional statuary but there is an oddity in the stubby south transept: a 1759 painting symbolising the union of Brittany and France, with the figure of Anne de Bretagne looking up at her husband Louis XII, king of France. It seems from the position of the figures and indications of peace and abundance to be based on the one now in the Louvre, *Allegorie du Bon Gouvernement* (1644), a reference to Anne of Austria's regime when she was regent for her little son, Louis XIV. But Anne de Bretagne struggled to keep Brittany a separate territory, despite her position as Queen of France, not to mention the fact that she and her husband Louis XII were both dead long before the merger happened officially.

Yet more of the road walking that characterises the route I'm following in south Finistère takes me eventually to the Oratoire de Saint Anne. This shrine sits on the edge of farm buildings and cultivated land. Set in a grove of magnificent beech trees, some having obviously been lost in the recent great storm, the little structure contains a huge statue of Anne and her daughter Mary, with no room for anything else. Someone is obviously taking great care of the place, but their patience with feckless visitors seems to be wearing thin. There are many forbidding notices, dogs appearing the main objects of wrath, although we all know it's always the owners to blame.

The spot is a tiny haven, with wooden benches arranged in a semi-circle outside for quiet contemplation in the beech grove, but all around the bounds of the sanctuary is debris, like rusting metal, piles of stuffed plastic bags, and electric fences. It is not a salubrious environment. A black bull bellows furiously in the field as I sit for a few minutes thinking about the contrast. When I go on towards Bannalec, a woman walking her dog stops to talk and tells me there's been trouble with the unruly dogs on the unkempt farm behaving badly with passing canines on their innocent way into the woods. This may explain those indignant interdictions at the oratory.

More roads lead into Bannalec, where a busy grey Saturday is bringing out more energy than I've ever seen here before. Not so banal as my persistent image of the place in the past. Around the church people mill and cars constantly manœuvre. The bar where I stop for coffee is welcoming and I'm happy to sit for a bit before heading on down to the station. The original passenger hall building still stands, somewhat modernised and with the word Ti-Gar (station house) emblazoned on the front below a blown-up reproduction of an old postcard of the station in its heyday after the inauguration in September 1863. The surrounding buildings from that time have all vanished. It is now a halt, with the TER train flagged down by passengers on the route between Quimper and Lorient.

My path initially follows the railway along a parallel single-lane road, dipping to a stream and then rising again to give views across the tracks to wooded hills. Turning over a rail crossing, I am soon on a track leading down into the valley of Moulin Neuf around the pretty Ster Goz stream, before emerging in a series of hamlets and small roads that will eventually lead to Trebalay. And now we are really in chapel country. A whole string of these blocks of faith stretches across the heavily worked land westwards, little blobs of respite from intensive farming. They seem to continue their own introverted life silently now, much reduced from a former role, while the world goes on around them.

The Roman road from Vannes to Quimper (the modern D22 taking a roughly similar line) provided a well-used pilgrim trail that could finance the building and the maintenance of some seriously sumptuous shrines. In the days when there was no need to lock chapels and tight-knit rural societies populated the countryside without constantly rattling about everywhere in cars for work, shopping and entertainment, they must have been surrounded by life. Generally, I found these expensively worked, imposing structures curiously bland and lifeless, depleted of the energy that must surely have thrummed once on this traditional pilgrim route. They look good, but some heart seemed lacking. Perhaps it is simply my own lack of Christian credentials.

This is my first time at the Chapelle de Saint-Tréfine in Trebalay, and I have a powerful experience outside the chapel. The calvary with a naif figure of Christ catches the attention at once. It looks like the totem of a primitive people, and no less commanding for that. What really stands out is a group of four yew trees forming a square with a little stone placed half way on each open side and a simple stepped cross in the middle. A curious line of rough stones higher up the slope seem to act as both barrier and portal to ritual space. I've never seen such a set-up, and walk round the outside slowly. Then I step into the square and at once I feel the strength of energy around me. Three times I make the circuit of the cross. The sense is constant rather than heightened, a warmth, gentle potency that draws me back into a distant past, an echo of another era. Perhaps it is a grave.

Roads, roads, roads, chapels, chapels, chapels. Only a couple of kilometres further on, the Chapelle du Moustoir is a total surprise. It is signed off the road, which is following the line of the Roman thoroughfare, and reached along an overgrown little path. Once in the presence of the chapel there is no sense of anything else as the large grey structure dominates an open green space with mature trees, setting off the west face with its magnificent and intricately carved double doorway. A figure holds up a cup like the Holy Grail, a Green Man peeps out from foliage, all the characters have expressive faces. It feels well away from the world, all alone in its grandeur, but still commanding in physical presence. Dedicated to Saint Maurice, a 12<sup>th</sup> century abbot of Langonnet in Morbihan, the building dates from the 15-16<sup>th</sup> century. The bell-tower was lost to a storm in 1937, leaving a strange cross-wall and stair-tower, now supporting only air.

The much more famous Chapelle de la Trinité, in the commune of Melgven, stands on the D22 road, also called the Route historique du Tro Breiz, and traffic almost scrapes along the south wall as it wraps round a blind bend. Cars shoot by dangerously close as I try to take photographs. Once again the position by a Roman road accounts for the chapel's development and grandeur, with plenty of pilgrim passage through the ages. It's imposing in size, but the great figure of God with Jesus' body across his knees on the tympanum of the west door left me cold, although it is an unusual subject, as we are more used to often very moving sculptural exercise of the Pieta, with Christ's mother holding her son's body. Perhaps grief on a human scale is more moving than a god's. The expense of the exquisite carving here must have been great, an investment of donated funds into a glorious façade. On the other side of the road, quite out of the way, are the *fontaine* and *lavoir*, with no statue but attractive stonework and plenty of green sludge.

My route now diverges from the main road and follows the line of a local lane which becomes a track and offers muddy walking edged by late spring flowers all the way to the Croix de Quinquis. Here there are stone benches for rest and contemplation, but right next to the main road. More tracks follow before a road joins the line of the same old route to a jewel in the Tro Breiz pilgrimage through southern Finistere, the beautiful little *enclos* of Locmaria-an-Hent. Quite a contrast with the grandeur of Melgven! Here all is simple and direct. The church is enclosed by a wall, and what a difference separation from the traffic makes, doing its job of creating a sacred precinct. Keep profane things like cars and motorists out at all costs. Then there's the calvary and a hauntingly lovely ossuary building, despite its macabre purpose of storing dead bones. The stone tracery of the four-arched opening is delicate, and the stoops bloom with plant life, like the light touch of an interior decorator to set off the greyness of the building.

After this, I've run out of time and have to opt for car transport on to Saint-Evarzec and a quick look at the church, which amazingly is open. A rather prim statue of the patron Saint Primel in deacon's robes doesn't fit well with his image as a forest-dwelling hermit with great healing powers. This Welsh monk is said to have lived near Saint-Thois when his friend Saint Corentin came to visit. Albert Le Grand, 17th century author of The Lives of Breton Saints, records the touching incident that Corentin prayed for a source of water closer to Primel's dwelling, as the ageing, lame hermit was exhausted from fetching it from a distance. One thump of the baton on the ground and water sprang forth. Another example of the importance that the saints showed control over man's most vital resource, an element held sacred from time immemorial: revitalising, soothing, therapeutic. By analogy, Primel is the patron saint of water-diviners.

Starting again from Saint-Evarzec another day, I cross the busy D783 and turn down a stream-lined path to the lake at Le Mur. The valley is full of the relics of the great storm with fallen trunks and piles of cut branches. It's a pretty route, but the lake seems to be private property. When I come out on the road again and realise there are many more kilometres of it before the edge of Quimper, my spirits droop. But there's not much traffic and views open out as the road rises towards the city. In a dip soon after entering Ergué-Armel, I find the secretive and rather beautiful *fontaine*, with a statue of Saint Armel behind a grill. There's a perfectly placed seat to enjoy the stone, water and tumbling flowers on the wall behind the spring, but loud music pulsing from the house beside the scene is off-putting, and instead I slog uphill to the church. This has a war memorial formed from a calvary inside a square of military shells, with the generic figures of a soldier and a sailor standing on the lower bar of the cross. An attractive grove of lime trees shades the precinct.

A short distance further on and I'm engulfed by the mad rush of Quimper, a crazy world compared with the rural route that's brought me here. It's a city I know well, but coming in the back way like this, and on foot, is completely disorientating and I have to follow written directions carefully to negotiate the endless roundabouts and junctions. Passing through the Bois de Kerandennec and round the lake in the industrial quarter of Creach-Gwen, I finally reach the grounds of the Château of Lanniron and some respite from the traffic. It's a fitting way to enter Quimper, in fact, because the route then curves round under the express-way and onto the banks of the Odet to come out in Locmaria, the oldest quarter of the city and the earliest religious heart, retaining every sign of its antiquity.

## 22 Soaking it all in: a miraculous fish, finding lost things, and a miracle

I pause at the medieval-style garden on the river bank before entering another of my favourite places in Brittany. The abbey of Locmaria is the oldest building in Quimper, founded in 1124, probably replacing an earlier monastery. The church retains that sense of the distant past in the history of worship, aided by the modesty of the Romanesque architecture. Attached are remains of the cloister and fragments of sculpture, with a later colonnade in light tufa stone. This side of the Odet was settled and exploited long before Quimper grew up across the water. The Roman settlement here was called Aquilonia, and before that the Celts were already using the local clay to make pottery, an industry Locmaria has become famous for. The Henriot brand, founded in 1690, continues in the quarter to this day.

Walking up the river to cross one of the many bridges into Quimper, the change of pace is evident. This modern capital of Finistère was in legend constructed at the impetus of King Gradlon (4-5th century), who was establishing a new power-base in the post-Roman Armorica. He was converted to Christianity under the influence of Saint Guénolé, the abbot of Landévennec abbey, who remained an important advisor. One day when out hunting near Menez Hom, one of Brittany's sacred hills, Gradlon's party came across a hermit, Corentin, who lived in a simple hut beside a little pond he had created by striking the ground with his staff. In this lived a single fish which he caught each day, cut off a piece for his sustenance and then returned to the water, where it miraculously regenerated.

Corentin was also able to feed Gradlon and his retainers in this way, and the king was so impressed he urged the hermit to leave his solitary life and come to the new city to become the first bishop. This involved sending him to Tours where Saint Martin performed the episcopal ceremony. A stained-glass window in his chapel in the nave of Quimper cathedral relates the legend of his discovery, complete with fish and frying pan! So Corentin is the seventh and last of our founding saints of Brittany. He was also the earliest, born c375, son of immigrants from Great Britain, and his stories are essentially fishy. One anachronistic tale has saints Patern and Malo (born c510) visit him and enjoy a meal of eels from the magic pond. (This is now associated with his *fontaine* by a 19th century chapel in his honour in Plomodiern, site of the original hermitage.)

Corentin's magnificent Gothic cathedral, full of light and dazzling space, was built in three phases from the 13th to early 15th century. The spires with their majestic equestrian statue of Gradlon were not added until 1856. The crooked nave is only one of many striking features, and is probably the result of this disjointed construction, when the foundations of other structures may have prevented a true line. A less likely explanation is that it represents the angle of Jesus' bowed head on the cross. At the time of the Revolution, the statues of the saints were taken out into the adjoining square and burnt - with revolutionary contempt, this took place on December 12th, Corentin's feast day - so many of current versions have been brought in from elsewhere. This is true of the fine triptych showing Saint Yves between a rich man and a poor man.

Records reveal that in 1424 a new money box for offerings was established in the cathedral, to be double-locked, with one key in the hands of an administrator and the other held by a religious official. The journey of the Seven Saints of Brittany is mentioned specifically, in the context that the money given must be used according to the conditions of the cathedral's statute of pilgrimage. This is a clear indication that the Tro Breiz was a well-established practice. Dom Lobineau in his *Histoire de Bretagne* (1707) says that there was an altar of the Seven Saints here in Quimper cathedral. Interestingly, he had given a list of the saints in the text with Saint Méen and Judicaël in place of Patern and Brieuc, but corrected this in the preface before publication. Further research had shown him that the Seven Saints referred to the first bishops in western Brittany, but clearly it was not a tradition he had immediately recognised in the early 18th century.

At the end of the southern aisle is my special spot, the place of Santig Du, the 'little black saint' of Quimper. His statue and the relic of his skull are fixed on the wall. Jean Discalceat (barefoot) was a Franciscan monk who helped the inhabitants assiduously in the turmoil of the Wars of Succession when the city was besieged, and during an outbreak of the plague in 1349. He himself died of the disease. Like Saint Yves he is always associated with the poor, but he has another facet, commemorated in the cathedral for hundreds of years. He is relied upon as a finder of lost things. It is still the tradition to pray to Santig Du for retrieval and, when successful, to bring a loaf of bread to place in the basket provided on a table near his statue. Anyone in need can come and help themselves. I have to say that Santig Du has never failed me and I cannot count the number of loaves I have carried with thanks into the building over the years.

There's a real sense of the last stage of my colossal journey as I leave the cathedral in Quimper after a heartfelt entreaty to Santig Du for good passage. Maybe this is not his forté, as things turn out. It's April and the weather is violently unpredictable. Gale force winds and a lot of rain are forecast for today, but it is the only time I have free to make progress on my Tro Breiz. I can already feel an uncomfortable sensation in my left eye as the air rushes into my face even as we are still sheltered by towering medieval houses in the rue Kéreon.

The streets of central Quimper are lined with ancient, often colourful dwellings decorated with little statues. It is a handsome city by any standards, even on a day like this. David has bravely agreed to accompany me on today's walk and we have left one car in Seznec, about 12km north, so if the walk proves over-ambitious for me, he can go on ahead and return with the vehicle. But there is no doubt that being on 'home territory' with the final goal of the Monts d'Arrée ahead is good for the morale, underpinnned by the knowledge that I will actually finish the Tro Breiz (barring accidents, as my father always said) albeit a little later than planned.

Quimper is moderately busy with locals going about their business. There is no obvious sign of tourists, even in the cathedral, this morning, nor in the Place Saint Corentin adjacent, where statues of the saints were burnt in 1793. Once at the Pont Médard, we are passing a significant boundary. The Steir ran along outside the medieval walls, giving an extra layer of protection, but there's more to it in Quimper. The bishop held sway within the old centre around the cathedral, with the remit of the duke only beginning across this little river. The elegant square Place au duc reflects this unusual limitation of power. The duke has his mills here on the Steir, where we soon pass a former mill-race, water hurtling down towards the confluence with the Odet. On a day like today it is not hard to credit the depth of flooding in modern times, indicated by little round markers on some shops. It is a powerful flow, streaming down from higher ground to the north, channelling its force through the city centre.

But the walk soon becomes much more peaceful, as a riverside path lined by willows leads gently out of Quimper, past the two springs of the Fontaine du Parc du Manoir, with its small square attached *lavoir*. We are already damp from a heavy shower despite stopping under a road bridge for brief shelter. The path moves from side to side of the river, sometimes through flooding. Although houses are all around, the walk feels rural already. Sodden tree bark and splodges of saturation on stone walls turn everything dark, clumps of moss swollen like pin-cushions. Daylight is low and grey. I feel a bit apprehensive about the way ahead in these circumstances, but it is not quite so daunting in company, which always makes the miles go by less laboriously.

There are roads to negotiate near the express-way and we see no more of the Steir for a while as the route climbs. After crossing the railway line, feeling confident that we are on right path in the pelting rain, we slog up a road with fast traffic and no pavements, only to lose sight of IGN® signs and hence confidence. Everything is harder in tough conditions. I don't think well, convinced we should be following the line of the river more closely, instead of going directly away from the Steir valley. We decide to retrace our steps to see if we missed a turning back down into the valley. The sky explodes into cutting slices of rain as we trudge downhill. The only possible side road is a dead end and the smiling house owner assures his unexpected bedraggled visitors that there is no footpath around there.

We sit in a bus-shelter, welcomingly waterproof although we are drenched already, and eat our lunch with a window on the dismal downpour inches away. David gets a signal on his phone and we decide from a better map than the one in the guidebook that we do need to go up the road again and across the top of the hill before descending to the river further on. It is an ordeal, but we have no choice. In fact there is to be no more river walking, just the wretched hard surface of the road that racks my joints with each footfall. Plod, plod, plod. It is quite difficult to think of anything except the next step.

The Steir valley here contains road, rail and river transport surging in parallel lines to and from Quimper. We cross over on bridges and then are on the up again, veering off onto a wooded footpath at last. This rises steadily and rises some more until I feel we'll emerge somewhere up in the sky, although that could be weariness talking. We chat intermittently, more to keep our spirits up than from having anything to say. I feel less and less inclined to communicate as every scrap of energy is needed to head into the driving rain. It is like being under constant enemy attack.

On finally emerging from the trees, it's just roads and more roads. Ironically my foot, the bane of my walking life, is hurting but not too bad for the moment. My hip on the other hand is killing me. David chivalrously offers to go on and get the car, but I am grimly determined and stagger on in silence. The little chapel of St Denis near Seznec is my reward, reached through a tunnel of verdure, a simple doll's house of a shrine with a pretty red door. Closed, of course. It seems to be growing out of adjacent farm buildings, like a stellar crop. As we do a quick circuit, the rain begins to lash down with more force than ever. We take refuge in the car, challenge over, for today at least. It's hard to imagine worse conditions than we've just had, but I am soon to find out that they do indeed exist.

We pick up the route another day, from the same spot. The weather is overcast and some rain is forecast, but it's a very pleasant start in the month of May. Bluebells now line the path to the chapel. A stony track leads away from the neighbouring farm and down into a stream valley, a pattern to be repeated several times this morning with increasingly steep gradients. After about two kilometres of cheerful walking, appreciating the long views of staggered hills and burgeoning trees, the promised rain begins. Gentle at first and not at all unpleasant, it gradually revs up as the kilometres pass until we are both soaked to the skin despite various layers of waterproofing.

Again we are forced to take refuge in a bus shelter and eat our lunch on a damp seat. After that there is no respite, even hail and a low growl of thunder at one point adding to the nuances of the downpour. It's a pity. This would be a lovely route in traditional Beltane weather, the start of summer, with the wooded hills above Locronan slowly getting closer and a series of rushing streams in the valleys. We stop to admire a water-course that has been trained by a line of boulders to turn at 90°, creating a wide space of swirling water, some threads turning complete circle in a doubling back before joining the main flow. A large concrete tunnel channels the stream under the track and we fool about sending leaves and a stick through but it's hard to make anything out in the spate that emerges.

The long stint of road walking after Kerven is dispiriting, adding a note of prosaic heaviness to the pounding rain on my head. We reach the Chapelle Saint-Théleau, which has more the air of a large parish church despite a very rural location, but there is no porch for shelter and after a moment to draw breath, we slog straight on up a steep narrow footpath behind the precinct, into the woods. Now even the bluebells are looking flat and joyless under the watery bombardment. The incline is increasingly challenging, aided and abetted by a torrent of water splashing down on us where the path should be, as we attempt to rise to the top. Three white horses in a field gaze gloomily as we finally reach the little road at Plas ar Horn, and there one of my favourite chapels, a tiny oasis on a dismal day.

The Chapelle ar Sonj (Chapel of Memory) is a fairly recent construction on this lofty sacred spot with far-reaching views to the coast and the Bay of Douarnenez. A huge ugly earlier version (1911) was torn down in 1977 and replaced by this minute softly low stone edifice that blends into the landscape. It has incredibly expressive stained-glass windows of abstract design by master craftsman Jean Bazaine. There is also a 19th century outdoor pulpit on the roadside, with a wheel-headed cross, drawing the attention of passers-by. The chapel was designed to be a focal point of a very special local Pardon, the Tromenie. It is the 10th

station, honouring Saint Ronan and making association with the Celtic month Lughnasadh.

Not dedicated to a saint, it nevertheless has a powerful voice of place and past, representing the blend of Christian and pagan traditions that surround Saint Ronan, as we shall see in Locronan down the hillside. Here on the 'mountain' top, even in today's sopping conditions, it has an unaccountable air of spiritual radiation, forging in all dimensions, a sort of volcano of the sacred. For me it has often been somewhere to linger and reflect, attracted by the sensation of strength, based on many lifetimes of faith and endeavour pulled together in one spot, and also an arcane ambience of sanctuary. Today I am looking forward to re-energising in its unassuming embrace more than I can express. The door is locked.

There is no way out of the rain. My 'water-resistant' walking trousers are now so heavy I am struggling to lift my legs to make forward progress. We are both so chilled that our muscles and sinews feel numb and lifeless. David nobly presses on downhill into the village of Locronan to fetch his car and come back for me, as I can hardly stand. Strange pains rack my arms and legs, but attempts to find a dry spot under a tree are hopeless in such relentless conditions. I start to totter downhill, not really in control of my limbs, trying not to fall into the path of the occasional speedy cars that pass, and eventually meet David, still on foot, coming back from a wrong turning... Hapless travellers. It is not our day.

We don't dwell in lovely Locronan. When I am alone back at my car in Seznec I intend stripping off and driving home in a dry jacket and little else. But my clothes are too wet and my hands too cold to perform the manœuvre. Two pristine pairs of shoes in the boot laugh at my futile attempts to unlace my boots. The sodden garments have formed a kind of straitjacket and I'm trapped. I find a large canvas bag, fling it on the driver's seat, squelch into the car and, rigid claws gripping the steering-wheel, grim in concentration on the road ahead, set off for home. Once there, I get straight in a very hot bath and lie for a long time, empty-headed, senseless, imbecilic. But something nags at me, some sense of absence and eventually I realise what it is. There has been a miracle. My foot is absolutely fine.

## 23  Feeling good: a difficult saint, the Breton Atlantis and moorland freedom

A miracle indeed. From that very day to this moment of writing, I have walked pain-free. After nearly 40 years of reactive arthritis, suddenly it's gone. There is no obvious explanation. I wish I could attribute the wonder to one of the healing saints, but I didn't even stick my foot in the hole in Saint Urlou's tomb in Quimperlé. Maybe it's a reward from some universal energy for my determination to finish this journey. The sensation of normality is bizarre and I find my gait changed, with no constant adjustment to alleviate the agony. There is no doubt that I am generally stronger and fitter after all my efforts over the last year or so, but this seems a sudden rather than gradual change. Only on the last walk a few days earlier, it was the same old suffering. I can't explain this transformation, but I've come to accept it, and slap my feet down freely like any walker rather than gingerly seeking the least painful angle for each step.

I don't think Saint Ronan would have been a lot of help anyway, as I return to his holy place, Loc-ronan, to pick up my route. He seems to have had a difficult personality that rubbed people up the wrong way. Arriving in the Age of Saints from Ireland on a stone boat in the bay of Douarnenez, he immediately accused the locals of being wreckers and threatened to shine an enormous light on their nocturnal activities. After this undiplomatic start, it was necessary to beat a hasty retreat inland, where he set up a hermitage in the Bois de Nevet. The wonderful church in Locronan has an attached chapel with the tomb of the saint (1430), and the details of his subsequent career are portrayed on the panels of the pulpit.

One day Ronan saw a wolf carrying off a lamb and prayed to God to save the helpless victim, which was immediately released at the saint's feet. The animal's owner was so impressed that he began to spend time with Ronan, learning about Christianity. This aroused the resentment of the man's wife Keben, who took against the incomer and accused him of many things, including the murder of her daughter. She presented her case to King Gradlon in Quimper and Ronan was arrested, but savage dogs set to attack him turned away, so that the king recognised a true man of God. Ronan told him the missing child had been locked in a chest by her mother and this proved to be the case. The child was dead after her incarceration, so the saint had another chance to demonstrate his powers by bringing her back to life.

Ronan eventually left Locronan after more accusations fomented by Keben, and went to the area around Hillion in Côtes d'Armor, where he lived as a hermit again and eventually died. His body was brought back on an ox-cart, which Keben, ever vengeful, encountered, striking off the horn of one of the beasts (hence providing an explanation of the place-name Plas-ar-Horn). This is shown in one of the coloured medallions on the pulpit in the church at Locronan, the spot where the cart stopped and his tomb was made. Keben herself, often presented as a witch or sorceress, was consumed in flames, a spectacular ending to their feud in which she had also accused Ronan of being a werewolf, a monster of double-form. He is certainly an unusual saint, perhaps with Druidic origins.

Locronan is a most beautiful village, a film-set (literally – Polanski's Tess (of the d'Urbevilles) and many others have had scenes shot there) of 18th century façades and floral decoration. Inevitably this has led to tourist-mecca status, with all the negatives (and commercial positives) that a surfeit of visitors brings to any small rural community. Generally I would avoid it in summer, but there is one occasion that is unmissable: the annual Tromenie (6km) in July, and every six years, the Grand Tromenie (12km). This religious festival, Ronan's Pardon or a Tro-minihy (journey around his sanctuary), sees a silent procession of hundreds through the countryside, on a route that Ronan himself was said to have walked, fasting, every week. It is an extraordinary occasion, with flowery cabins set up along the route to honour different saints, and access to sacred rocks where Ronan paused to meditate. Many regard his ritual walking around specific natural features as marking out a Celtic *nemeton* or sacred space, with possible cosmological significance. The quadrilateral shape of the mini-pilgrimage may be connected to the four pagan solstice and equinox festivals. Certainly when walking it, one feels that the purpose lies in the landscape.

The weather is good (by which I mean simply not raining) on the day I'm back alone for the next stage of my walk, but there's a major VTT or mountain-bike event going on in the area and I arrive to find the unwelcome signs of safety monitors at their stations whenever a foot-path touches the main ring-road. Praying that my route won't coincide with the cyclists, I leave the centre of Locronan on foot via the pretty Chapelle de Bonne Nouvelle with its *lavoir* banked by colourful shrubs, before a stint of road-walking through hamlets to avoid the busy route to Douarnenez. Finally over this, I move towards the Bois de Nevet via Le Mez. A single track serves the few houses in this rural retreat (one rather oddly with a huge anchor propped up against the gateway) before entry to forest at Kergoat Nevez. Here I pass a garden where a ginger-coloured dog on a chain bounces up and down impressively, barking his head off at the sight of a stranger. The owner comes out, mildly chiding the dog, and shrugs expressively at me. We exchange that wry complicit smile of dog-lovers.

The wood is beautiful, a vibrant green glow, with little sign in this part at least of the terrible storm damage that blighted the forest where I live, 50km away. The path skirts the edge, shady and bright at the same time. The wood is a mass of thin trunks as if the trees are still young, with the mossy bases of tangled others lining the route. It's early and there are few people about. The temperature is a moderate 18° and this is shaping up to be a lovely walk. Gone are my fears about not being able to make the final pick-up point, and the removal of this constant anxiety lightens my step. When I reach the large parking-area on the opposite edge, I feel refreshed and made lively by a surge of plant-channelled energy.

Following the main footpath signs into the grounds of Vieux Château, there's an ominous trickle of cyclists coming up behind. Suddenly, I am on the narrowest of earth paths with little room for manœuvre on either side and bikes constantly nibbling at my heels. Some are aggressive and arrogant, forcing me out of the way with little regulation of speed, others considerate and calling to their fellows to slow down. Seeing that this is a major walking route and a fair Sunday, they should surely be prepared. One young man stops to speak to me and warn me that many cyclists are coming. I say rather pointedly that I'm happy to share the path with them. He laughs, says Fair enough, and goes on.

When I can't take any more of this unquiet path, I go straight on where they all rush right downhill, simply for some respite, and wander along in peaceful woodland, eventually finding a log to sit on and rest. Fortunately this turns out to be my route and I avoid further tussles with the mountain-bike men. A blessed relief. Emerging from the wood, a little road leads to Kerbellec, with a pretty decorated house, and then up a narrow side road signed Bellevue. Going ahead on a grassy track, I soon learn why. Never was a name better deserved. Once a couple of galloping horses and their young riders have disappeared into the distance, I find myself in paradise. A tree-shaded picnic table is the perfect place to stop.

Below is a broad valley lined by fields and studded with trees of all shapes and sizes. The meadow beside my seat is bright with ragwort, sorrel and lady's smock, grasses undulating in the breeze. The view is indeed lovely. At the bottom of the hill is the lake my route will soon pass, and in the distance I can see the port of Douarnenez and the sea. The rare conditions of the day – no pain and no rain – combine to allow total immersion in the picture-perfection of the scene. Going on slowly to enjoy it, I continue as the track curves round the edge of the wood and then the spire of Kerlaz church comes into view to add to the glorious manifestation of the view. The openness and beauty are powerful stimulants. I feel the rattled pieces of my interior world come back together, and the empowering joy of walking freely on a sunny day.

When I get to Kerlaz, the church of Saint Germain is closed. Even on a Sunday morning. I was hoping to see the 1917 stained-glass windows of Gabriel Léglise showing scenes from the parish past, both legendary with a memorable episode from the Breton Atlantis story, and historical, like the refusal of local priests to swear allegiance to the new Republic at the time of the Revolution. There is also a small illustration of famous missionary Père Julien Maunoir preaching here in 1658. Earlier in his career, he had composed a canticle in honour of the Seven Founding Saints of Brittany, as part of a revivalist programme directed at ordinary people.

At least the exterior of this parish close is appealing, with a proper triumphal entrance gate, the calvary of 1522, a handsome south porch decorated by animal carvings, and a little roofed ossuary tucked into the side. But I am attracted out into the street again by something even more fascinating: a man walking towards a machine in the car-park opposite. I watch with eager attention. He puts in his coins and out pops a fresh baguette. As miracles go, this is a good one. I have often wondered a) if these machines really work and b) if anyone ever uses them. It feels rather thrilling to see it in action. Beside it is another offering fresh milk. All that's lacking is an egg dispenser to wrap up Sunday refreshments.

Saint Germain's *fontaine* is sited in a deep hollow on the way out of Kerlaz, rather domesticated in appearance, with garden shrubs dotted about the steep banks. It looks like a stone chair with two protruding arms and a tall triangular slated roof. A sad statue of the saint is kept in check by a stout iron grill. Apparently it was chucked into the basin a couple of times in 1907/8, the second causing the head to break off, hence security measures were taken. After a fragrant pause beside the spring, it's a long hike on the tarmac down to the coast at Treizmalaouen. Here steep steps lead down to the beach. Past a cordon of pebbles, the vast damp orange sands are striated by gleaming swathes of light water left by the receding tide. There is hardly anyone in sight, a dog-walker, two wind-surfers struggling in the small grey waves and a couple roaming in the distance. The scene is all glitter and shade under heavy clouds which have replaced the sun, as the weather starts to close in for the ten days of rain we are promised in Finistère.

The Baie de Douarnenez is a huge soft space, the shallow bay embraced by two long arms of land. The town of Douarnenez with its three ports is tucked into the corner to my left, with Cap Sizun starting to stretch away beyond into the Atlantic. Opposite I can see the Cap de la Chèvre ending the hazy line of the Crozon peninsula. The land near and far is all dark contours against the luminous strand, sparks of reflection on the wet surface dancing off into the distance. Walking along the beach, I have to wade through a strong stream pouring down over the sand to create its own delta, before climbing up steeply through the pricking gorse to the stepped memorial cross on the point Beg ar Garrec.

It's a good place to sit and look over this spectacle of legend, reminding me that imaginative connection with the land is forged through a physical one. Quite apart from Saint Ronan's grumpy arrival, this is the location of the city of Ys and the seminal tale of Brittany's own Atlantis. There is indeed something theatrical in the very setting. And framing is vital to this story, still performed by *conteurs* (story-tellers), and so with a meaningful life not confined to words on the page, which is appropriate, as it strikes deep into the heart of Breton-ness.

The daughter of Gradlon, king of Quimper, was ruler of the city of Ys, a settlement integrated in the tides of the bay, cleverly designed with gates that opened and closed as water levels changed. Her father had entrusted this important centre, perhaps on maritime trade routes, to Dahut, who was highly regarded by her people. Or was she the spoilt princess of dubious moral character, tired of the limits imposed by the regulation of life under the new religion of Christianity? Certainly her father was heavily influenced by Corentin, the former hermit of Menez Hom, and abbot Guénolé, both stalwarts of morality, who were helping in the creation of his new capital on the banks of the Odet. (It's worth noting that saints here have taken over an older Druid role in advising leaders.) Had she persuaded Gradlon to build her a city in the Bay of Douarnenez to be a place of liberty and licentiousness?

Rumours flew as far as Quimper of the princess's wild partying and sexual activity in the city of Ys, symbolically placed away from the conventions of *terra firma*. The monks who advised Gradlon urged him to put an end to this travesty of religious tenets. Eventually he rode out across the sands with Saint Guénolé in tow to see his daughter's situation for himself. The visitors ended by spending the night in the walled city. Dahut, as usual, enjoyed her evening entertainment, dancing flamboyantly with a masked man dressed in red. To this stranger she divulged the existence of a key to the city's protections, which was in her father's keeping. When night fell and the king slept, it was mysteriously stolen and the gates opened to admit the rising tide.

Higher and higher the waters rose as the city awakened in panic, too late to be saved. Gradlon and Guénolé rode out on strong horses to beat the flood and gain the shore. They saw Dahut, struggling in the sea, calling to her father for rescue. Guénolé told the king to resist these pleas, but Gradlon could not and pulled his daughter up behind him. The horse began to lose speed and escape seemed impossible. Again the saint fiercely exhorted the king to hurl Dahut down into the waves, a necessary sacrifice for survival. Finally he did so and she tumbled away, soon lost in the turbulent waters. King and advisor made the shore and turned to see the city of Ys disappearing under the sea, never to rise again.

It is a story that can be spun in many ways, from simplistic moralising of bad behaviour rightly punished, the individual sacrificed for greater good, to a nuanced weave of unresolved issues in Dark Age society. It can tell of Christianity versus paganism, convention against freedom, the importance of women in Celtic communities stamped out by the church, or even the imposition of outsiders on locals. Maybe a better criterion for judgement is the aftermath, for the sting in the tale is that in Breton legend Dahut did not die, but was transformed into the sea spirit Ahès, creating her own lasting legacy in oral culture. Two separate traditions may have been welded together here over time, as other versions tell of Ahès the 'fairy-builder' (like the more famous Mélusine), a siren figure often associated with road-construction in western Brittany. One such *Hent Ahès* or Road of Ahès led to the Baie des Trépassés, not too far from here, legendary bay of the dead, haunted by the spirits of unburied victims of drowning at sea.

Dahut has other stories emphasising her individual right to freedom or moral turpitude depending on the teller's point of view and the purpose of relating the tales. These days it is often more about the entertainment for tourists that has undermined and trivialised the wider significance of myth and legend here. At Huelgoat, which she is said to have reached from the Bay of Douarnenez by underground tunnels, she took a different lover every night on the rocky height above the chasm of the Gouffre. The men were given masks to wear, tortuous devices that later tightened into strangulation. Servants threw their bodies into the depths next day and their despairing cries are still carried in the tumultuous tune of the rushing water. Is this story of the power of women, strong in their sexuality, designed to provoke admiration or fear?

And do such legends echo the changing balance of the sexes from Celtic society, where women enjoyed a certain equality and may even have participated in the ritual of the early church in Brittany, to the relentlessly male Catholic dominance of the Church of Rome? Perhaps, but in the triumphant survival of Dahut there is also something more subtle and very Breton: the victory of the people against authority, the ordinary man and woman emerging defiant against strictures laid down to limit their lives by faraway officials who do not share their values or their language. This is a theme that resonates through Breton history.

A lot to think about as I take the coast path north to Saint-Anne-la-Palud, a *haut-lieu* of Catholicism, where another legendary woman made her mark on religious and social life in Brittany in a very different way. This place is often regarded in legend as Saint Anne's 'home', where she revisited later in life with her grandson Jesus. He is said to be responsible for the spring with its strong stone surround across the grass from the chapel. A whole series of sacred buildings have graced this spot over many centuries, the earliest perhaps even situated where the beach is now. The latest is 19th century, with an exterior oratory added in 1903.

The legend of Saint Anne has a powerful grip here, as the area is claimed as her birthplace and residence until an abusive marriage forced her to flee and settle for a time in Judea, before a late return to Brittany. This sets the Breton faithful closest to the heart of the Holy Family itself, and statues of Anne and her daughter Mary illuminate the space here at the entrance to the precinct, together with Saint Hervé and his wonderful grinning wolf companion, both couples tenderly depicted in dark kersanton stone. Inside the chapel, golden crowns and rays light up the shimmering spectacle in reds and blues of a mother teaching her little daughter to read, the ubiquitous set-piece of Anne and Mary in Breton shrines. The Petit Pardon is held here each year at the end of July but the main event is the hugely well-attended Grand Pardon on the last weekend in August, a feast of Breton religious and cultural celebration.

The close association of the chapel and the sea brings all those early journeys of saints to mind again. In her case, it was to flee danger rather than arrive on these Atlantic shores. One story says that Anne disappeared on death only for her body to be found much later in the waves, encrusted with shells. I try to imagine that spectacle as I walk along the sand. Much of the coast path here can be exchanged for the beach except at high tide. A cordon of pebbles protects the Marais de Kervijen, a project begun twenty years ago to use reed beds to filter harmful substances from the water of the Kerharo stream as it passes through to the sea. It was one way proposed to alleviate the problem of noxious green algae polluting many Breton beaches. This would make a good healing job for an incoming saint.

My route turns inland before the vast expanse of yellow sands at Pentrez, and pursues little roads all the way up to the foot of Menez Hom and the famous Chapelle de Ste Marie de Menez-Hom. I like this place very much, not least because it is always open. But there are other reasons in the interior, where I enjoy the crazy contrast between exceptional baroque bling in a line of three altars (official Catholic saints) and the plainness of the rest, apart from some magnificently sculpted beams, not noticed by many visitors, and an old statue of the blind Saint Hervé, probably my favourite saint.

David joins me for the hike from here up to Menez Hom next day and comments on the 'Turkish' air of the church tower. Our last view shows it beautifully framed through an arched gate in the precinct wall. Down the road we hesitate over a stony path heading straight up towards the summit of one of Brittany's seven sacred hills, but decide for once to stick with the planned route and to go on to a split in the road, and then up the incline on a well-marked track. My dog is delighted to get to a point of freedom. When we come out of the trees we are surrounded by bleak moorland, with many stunted and dead pine trees, their jagged trunks still standing stripped of foliage, poignant souvenirs of pre-storm days.

This is a lengthy zig-zagging path constantly ascending the far side of Menez Hom and then turning back towards the summit, over the shoulder and on to the table of orientation at the top. It's a long way round, but there are wonderful views east and north, with occasional glimpses of sea to the west. A limitless pattern of hedged fields and wooded hills is folded across the landscape, a striking contrast with the raw heathland tracks we are on. The slopes of the Aulne valley below us are fertile soil. Near the top of the climb, we at last see our goal of the bridge over the wide river a long way off, with its distinctive cabled curves over a silver streak of water.

We stop to have our picnic lunch on the summit. Few people are about, but a group is operating their radio planes, a hobby for which this site is famous. The Atlantic swells out to the west, with views over the Bay of Douarnenez and a satisfying sense of all the distance I have covered. But what comes up must descend, and it is tough: a narrow path and then very steep steps, not a good height for my stretch, but the step-less path people have forged on the left to avoid them is quite precipitous and eventually I go back and take the steps very slowly while David waits at the bottom. Most walkers just take things like this in their stride, quite literally. I can't easily adjust from the habit of being extremely cautious in my new-found post-miracle state. Red, white and blue windsocks flap from one or two of the sparse trees. Then we swing across the moor and into spruce woodland on a disintegrating and uneven path with deep holes. It makes for uncomfortable walking.

Finally after what seems an age (as hard bits always do) we get to a road, continue on another track past Kerfréval, then down a beautiful valley with barley fields, the crop dark green at the base with feathery light tops. On the hills opposite, a whole nuance of greens ripples in the dense woodland. May is the best month for trees. We reach the main road D60, which proves the worst bit of the whole walk. It is quite narrow with no place to walk alongside, so potentially dangerous, especially with my dog who sometimes leaps at passing cars if given half a chance. I feel anxious and weary on this bit, longing for an end to road walking. After a very long kilometre, we turn towards the hamlet of Coat Carrec, then more road walking. Finally when I can hardly go on through aching muscles (but with no familiar pain), we reach Kerfanc, where a welcome picnic table on the roadside offers views of the river ahead, and a friendly dog comes out to join us as we rest for five minutes.

The last section of the walk is a restorative delight. A track lined by over-arching trees gives views of the tributary to the Aulne and then the wide river itself, such an impressive sight, this major waterway, as we turn towards the Pont de Térénez. This path takes us all the way to the parking by the bridge where David's car is waiting to transport us back to mine at the chapel where we started below Menez Hom, many hours ago. It has been a wonderful day, with the sort of walking I like best, hilly moorland with great long views over land and sea.

## 24  Connecting things up: curvaceous bridge, encounter with a snake and Druid blood sacrifice

I'm looking forward to this walk from the bridge up to Le Faou. It's a sensational start to cross the Pont de Térénez (2011), a curving wonder of towers and metal cables supporting the deck, with a wide pedestrian walkway on each side below the traffic line. Remnants of the old bridge, which I remember crossing many times on my way to Landévennec, are now viewing platforms. I choose the eastern side looking upstream over the mighty Aulne, imagining the Vikings on an exploratory raid up this broad and winding expanse of river. The beacon point at the Roche au Feu many miles inland is said to have been lit as one of a chain to warn of their approach.

At the far end, the footpath ascends steeply between foxgloves through the woods, with views down onto the bridge from on high. Then it evens out to follow the contours above the water for some distance. This is beautiful shady walking, but after shifting away from the river and crossing a stream, I emerge on a track with a strip of grass in the middle for the long incline up to the hamlet of Kergadalen. Towards the top I stop sharply when I realise I am sharing the path with a large snake.

It is on the other side of the central green line, head down on the ground and completely motionless. It has distinctive rings on the back of the neck so I assume it's a *couleuvre à collier*, a type of grass-snake, although I don't get a lot of practice for snake-identification, except a few vipers under the rocks of the Monts d'Arrée. I wonder if it is dead, and then just admire the natural grace of the sinuous body lying in curls that merge into the grass. The second I start to reach for my phone to take a picture, the head rears up and we look each other in the eyes. Then it turns with a flick and slithers away out of sight.

The route skirts the hamlet and gives fantastic views to Menez Hom across the fields, but soon I am plunging down a tiny degraded path overhung by tall grasses laden with seed into a narrower world. There are shiny new Mon Tro Breizh waymarks pointing the route. At the bottom, the stream is alongside, with rings of tree-trunk recently laid (and not entirely stable) and wooden walkways to cross the wettest bits. The sensation is of walking through a verdant tunnel. At the other end I discover from noticeboards that this is the *sentier botanique de Kervezennec*, with information distinguishing between the humidity-loving ash, hazel and willow around the stream-bed, and oak, pine and ivy flourishing in acidic soil higher up. It is certainly a very welcome wildly natural section of my journey.

The path emerges to a grassy track between fields, one newly ploughed with rich soil, offering distant glimpses of the Faou river to the left. A mixed herd of cows busy themselves feeding on lush grass, with a backdrop of the estuary and then distant hills. There are woods ahead and soon the path is narrow again and muddy. A group of women in walking gear comes towards me, chatting cheerily. We exchange merry greetings and then the last one stops to ask if I've seen any snakes – well, yes! I can hardly believe the co-incidence. Her reaction is one of horror, but when I point out that this is nature after all, the others all agree and try to laugh her out of her fright. I think any self-respecting snake will get well out of the way when it hears them coming. And that will be well in advance.

There is more evidence here of trees felled by the storm. I stop by a huge tumbled oak across the path to empty stones from my boots and drink coffee from my thermos. It is all going so well. Heading into the next wood, I am distracted by a white van parked as if concealed in the trees ahead, stirring an inevitable sense of caution on these little walked paths a long way from houses. So I manage to miss the footpath to the right on entry. Ploughing straight ahead through tracks churned up by logging, I am soon struggling over fallen trunks and great branches searching for the way, convinced that the waymarks are lost on fallen timber. After a wasted half hour of searching for a path, I retrace my steps, and immediately discover the right way. This pleasant woodland trail leads to more open country and a spell of pushing through long grass at the edge of a field. I descend to the road at Toul ar Choat (wooded hole) and then off on another track, this time with great views over the Faou valley, when high ferns permit. The tide is up and I can see houses on the edge of Le Faou, my immediate goal.

From the end of the track, it's road walking all the way down into the town, a comely place. The homogeneous appearance of the houses, many of them listed as historic monuments, is enhanced by the richly toned ochre coloured stone of Logonna or *pierre du roz*, quarried at nearby Logonna-Daoulas. The position of Le Faou on both the Rade de Brest and a major road route from Brest to Quimper led to economic prosperity, a commercial development to be seen in the quality of the domestic architecture. Many of the formerly half-timbered facades are faced with slate, a striking contrast with the yellow stone.

I cut down behind the central street straight towards the river, where the church of Saint Sauveur beside the water has a very tall bell-tower with tiers of open galleries, topped by a Renaissance style dome. Brightly painted 17th century wooden statues of apostles can be seen in the porch, unusually with their names in Breton - Per, Jakez, Filip, Yann. The door stands open, so I can go in to admire the baptismal font, a very original curiosity, which may have been part of a *fontaine* when created in the 16th century. Made of kersanton stone, it is oval in shape with sinuous decoration, snakes, birds and cherubim, once in glowing fiery colours. One side has been defaced, probably to remove a noble coat-of-arms at the time of the Revolution. An inscription refers to the four rivers of Paradise. I have never seen anything quite like it before.

Outside, I lean on the precinct wall overlooking the mud-banks of the estuary, thinking about the very last stages of my Tro Breiz which lie ahead. It is true that I feel more comfortable back in an area I know well, my long walk deepened by familiarity. I anticipate the passage through a great forest that will lead me back to the high moors and the chapel where this all began. I can already feel the scenery wrapping itself around me like a security blanket. Many of the actual paths will be new, but there is only excitement and satisfaction in the idea of returning to a known world.

The amazing change in my physical capacity is mirrored internally not by any sudden great revelation, but by a profound new clarity about the nature of my settling here in my place. Looking back on my whole life from this distance, one insight pops up to the surface: where I have always felt coherence is in my own endeavours. The path has been a good one. I have come to realise on this pilgrimage that I fit in with myself, and that that is the key to contentment and personal surety. And while the landscape here holds my heart, there is nothing more to be sought.

Pilgrimage is a connecting line on many levels, joining places in a narrative that embraces periods of time and a huge assembly of disparate people. It sits in my imagination at this late stage of the journey like a pack of cards, a multi-coloured unit that can be constantly shuffled and dealt out in different patterns, as I mull over all the sights, voices and echoing sounds of the past and present that have filled my thoughts, waking and sleeping, for so many months. From staccato bursts, my progress has become rhythmic, like the energy of the tidal estuary before my eyes. The grey expanse will soon be filled by the surge of the sea, all will be the same and yet completely transformed. An emptiness will be filled by the eternal flow.

My next excursion starts just down the road at Rumengol. I am going to walk with friends Julia and Phil (and my dog) through the Forêt du Cranou, but first we must pay tribute to the splendid church Notre-Dame de Rumengol, a famous site of pilgrimage. In 1880 an additional outdoor chapel was added to cater for the huge numbers attending Pardons here. Two are still celebrated (Trinity Sunday in late May or early June, and August 15th, the Assumption) and once there were four, suggesting echoes of more pagan rituals around the solstices and equinoxes. And paganism has a big role here in the church. The stained-glass window above the High Altar, dating from 1886, reflects a toponymic legend promulgated by the Chevalier de Freminiville, a naval man, indefatigable antiquarian and notorious cross-dresser, who liked to go to the opera in Brest in full feminine regalia.

In a publication of 1835, at a time when the megaliths were still regarded as the work of the Celts and their Druid leaders, he presented his explanation of the name Rumengol: red (ru for ruz) / stone (men) / lights (goulou). The story to back it up involves Saint Guénolé, Saint Corentin and King Gradlon seeing smoke from the top of Menez Hom, and being outraged on finding out this marked the fires of Druid ritual in the forest of Cranou, where human sacrifice was practised. The focus was a megalithic monument, said to glow red with blood. The upholders of Christian values dashed over to the spot and put an end to such degenerate pagan practices, with the stone destroyed and a church built in its place, origin of the current one here in Rumengol. In other words, de Freminiville created a foundation legend.

The window shows the Virgin Mary sitting on a dolmen, a neolithic burial place, beneath a great oak, sacred in Druid lore, with Saint Guénolé admonishing the people, whilst Corentin and the king, holding a model of the church he has vowed, stand before her. The inhabitants watch uncertainly from the trees, a figure lies prostrate as if begging forgiveness, and in the corner a richly clad Druid

languishes, harp rendered useless, a tear on his cheek. I'm surprised the whole thing hasn't fallen down under the weight of symbolism. The mix of pagan and Christian traditions behind all this is typically Breton, and the potential vagaries of oral culture are exposed. The church records suggest a much more prosaic explanation of the name Rumengol: Notre-Dame of all Remedies (Remed-oll).

The sacred space of this compelling church is graced with a high quality of decoration (16-18th centuries), from the sun dial, tympanum of the Magi and apostles of the porch, to the sumptuous interior altarpieces which illuminate the shortened nave. Statues include saints Corentin and Guénolé, who are said to check up on the faithful at each Pardon of the Trinity, seeing that they have not lapsed into their pagan ways. (The vantage point of Menez Hom can actually be seen in the distance from the precinct.) There are also some finely obscene gargoyles on the roofline for those with good eyesight or a zoom lens.

Leaving this extraordinary place, we turn off the main road opposite the *fontaine*, and soon see a rare example (on the Tro Breiz) of pilgrimage art: a tree with Compostela trail sign and a huge heap of scallop shells creatively arranged around the base, presumably by the owners of the house nearby. It immediately conjures images of pilgrims sharing the way, of others persevering along their chosen routes. It boosts my spirits in a wider sense than this beautiful walk on a sunny, warm day. I think about it still as we follow hard tracks through undulating countryside and a profusion of foxgloves as tall as me, with views of the Forêt du Cranou to the north.

At Ty Kerneis we take a secluded path parallel with the railway. A large dog, with soft brown and white fur and blue eyes, joins us for a little while, although mine, in typical terrier fashion, quickly loses interest in having a canine companion. At the road we cross the railway bridge over a deep cutting and search for our expected path on the left. When we eventually find it, fallen trees block the route and we consult the map to find another option. It seems best to go back over the railway and round by roads to access the forest path we want at a different location.

But beside the railway there is a tempting bridleway, bemired but clear of detritus. We all agree to chance it and continue ahead happily into the woods until we reach a wide, deep stream at the bottom. No problem for a rider on horseback, as the muddy banks show, but no obvious crossing for us. We discuss and decide we must go on, as the track we want to follow right through the forest is actually visible on the other side, so I take off my boots and begin to wade across gingerly. It is very slippery underfoot and the water is rushing, so progress is slow, but the cool water is invigorating.

The dog is frantic. He does not like water and is torn between the need to follow me and his fear. Twice he puts a paw in and twice leaps back in alarm. Meanwhile Julia and Phil are investigating a tree-trunk across the water further downstream. The dog runs back and forth between us, squeaking with anxiety. I have to concentrate on keeping my balance, but when I next look up, Julia is sitting astride the tree, inching her way across, the dog is behind her and Phil is still wondering whether to risk it. Eventually we are all reunited on the far bank, to great canine relief. I am the one covered in mud.

The forest is huge and beautiful, despite the damage. Oaks, beech (*faou* in Breton) and evergreens mingle on the hillsides that stretch away on all sides. It was once an important source of timber for naval boatyards in Brest, with logs shipped across the Rade from Le Faou. We have not come across as many fallen trees from the great storm of last autumn as expected, but in certain places, there are swathes of casualties as if a tornado has blown through. We see no-one else on our passage, but the weather has turned and there's a heavy shower, a few growls of thunder and very threatening skies. Someone must be throwing water onto Saint Conval's head. According to an account of 1890, this was a ritual to bring rain, carried out at his *fontaine,* which is still there, deep in the forest.

It's an other-worldly place, green and grey, silent but for the trickle of water. Conval sits behind a grill, eternal icon of a special sylvan landscape. His spirit is abroad in the forest, here where he found somewhere safe to settle, enduring even until now, through centuries and the transformation of the outside world on many levels. Saints live on in the mind and memory of the people: such is the nature of oral tradition which ensures survival, even perpetuity. They still shine like little sparks of light across the countryside. A Breton friend told me the saint's story the first time I visited Conval's patch here. It reflects yet again the close relationship between saints and the qualities of the land.

According to local legend, Conval tried first to find a home in the Bois du Gars but the local lord had him chased off when he cut wood for his cart. Welcomed in Cranou, the saint mouthed what amounted to a curse, and a neatly rhyming one at that: *E Coat-ar-Harz / Biken goal-kar n'vo kad ebars / E coat ar C'hranou / Birviken coat na vankou.* Rendered inelegantly in English, apparently it means the forest of Gars (Harz) will never produce wood to make the shaft for a cart, but such timber will never be lacking in Cranou. Continuity through the passage of time is the currency of the Breton saints. He once had a chapel here too, but it was dismantled in 1942 and transferred elsewhere, deemed inconveniently placed for services. The shaft of the former calvary still stands on a crossroads of paths, with an inscription R.DORE MA FAICT, Roland Doré (a famous sculptor), made me. It is dated 1627.

We follow a broad straight track cutting right across the forest for a few kilometres, via the deserted Maison forestière de la Roche noire. Pine trees become more and more frequent. The route gradually climbs more steeply as we move out of the main forest. My walking is slower and slower with a painful right hip making me lopsided. Perhaps my body is compensating for the lack of pain on the other side, or more likely it is the humidity bringing out rheumatic twinges. The last bit of path we need to cover seems blocked, so Phil goes to investigate whilst Julia and I sit on a damp bench. He reports back that many trees were down over the path in a stand of conifers, but there seems to be a way forced round by other walkers. We manage to get through and up to the road where we have a car waiting. It's good to be finished for the day, but we've had a very satisfying walk and the end of this great endeavour is almost in sight.

## 25  Reaching the end: a hidden valley, the presumption of ignorance, ridiculously lost

When I come back to pick up the trail soon after, it turns into the most stunning walk of the entire Tro Breiz pilgrimage, challenging but memorable, as such a journey should be. David and the dog are my companions, and we start on a gravelled path through moorland vegetation of gorse, broom and ferns. Soon we have incredible views of layers of high hills and very steep-sided valleys ahead, stretching away into the distance. Lots of the arboreal cover is pine here, although there are signs of trees fallen in mass in the storm and only gradually being cleared. David said the extraordinary vista reminded him of the Alps, I thought of the Tatra Mountains in Poland. I've never seen scenery like it in Brittany. The path is very eroded and extremely steep downhill into the squeezed valley of the Squirriou. When we lose the wide views, the river environment is stunning, with mini-cascades and a lively flow in cool, dim light. There's a sense of remote loneliness, of being deep in the folds of earth. The only person we see all day is a surprise later on, a photographer carrying his gear.

We follow the river some distance round behind the invisible Nivot agricultural college, and past a fish-rearing establishment that looks deserted. It is hard to believe that any other human beings set foot in this world apart. The path is soon blocked in several places by fallen trees, revealing their massive ripped up roots, some even full of large blocks of stone. We have to be inventive to get through with little detours, but finally make the site I had been looking forward to most: a remarkable oak of supreme size and shape. Later I learn that it was known as the *Chêne tipi* or teepee, for the distinctive outline. It is marked by noticeboards, but the tree itself has been destroyed by the storm. A hollow trunk like a little volcano remains, a tangle of huge, thick branches lying prostrate, mingled with other foliage. The froth of leaves is like green blood at a murder scene.

After this sadness, the path is clear and we enjoy the river, stopping at little pebbly beaches beside the water, constantly amazed at the beauty and deep peace of the setting. When we sadly must leave this discrete environment at a bridge to turn onto a stony track, we discover that David has left the dog's lead where we stopped for lunch by piles of cut timber long ago. He sets off to run back and I have trouble keeping the dog from running after him, and can only do so by physically blocking the entrance to the footpath and repulsing his repeated attempts to push past me. Terriers are worryingly assiduous. He never lets up trying until David returns with the lead in hand. I feel as if I've survived a long bout of some physical combat sport.

At the access road to the college (still invisible) we turn away down to Kerfranc, past the Moulin de Squirriou and finally join a road past Sternfars. We pause at the Chapel of Saint Sebastian, a pretty little building in a walled enclosure, then still more road walking before a lovely long footpath rising steadily with long views behind. And at last we look back across the valley to see the college of Nivot perched on a hill. It is a grand complex of buildings, impossible to imagine when we were down by the river. Emerging at the top of the slope, we can see our goal of Brasparts church across another valley.

In the farming hamlet of Botquest, we turn past out-buildings onto a grassy path through fields. It becomes narrower and stonier, eventually turning into an atmospheric *chemin creux* (sunken way) down into the valley and then endlessly up towards Brasparts over great slabs of slate. It is easy to imagine weary pilgrims toiling up here towards their next spiritual halt, forced to walk in single file, slipping and sliding as we are on the wet terrain. The thought of the wild Monts d'Arrée crossing lying ahead, fraught with dangers, must have been daunting. That's the bit I'm looking forward to, but for the moment I am really tired, although when we finally come out by the church, we think ourselves lucky to have enjoyed such a walk.

I lived in Brasparts at a very difficult time in my life, when impecunity forced me to accept the charity of a Breton friend for a roof over my head, albeit one belonging to an un-renovated hovel with mice, holes in the wall and no proper heating. Within days of arriving, as I slept on the floor downstairs, my car a few feet away outside was smashed up with a hammer. When the police came next day, they asked me if I had annoyed anyone. Give me a chance, was my reply. Someone later told me, in a perfectly conversational manner, that it was a local who resented 'English' people taking Breton houses. With a few notable exceptions, this was an attitude I encountered many times during the four years I endured those living conditions, including the terrible winter of 2010. My health and spirit were broken by Brasparts, as well as my car.

It is not easy to be a woman alone here in Brittany, and a perceived foreign outsider as well. This is in general because society is strongly family or couple based. And my natural solitariness probably gives off an aura of being determinedly separate. In terms of my work, a common automatic presumption of ignorance is very hard to bear. Natives have trouble accepting an outsider's expertise. Twenty-five years of dedication to Breton history and landscape have given me a considerable overview of the country I love with such passion. It seems a natural path for a creative loner like me, rooted in historical enquiry, who relates to places before people, who is free for total immersion in the theme that has come to dominate all my work, whether historical writing, novels or poetry. The spirit of place. Isn't the essential lesson of the Breton saints that incomers have something to offer?

Back in Brasparts today, the small past is forgotten. I believe myself fortunate to be here in Brittany and to be me, settled in myself and in the long history of my land. The church is well worth seeing, and David hasn't been before, so we take the time. Église de Notre-Dame et Saint Tugen has plenty of architectural merit, but the greatest attraction is that it is usually open. We enjoy the horned man in the porch. Saint Tugen is one of those Breton saints often described as semi-legendary, as if only half of him was real. He is associated with dogs and the cure for rabies, after apparently claiming it was easier to control a pack of rabid dogs than one woman, when he failed to keep his sister safe from an unsuitable young man. The voice of God was heard at once: then go off to Armorica and protect the Bretons from the fangs of mad canines.

Inside the church there are graphic statues – like Saint Andrew crucified on a saltire cross, Saint Eloi the blacksmith, plus horse, and a cow making eyes at Saint Herbot. My favourite detail is outside on the ossuary, where a skeletal Ankou the Grim Reaper, rather ravaged by time now, wields his spear on the gable end.

On a fair weather day with gusting wind I set out for the last leg of this incredible journey. Squaring the circle of my Tro Breiz. The beginning is marred by the fact that I have no map (the person giving me a lift to the start in Brasparts again printed it out for me but has forgotten to bring it) for the Bois d'Isle just outside the village, which I know is a mishmash of paths where I have aimlessly wandered before now. I begin on familiar ground, passing behind houses, including the hovel I used to live in, down a narrow footpath. It's tricky underfoot, swimming with water after a recent rainy period. The rather sad *fontaine* of St Edern has not been cleared since storm Ciaran and the hollow where it lies is a mass of fallen branches.

I go ahead through fields and into the wood, soon seeing the little river ahead. In my day, there was a rickety log crossing, but now I can use a new *passerelle*. I keep the water on my left and manage to follow the path, despite having to clamber over storm debris in places. When I come to a junction of paths and a bridge, I stop uncertainly. The map I prepared showed a confluence of streams, but that is not clear here. Perhaps I haven't gone far enough yet. I cross over to look at the way on the other side, but the path soon turns in a completely wrong direction, so I go back and continue along the stream. The terrain underfoot gets increasingly difficult and is obviously less walked, a bad sign, with piles of branches to negotiate. The dog struggles with this, being low to the ground. I realise from a gentle appearance of the sun that the valley has swung south east, with a very steep hill across the water, and that I am off course.

I go all the way back to the bridge, cross and spot a small path I ignored before because it goes uphill where I was expecting to stay close to streams. It feels the right direction. Once I've plodded up for a while something drives me on even though I know it can't be right. I can only describe it as a perverse determination not to be beaten by the route on this important day, although that's exactly what is happening. We are climbing the steep hill that looked so daunting from the other side of the stream. The land is more and more demanding, the path diminished to nothing. My poor dog is having trouble with brambles and hard winter stalks at his eye level. We are lost on our last walk. In a relatively small wood. How ridiculous! I think the tense expectation and surfeit of emotion bound up in the occasion has frazzled my brain.

When I can go no further and that niggling pain in my hip is setting in, I force a way through the trees to the precipitous edge and sit down. Luckily I am carrying a thermos and the coffee pulls me together to focus on finding a way out of what has become the worst situation of the entire Tro Breiz. Only a few miles from home! The onerous route has sapped so much energy, I don't feel going back is an option, but by observing the prospect through the trees, eventually I pick out the line of what must be the main road up to the top of the Monts d'Arrée, although cars are intermittent. It is high on a hillside a long way off, but it confirms my general sense of orientation is correct. The problem is that there's no obvious way off this hill-top, vertical slopes or dense brambles bar the two directions that might help.

We make very slow progress along the edge of the drop and then a painful plunge through thorns brings us into a space of luscious grass. The dog goes mad, doubtless itching from a million scratches, and rolls on his back every couple of steps. I see buildings some way below and a small road off to the left. Moving downward, at last we come into fields, those nearer to the farm with electric fencing, and I realise I am clearly trespassing, way off any footpaths. There may well be loose dogs too in such a remote place, so I don't want to risk going onwards.

I tack back across another field and re-enter the tree line, unsure what to do next. Then like the song of angels, the sound of voices carries up to me, and far below, down an almost vertical slope, I glimpse a woman and young girl passing along with a dog, on what must be a track. The track I should have been on all along. The only option is to go straight down and we start incredibly slowly. The dog is pulling me and I begin to fall several times, only saved by grabbing at branches. At the last sheer section of banking I have no choice but to let him off the lead to fend for himself and I slide down on my bottom.

After this, the route is no problem. Turn left at the road, cross the stream and continue uphill as far as a single house where a track will lead off heading all the way to the main road I glimpsed earlier. That bit of the map is clearly fixed in my mind. It all works out as expected, and the views are stunning, looking back as far as the Montagnes Noires to the south. I sit on a log for a while to recover and then toil up to the road. There's the lay-by where I used to park daily to walk up onto the Monts d'Arrée when I lived in Brasparts. There's the track leading up to the security of the moors.

Once the way is familiar my body feels lighter and less stressed. At the top of a long pull uphill there's a happily remembered picnic table with marvellous views across the moors to Mont-St-Michel-de-Brasparts. The chapel on the hill-top is where all this pilgrimage started such a long time ago. Everything is bleached pale colours by the forceful winds and intermittent sunshine. It's a raw and ancient landscape. We sit for a long time to let it all soak in, and I drink the rest of my coffee and share the remains of a croissant with the dog. I have difficulty getting up again after and in urging my exhausted joints into action, but we go on, down a flowing stream covering the narrow path towards the big junction of walking routes I know so well.

From here we are in effect starting the last long ascent. The stony surface jars and probes my weary limbs, but I revel in the open landscape and long views. At the access road to the car-park below the summit, we cross and start to ascend a huge ladder of steps climbing steeply into the sky, or so it looks from the bottom as the curve of the hill hides our destination. My knees scream with all the volume of their age and wear, but this is where that dog maxim proves its worth: dangerous for down, useful for up. He pulls me enthusiastically all the way to the top. Then we round a short curve to the chapel approach. I see people ahead playing at being driven about by the force of the wind. Then I realise they are not joking. I can hardly stand against it and imagine the dog sailing up into the air with the lead trailing, like a balloon on a string.

I intend taking him into the chapel, which is open every day, even if I have to carry him. A year ago they were renovating and there was no entry, so we are definitely going in this time. I am longing to see the new interior. I've saved it until now, although many people I know have been and admired the slab of altar stone and modern metal work sculpture, calling it moving, elemental and deeply spiritual. I'm full of anticipation for finishing on such a note, and for saying a few words there of farewell to the Seven Founding Saints and the Tro Breiz. But first I want to take a moment to look across this landscape that means the whole world to me, and stand on the spot where this journey began.

We fight round to the north-east face where there is a modicum of shelter from the onslaught of rushing air. It's a relief. It's all a relief, being here, being finished, surviving, fitter and stronger than I was a year ago despite today's fiasco. Overwhelmed by the occasion and the frustrations of the day, I start to cry and then find it hard to stop. I think of the two spirits that have been with me all along the journey and honour them again at the end as at the start. It's hard to believe, but I've done it. Now I can savour the reward. We struggle against the weather round to the door, noting that everyone else has gone, and my faithful dog and I are alone on the summit for the final magic moment. The chapel is closed.

Three months later, I go to the Pardon on the last Sunday in August at the Sept Saints chapel near Erdeven. The President of the Association is welcoming, rightly proud of the group's achievements of restoration. Now I see inside, it's a pleasingly plain space with statues and stained-glass of the founding saints, and the processional banner for their special day.

About a hundred people attend the mass, mostly old but a few youngsters. The mood is relaxed, almost jovial. The locals have pride in their habitual roles, and the celebrants give every appearance of enjoyment. After, we process behind the cross, banner and a gilt reliquary into the trees where the *fontaine* lies. The priest offers benediction, and we all get the lightest spray of sacred drops as he dips the leaves of a bay twig in a bowl and shakes them around the crowd.

The ritual and sincerity of the celebration were truly moving, although the sermon was heavy-handed sophism claiming Paul of Tarsus didn't really mean women should be submissive to their husbands. A tedious apostle rather than Pol, Tugdual, Brieuc, Malo, Samson, Patern and Corentin. I would like to have seen them given pride of place, celebrated for their unique role and the legacy that has brought us all here today. The priest stumbled over their names and didn't know which cathedral Tugdual and Samson represented. Or pretended he didn't, to involve the audience. It did indeed all seem a bit of a performance.

With the picnic underway outside, I go back into the chapel to bid farewell to the seminal saints. I have been working all summer on this book, now nearly finished, so soon there will be no reason to spend any more time with those seven founders of Brittany and all they still represent. This makes me very sad until I remember one important fact. The Tro Breiz is a circular journey, and therefore never-ending.

## Main Places on the route

## Saints in Brittany